BENJAMIN FRANKLIN

Other Titles in the
People Who Made History Series

BENJAMIN
FRANKLIN

Tanja Lee, *Book Editor*

Daniel Leone, *Publisher*
Bonnie Szumski, *Editorial Director*
Scott Barbour, *Managing Editor*
Stuart B. Miller, *Series Editor*

Greenhaven Press, Inc., San Diego, CA

Every effort has been made to trace the owners of copyrighted material. The articles in this volume may have been edited for content, length, and/or reading level. The titles have been changed to enhance the editorial purpose. Those interested in locating the original source will find the complete citation on the first page of each article.

Library of Congress Cataloging-in-Publication Data

Benjamin Franklin / Tanja Lee, book editor.
    p. cm. — (People who made history)
   Includes bibliographical references and index.
   ISBN 0-7377-0898-0 (pbk. : alk. paper) —
ISBN 0-7377-0899-9 (lib. : alk. paper)
   1. Franklin, Benjamin, 1706–1790. 2. Statesmen—United States—Biography. 3. Scientists—United States—Biography. 4. Printers—United States—Biography. 5. Inventors—United States—Biography. 6. United States—Politics and government—To 1775. 7. United States—Politics and government—1775–1783. I. Lee, Tanja. II. Series.

E302.6.F8 B452   2002
973.3'092—dc21   2001023478
[B]   CIP

Cover photo: © Philadelphia Museum of Art/Corbis
Library of Congress, 13, 26, 63, 75, 82, 177, 195

Copyright © 2002 by Greenhaven Press, Inc.
PO Box 289009
San Diego, CA 92198-9009
Printed in the U.S.A.

CONTENTS

use of questions introduced a new approach to scientific research. The *Opticks* also differed from Newton's earlier phenomenal work, the *Principia*, in that it was written in English instead of Latin, which meant that a greater number of people had access to the work, including Benjamin Franklin, whose experiments with electricity were directly influenced by Newton's studies.

Chapter 2: The Legendary Ben Franklin

Chapter 3: The Political Career of an Eighteenth-Century Activist

changes while in the role as a diplomat with full authority: a plenipotentiary. In order to obtain a greater number of British prisoners, which would allow for a retrieval of an equally greater number of American prisoners, Franklin began hiring privateers—privately owned armed ships that were generally used against enemies in warfare and sometimes for pirating.

Chapter 4: Dr. Franklin's Legacy

FOREWORD

In the vast and colorful pageant of human history, a handful of individuals stand out. They are the men and women who have come variously to be called "great," "leading," "brilliant," "pivotal," or "infamous" because they and their deeds forever changed their own society or the world as a whole. Some were political or military leaders—kings, queens, presidents, generals, and the like—whose policies, conquests, or innovations reshaped the maps and futures of countries and entire continents. Among those falling into this category were the formidable Roman statesman/general Julius Caesar, who extended Rome's power into Gaul (what is now France); Caesar's lover and ally, the notorious Egyptian queen Cleopatra, who challenged the strongest male rulers of her day; and England's stalwart Queen Elizabeth I, whose defeat of the mighty Spanish Armada saved England from subjugation.

Some of history's other movers and shakers were scientists or other thinkers whose ideas and discoveries altered the way people conduct their everyday lives or view themselves and their place in nature. The electric light and other remarkable inventions of Thomas Edison, for example, revolutionized almost every aspect of home-life and the workplace; and the theories of naturalist Charles Darwin lit the way for biologists and other scientists in their ongoing efforts to understand the origins of living things, including human beings.

Still other people who made history were religious leaders and social reformers. The struggles of the Arabic prophet Muhammad more than a thousand years ago led to the establishment of one of the world's great religions—Islam; and the efforts and personal sacrifices of an American reverend named Martin Luther King Jr. brought about major improvements in race relations and the justice system in the United States.

Each anthology in the People Who Made History series begins with an introductory essay that provides a general overview of the individual's life, times, and contributions. The group of essays that follow are chosen for their accessibility to a young adult audience and carefully edited in consideration of the reading and comprehension levels of that audience. Some of the essays are by noted historians, professors, and other experts. Others are excerpts from contemporary writings by or about the pivotal individual in question. To aid the reader in choosing the material of immediate interest or need, an annotated table of contents summarizes the article's main themes and insights.

Each volume also contains extensive research tools, including a collection of excerpts from primary source documents pertaining to the individual under discussion. The volumes are rounded out with an extensive bibliography and a comprehensive index.

Plutarch, the renowned first-century Greek biographer and moralist, crystallized the idea behind Greenhaven's People Who Made History when he said, "To be ignorant of the lives of the most celebrated men of past ages is to continue in a state of childhood all our days." Indeed, since it is people who make history, every modern nation, organization, institution, invention, artifact, and idea is the result of the diligent efforts of one or more individuals, living or dead; and it is therefore impossible to understand how the world we live in came to be without examining the contributions of these individuals.

BENJAMIN FRANKLIN: "IN ANY AGE, IN ANY PLACE"

He was never a president of the United States, nor did he lead any army in battle. He had no talent for public speaking, preferring to write out his thoughts on scraps of paper to be read aloud by others. Yet in his day he was certainly one of the most well known celebrities, beloved in both the United States and throughout most of Europe.

A RENAISSANCE MAN

Benjamin Franklin was a true Renaissance man—the sort of person who is interested and gifted in many areas. He is known as one of the founding fathers of the United States. His contributions in the writing of both the Declaration of Independence and the Constitution are very important. Many historians believe that the American colonies could not have won the Revolutionary War without the assistance of the French. And the key American sent to Paris to enlist their support was Franklin.

But Benjamin Franklin's interests and achievements extended far beyond politics. He was a man who loved to explore ideas; he was constantly looking for new ways of doing things. From this passion grew such concepts as the first public library as well as the first city fire department. And his scientific pursuits—notably his contributions to the study of electricity and inventions—such as bifocals, the odometer, and the glass armonica—are legendary.

Finally, he was a very talented writer. His *Autobiography, Poor Richard's Almanack,* and hundreds of editorials on a great range of topics establish him as one of the most widely read authors of the eighteenth century.

EARLY GLIMPSES

Though Philadelphia would later claim him as a native son, Benjamin Franklin was actually born and reared in Boston.

Born on January 17, 1706, he was the fifteenth child in a family of seventeen children. His father, Josiah Franklin, was a soap and candle maker who, like many others in the American colonies, had left England seeking religious freedom.

Young Benjamin later recalled his childhood as a very happy time. It is also easy to see glimmers of his future talents in some of his activities as a child. For instance, as a strong and capable swimmer, he set himself to devising a way to swim even faster, and arrived at one of his first inventions—swim fins. He later wrote of these wooden contraptions, "They much resembled a painter's pallets. In swimming I pushed the edges of these forward, and I struck the water with their flat surfaces as I drew them back."[1]

His interest in using time more efficiently was also evident as a young child—although perhaps motivated more by impatience with saying grace before meals than intellectual analysis. Young Benjamin had been helping his father as the elder Franklin salted and cured large slabs of meat. The meat was placed into a large cask, where it would be preserved for the winter. The boy's suggestion became an often-repeated family story. "I think, Father," said Benjamin, "if you were to say Grace over the whole cask—once and for all—it would be a vast saving of time."[2]

A PRINTER

Like other boys at that time, Benjamin was expected to decide on a career by age nine or ten. Based on his idea for the cask of meat, his father was certain that the boy was not suited to the ministry. Benjamin tried working in his father's shop making soap and candles, but he did not enjoy it. Eventually his older brother James offered to take him on as a printer's apprentice.

Though the work was difficult, Benjamin liked it and learned quickly. He was a voracious reader, and the print shop offered a wide variety of material to read, from pamphlets about raising livestock to historical essays on ancient Rome. Whenever he could save a little money, it almost always went to buy books.

Sometimes he chose to buy books on subjects he knew nothing about just to teach himself something new or difficult. For example, he had never done well in arithmetic, and decided to tackle it on his own. "I took Cocker's book of arithmetic," he later recalled, "and went through the whole by myself with great ease. I also read Seller's and Sturmy's books of navigation."[3]

During his time as a printer's apprentice Franklin began studying the art of writing. His "textbook" was a copy of the *Spectator*, a London newspaper famous for its satiric essays. He read and reread an essay in each issue and diligently took apart each paragraph to understand what made the writing so good.

A few days later, he would try to write the essay himself, imitating what he had learned. The results, he later recalled, were interesting: "I discovered many faults and amended them, but I sometimes had the pleasure of fancying that . . . I might possibly in time come to be a tolerable English writer, of which I was extremely ambitious."[4]

As it turned out, he had an opportunity to use his new writing skills sooner than he might have imagined. In 1721 James started a newspaper called the *New England Courant*.

While working as a printer's apprentice, Benjamin Franklin studied the art of writing using essays from a London newspaper.

Although other newspapers in Boston competed for readers, James and his friends sparked interest in the *Courant* by including essays and articles criticizing various political and church leaders. They wrote under various aliases, such as Ichabod Henroost, Fanny Mournful, and Tabatha Talkative.

Benjamin wanted to try his hand at writing an essay, too. Knowing his brother would probably refuse to allow it, Benjamin wrote a humorous letter to the paper from a woman he named Silence Dogood. To his delight, James and his friends spent hours in the shop discussing how well the letter was written—although when Benjamin finally told James the truth, his brother was not at all pleased. "I began to be considered a little more by my brother's acquaintances," he later recalled, "and in a manner that did not quite please him, as he thought, probably with reason, that it tended to make me too vain."[5]

ON TO PHILADELPHIA

Benjamin and his brother did not get along well after that, and he grew restless working in the print shop. At age seventeen, Benjamin sold a few possessions and set out on his own. After a brief stay in New York, he moved on to Philadelphia, where he established himself as a printer's assistant, and not long afterward, ran the shop himself. Eventually, by 1728, Franklin and his friend Hugh Meredith had established their own printing house.

Business was slow for printers in Philadelphia at that time. To increase business, a creative printer turned to publishing his own writing. Benjamin recalled the excitement he had shared working on his brother James's paper, and decided to start one of his own. The city had one newspaper already, but it was, in Franklin's words, "a paltry thing, wretchedly managed, and no way entertaining; and yet profitable [to its publisher]."[6]

Franklin called his newspaper the *Pennsylvania Gazette,* and with a mixture of humorous articles and thought-provoking essays on life in Pennsylvania, the *Gazette* quickly won a loyal readership. He also took on many well-known politicians, including the royal governor of Pennsylvania. Franklin wrote editorials applauding the members of the colonial assembly who were refusing to pay the governor a fixed salary, maintaining that they would prefer to pay him according to the quality of his work.

Although his support of the colonial assembly over the English representative ruffled feathers among some prominent citizens, many others were interested in reading the entertaining, well-reasoned editorials. And just as modern newspaper editors have influenced their communities, writes one historian, "so did the *Gazette* steadily bring Franklin to an influential position in Pennsylvania."[7]

"MY PLAIN COUNTRY JOAN"

In 1730 Franklin married Deborah Read, a young woman he had met on first arriving in Philadelphia. She had been married before, but her husband had deserted her after taking the dowry her parents had provided. It was believed the man had moved to the West Indies and had remarried.

The bad marriage had taken a toll on Deborah's self-esteem. She seldom smiled and was painfully shy. Even so, she was extremely happy in her new life with Franklin. Within a very short time, the two set to work expanding his printing business. They added a small shop that sold a little of everything—"from the salves and ointments concocted by Deborah's mother . . . to the crown soap made in Boston by Franklin's brother John according to a secret recipe."[8]

Besides working in the store, Deborah ran their household, made all their clothing, and virtually ruined her eyesight spending long hours by candlelight hand-stitching bindings for the various books published in the print shop. Franklin loved her, and in a song for her called "My Plain Country Joan" (the word *Joan* meaning "woman"), he wrote:

> Of their Chloes and Phillesses Poets may prate
> I ding my plain country Joan.
> Now twelve years my wife, still the joy of my life,
> Blest day that I made her my own, My dear friends.[9]

POOR RICHARD

At the time of his marriage Franklin began a project that over the years earned him both great fame and wealth. The ongoing work was a book, which he called *Poor Richard's Almanack;* from the ages of twenty-six to fifty-two, he wrote, revised, printed, and sold the book.

Almanacs were popular in the eighteenth century—plenty were published in Philadelphia at the time. But Franklin knew he could make his special, just as he had made his newspaper special. He would include what people expected from an almanac, such as calendars, descriptions of touring itineraries, schedules of tides and changes of the moon, and even jokes and trivia. However, in *Poor Richard's Almanack*, Franklin took on the persona of a poor, henpecked astrologer named Richard Saunders—a man who was tired of being nagged by his wife to get "a real job" and stop gazing at stars to tell the future. Besides offering tidbits about his own life, Saunders gives advice on both marital problems and those of bachelors.

In addition to this somewhat "racy" material, astrologer Richard Saunders declared the exact date and time of the death of Titan Leeds, Franklin's business competitor! Of course, the predicted day came and went, and Mr. Leeds remained perfectly healthy. But Franklin enjoyed the abundant publicity the stunt aroused in Philadelphia—and the boost in sales of *Poor Richard's Almanack* reflected it.

THE WISDOM OF MANY AGES AND NATIONS

More than ten thousand copies of *Poor Richard's Almanack* were sold each year, making it a runaway best-seller in today's terms. Each year Richard Saunders would thank the public for buying his book, saying that his wife had stopped nagging him, that he had been able to buy her many new clothes, and that, he wrote, she "has been enabled to get a pot of her own, and is no longer obliged to borrow one from a neighbor."[10] The continuing story of Richard Saunders kept the almanac's customers coming back for more year after year.

But Franklin's almanac was innovative in another way. He later wrote in his autobiography that since most colonists could not afford books and had limited education, he thought it a worthwhile purpose to educate them by, he said, filling "all the little spaces that occurred between the remarkable days of the calendar with proverbial sentences."[11]

Some of Franklin's proverbs have survived as well-known sayings, such as "Early to bed and early to rise, makes a man healthy, wealthy, and wise." Many were borrowed from biblical verse and proverbs from various cultures. These he simply reworded for brevity and clarity. For instance, the proverb "Fresh fish and new-come guests smell, but that they are three days old" was streamlined to "Fish and visitors stink in three days."[12]

Throughout his twenties, Ben Franklin worked hard at his writing and his business. And if that segment of his life was focused on private enterprise, Franklin in his thirties was a man with a wider view. Instead of concentrating solely on his business, he took a long look at Philadelphia to see how to help the city prosper, as well.

Some of the credit for his wider perspective was due to the Junto, a club he had formed in 1727. Its purpose was good conversation and self-improvement, its name taken from the Spanish word *junto,* meaning "together." But the club was commonly called the Leather Aprons, a reference to the fact that its twelve original members were tradesmen—carpenters, shoemakers, clerks, or printers, like Franklin himself—and wore such garments when they worked.

At weekly meetings, over glasses of wine, the members of the Junto discussed philosophical questions such as "How shall we judge the goodness of a writing?" or "Which is best to make a friend of—a wise and good man that is poor, or a rich man that is neither wise nor good?" Members of the club wrote essays themselves and took turns reading them to the group.

A Wealth of New Ideas

One of the most remarkable things about the Junto was the wealth of new ideas for projects that came from its members. Franklin himself proposed several important firsts, including America's first public library. Libraries did not exist in any city in the colonies; in fact, books were extremely rare. Franklin suggested that since the members owned books, they might combine them so that they all could enjoy them.

They put together a list of other people who might wish to belong to such a library club or, lacking books to contribute, to donate money toward purchasing books. The Junto members took turns housing the library. Any citizen was welcome to read the books, but only members could check books out. Soon the idea was borrowed by other cities throughout the colonies.

Franklin also proposed the formation of a city fire department. (At the time, one had to rely on neighbors' help in the event of a fire.) He persuaded thirty men to join him, starting the Union Fire Company. Besides guaranteeing a well-trained brigade of firefighters that would rush to any citizen's aid, the company also publicized tips on reducing the risk of fire in the home.

Franklin suggested a host of other projects, from a city police force to garbage removal systems. Anxious to avoid hurt feelings or resentment in others over the sheer abundance of his own suggestions, he often told people that a certain idea was not his, but rather a friend's. Things went more smoothly, he realized, when he did not immediately claim credit for everything he did. The truth would eventually become known. He wrote, "The present little sacrifice [to my] vanity will afterwards be amply repaid."[13]

SCIENTIST

If his thirties were devoted to civic duty, Franklin's forties were marked by his attention to invention and science—or "natural philosophy," as it was called then. He had always had an inquisitive mind, and was eager for explanations of any phenomenon. At forty-two he retired; he had more than enough money, and he looked forward to reading and learning more about things that interested him.

Electricity was especially fascinating to Franklin. A few people had done experiments with static electricity, but very little about it was understood. Even among educated people, the sparks and shocks caused by electricity were frightening. To the uneducated, they seemed magical.

Franklin bought equipment with which he could duplicate some of the experiments he had witnessed by visiting lecturers. For months afterwards, he later wrote, he was engrossed in a way he had never before imagined:

> I never was before engaged in any study that so totally engrossed my attention . . . for what with making experiments when I can be alone, and repeating them to my friends and acquaintances who, from the novelty of the thing, come continually to see them, I have during some months past had little leisure time for anything else."[14]

HIS OWN EXPERIMENTS

He eventually tired of merely repeating the experiments of others and set to work on some of his own. As usual, Franklin was eager to understand what made things work and was able to answer questions that other researchers in the new field had not even asked yet. It was Franklin who discovered the existence of positive and negative charges and who first explained how a condenser worked. It was Franklin, in fact, who was responsible for much of the vocabulary of electricity: condenser, conductor, battery, and electric shock.

His most well known experiment was, of course, with lightning. A terrifying, mysterious force to people in the eighteenth century, lightning seemed to Franklin to be electricity. His method of proving it was to draw lightning to a long iron rod during a storm. Once the rod was struck by lightning, Franklin's assistant ran to the base of the rod and touched it with an electrical condenser. The bluish-white glow of electricity being conducted from the rod to the condenser was proof that Franklin was correct.

Once he understood lightning, Franklin, in his usual way, went looking for a practical use for his knowledge. One was the lightning rod. By attaching a tall metal rod to a building, and then connecting a wire from the rod to the ground, people would no longer have to fear that the lightning would burn their homes and stores to the ground. Instead, the lightning's charge would be carried harmlessly to the ground.

Lightning rods were erected on church steeples, barns, houses high on hills, and even on the masts of tall ships. And from cities all around the world came letters of praise and thanks to the scientist who had lessened lightning's terrible threat.

TAKING UP POLITICS

Of course, Franklin contributed dozens of other inventions, too—bifocal glasses, the energy-efficient Franklin stove, and the odometer, among others. But an age of political turmoil was fast approaching, and Franklin soon would become a key player.

In 1754 there was trouble in the colonies. The on-again, off-again hostilities between England and France had flared into war, and the war spilled over into the American colonies. The French had strongholds throughout North America, including Pennsylvania. Fearing the loss of their profitable fur trade, the French were building forts and military outposts, ready to do battle with the English settlers. In addition, the French were calling on their Native American allies to wage brutal attacks on the settlers.

The British government feared the French and Indian alliance and urged representatives from the various colonies to meet and decide how best to handle French aggression. Held in Albany, New York, the meeting would include representatives from seven colonies. Since he had served as an assemblyman from Pennsylvania in the past, Franklin was chosen as a delegate to the Albany Congress.

AN IDEA AND A CARTOON

At the congress, Franklin pointed out to the other representatives that the colonies were at a distinct disadvantage against the French. There was no history of colonial cooperation, and disunited defenders could be easily defeated.

He had an idea for strengthening the colonies, based on a Native American union he had dealt with as an assemblyman in western Pennsylvania. There the six native tribes in the area had organized themselves into one large association, known as the Six Nations of the Iroquois.

Franklin proposed that the colonies join in a large federal government—the first time such an idea had ever been proposed in America. The government would be composed of all the colonies, said Franklin, but "within and under which government each colony may retain its present constitution."[15]

However, the colonies could not get along with each other well enough to do as Franklin proposed. The larger ones did not want to limit their power, while the small ones were worried about being swallowed up in the wishes of the larger ones. Irritated, Franklin created what was the first political cartoon ever for the *Gazette*—a sketch of a snake broken into eight pieces. Each was labeled with the name of a colony. The headline read, "Join or Die." It was an idea whose time had not yet arrived—unfortunately for those English settlers who were the objects of attack by the French.

A MISSION IN ENGLAND

Over the following months, grisly stories began surfacing about French raiders, together with their Indian allies, making bloody attacks on settlements on the Pennsylvania frontier. And as the war with the French and the Indians continued, the Pennsylvania assembly continued to raise taxes to pay for the defense of the colony, primarily levied on personal and real property. But the largest tax base for such revenue—the vast lands owned by the Penn family—remained off-limits.

William Penn had been given the colony by King Charles in 1660. Since that time, the Penns had been like absentee landlords, collecting rent on the millions of acres they owned. Penn's descendants now lived in England, and their colony was overseen by a royal governor.

After trying unsuccessfully several times to levy taxes on the Penns' land, the assembly sent Franklin to England in 1757 as an agent. He would talk with the Penns about changing the rules; the colony simply could not raise enough tax money without it.

Franklin was excited by the prospect of visiting England. Deborah did not wish to go, but their son, twenty-seven-year-old William, accompanied him. The couple's daughter, thirteen-year-old Sally, stayed at home with her mother.

FAILURE

But Franklin was not successful. The Penns knew him by reputation, and were angered by his work on tax reform. Even before Franklin arrived in London, Thomas Penn wrote to a friend, "Mr. Franklin's popularity is nothing here. . . . He will be looked very coldly upon by great people. . . . There are few of any consequence who have heard of his electrical experiments."[16]

When he arrived in London, Franklin was met with rudeness and hostility. The Penns met with him a few times, but were unwilling to discuss the tax issue. They instructed him to submit his proposal in writing and then took more than two years to answer it. Finally, however, a compromise was worked out, although it was a sorry one. A small portion of the Penn land could be taxed, but only at the lowest possible rate. He would have very little good news to share with the assembly when he returned.

On the other hand, there was much about Britain that Franklin loved. He had made interesting friends, and looked up relatives from both his and Deborah's families. He even enrolled William in an English law school. But most of all, Franklin enjoyed the activity and intellectual excitement of London. "Why . . . should that little island [Great Britain] enjoy in almost every neighborhood," he wrote to an English friend, "more sensible, virtuous, and elegant minds, than we can collect in ranging one hundred leagues of our vast forests?"[17]

THE STAMP ACT

In 1764 Franklin was asked to return to England as an agent. This time, he was to meet with the British government to request an end to the proprietary government they had with the Penns. This time he would say good-bye to Deborah for the last time. He would be gone more than ten years; she would die before he returned.

His requests to the British government were put on hold, however; almost immediately more pressing business arose. The problem was Britain's lack of funds. Waging war against the French in America was draining huge sums of money from the royal treasury.

To raise money, British politicians proposed a new tax on the colonists, called the Stamp Act. It required that a special seal, or stamp, be affixed to all official documents, diplomas, and licenses, even playing cards. The stamp added an extra cost to the item, ranging from a few pennies to several pounds. In all, fifty-five items commonly purchased in the colonies would require such stamps.

Franklin knew the colonists would object to yet another tax by the British government, and tried to intervene. He was unsuccessful, however, and the Stamp Act became law in 1765. He then turned his attention to the colonies and wrote them, advising acceptance and calm. To one Philadelphia friend, he wrote: "A firm loyalty to the Crown and faithful adherence to the government of this nation, which it is the safety as well as the honor of the colonies to be connected with, will always be the wiser course for you and I to take."[18]

FROM GOAT TO HERO

Franklin underestimated the colonists' reaction, however. In several cities there were riots and angry demonstrations. And because Franklin had not openly denounced the tax, a great deal of anger was aimed at him. He was called a traitor, and a mob in Philadelphia threatened to storm his house.

Now Franklin understood the depth of the colonists' frustration and set to work trying to get the law repealed. Addressing the British House of Commons, he argued that the Stamp Act would do nothing except cause hostility. He also reminded Parliament that the colonists were more than willing to boycott British goods if they were pushed hard enough.

Franklin's efforts were successful, and the Stamp Act was repealed in February 1766. Throughout the colonies people cheered his name, drinking toasts to his diplomatic genius and brave spirit. In Britain, however, Franklin was far from euphoric over his "victory." He knew that the tax was not really the issue. The British government still maintained it had the unlimited right to tax the colonies, even though they had no representation in Parliament. That was the issue that had not been solved.

"SO MANY INATTENTIVE HEADS"

Franklin wanted to return to Philadelphia, but the assembly asked him to stay on. Other issues needed a colonial advocate in Britain, and as a figure of some status in England, Franklin was the perfect choice. In fact, he was asked by three other colonies—Massachusetts, Georgia, and New Jersey—to be their agent in London, too.

Franklin agreed, but soon found himself wondering if his work was even useful. New British demands—such as the Quartering Act, which required the colonies to house and pay for the expenses of a British standing army in America—were met with fury on the part of the colonists. And Franklin's attempts to dissuade the British from such measures fell on deaf ears. In a letter to his son William, he wrote, "I am weary of suggesting [ideas] to so many inattentive heads, though I must do it while I am among them."[19]

He wrote some tongue-in-cheek letters to the London newspaper editorial pages—under an assumed identity, as he had done in years past—but his attempts at getting the British to understand the colonists were largely unsuccessful. By 1774 the fragile relationship he had been trying to maintain between himself and the British government had been utterly destroyed.

THE HUTCHINSON LETTERS

The cause was a group of letters that had come into Franklin's possession while in England. The letters had been written to a British official by Thomas Hutchinson, the royal governor of Massachusetts. In the letters, Hutchinson maintained that the colonists had too much freedom, and he called for "an abridgement of what is called English liberty."[20]

Furious that an American would be collaborating with the British against his fellow Americans, Franklin sent the letters to Samuel Adams and other colonial activists. His hope was that the colonists would realize that it was not just the British who were the villains. Franklin also intended to present a petition to the British government from the people of Massachusetts to remove Hutchinson.

But before that petition could be considered, word arrived in Britain of a rebellious "tea party" in Boston Harbor in 1773.

Angered by more British restrictions, a group of colonists calling themselves the Sons of Liberty stormed onto British cargo ships in the middle of the night. The ships held crates of tea, which Britain ordered the colonies to pay taxes on. Rather than accept the burden of a new tax, the colonists dumped the tea overboard into the waters of Boston Harbor.

A POWDER KEG

As supportive of the colonies' rights as he had been, Franklin outspokenly criticized the Boston Tea Party. He worried that it would make reconciliation and compromise that much more difficult. He even offered to pay for the tea himself, on one condition: He demanded that Parliament repeal some of its strict new laws against the colonists. The British government was not interested.

But Franklin's good standing in Britain would soon come to an end. It was learned that upon receiving the Hutchinson letters, colonial leaders published them in the *Boston Gazette* for all the colonists to see. The reaction throughout America was one of outraged betrayal. John Adams, one of the colonial leaders, wrote in his diary about Hutchinson, "Cool, thinking, deliberate villain. Born of our bone, born and educated among us . . . vile serpent."[21]

The British were furious, too—but at Franklin. Called before Britain's elite Privy Council and barred from speaking, Franklin was mocked and humiliated. One lawyer pounded his fists on the table and screamed at Franklin for sharing the letters with the colonists. "I hope, my lords," he shouted, "you will mark and brand this man for the honor of this country, of Europe, and of mankind. . . . He has forfeited all the respect of societies and men."[22]

A BLEAK TIME

Franklin was finished in England; stripped of his position as deputy postmaster of the colonies, he sailed back to America early in 1775. Before arriving home, he learned of Deborah's death; that blow and his dashed hope of reconciling Britain and American differences left Franklin in despair.

But there was much to do back in Philadelphia; historians agree that the work of the colonies must have helped him deal with his grief. Indeed, a great deal of work seemed to require Franklin's touch. Ultimately, it is hard to overstate Franklin's role in the American Revolution.

He was unanimously chosen to represent Pennsylvania in the Second Continental Congress, a body formed from individual colonial assemblies. He was asked to be one of three commissioners who would meet with Canadian officials to gain their support for a colonial revolution. He designed paper currency for use in all the colonies, and worked with John Adams and Thomas Jefferson in creating the Great Seal, to be used on all official American documents. Franklin even met with General George Washington to help plan the new Continental army.

He also served as the sole editor of the Declaration of Independence. Franklin might well have been assigned to write the document, but his own sense of humor prevented that. Thomas Jefferson, who wrote the document in 1776, mentioned in his diary that the only reason Franklin was not asked to write the document was that nobody could trust him not to put a joke in it.

But while many in the Continental Congress relished his wisdom and admired his humor and energy, others were peeved by his popularity. John Adams complained in his diary that Franklin's role in the Revolution was bound to be exaggerated, telling the story that "Franklin's electrical rod smote the earth and out sprang George Washington. . . . Franklin electrified him with his rod—and thenceforth these two conducted all the policy negotiations, legislatures, and war."[23]

"AMONG THE POWDERED HEADS OF PARIS"

Without a doubt the most time-consuming aspect of Franklin's work during the Revolutionary War was enlisting the aid of France. The Continental Congress was well aware that without outside help, the colonies could not afford to maintain troops in a long war. The French government, a longtime enemy of Britain, was America's best bet. At age seventy, Franklin was once more enlisted to sail to Europe.

His was a difficult diplomatic mission, for while the defeat of Britain would please France, its foreign minister, Comte de Vergennes, wanted some assurance that the colonists had a good chance of winning the war. If they lost, and France was known to have helped their cause, Britain would quickly turn on the French. Franklin met regularly with Vergennes, reassuring him and reminding the minister of how valuable a trading partner America would be once the colonies were free of British restrictions.

A lady of the French court teases Benjamin Franklin for not wearing a powdered wig.

Franklin at first felt somewhat self-conscious about his appearance, for while the French diplomats dressed very elegantly, he arrived for his meetings dressed in his everyday drab coat. "Figure me in your mind as jolly as formerly," he wrote to a friend, "and as strong and hearty, only a few years older; very plainly dressed, wearing my thin, gray, straight hair that peeps out under . . . a fine fur cap, which comes down my forehead almost to my spectacles. Think how this must appear among the powdered heads of Paris!"[24]

But his appearance actually worked to his advantage, its eccentricity endearing to the French people. Franklin was adored by the French; they gathered outside his rooms, hoping to catch a glimpse of him or touch his coat. His fur hat became a sort of symbol of the odd but charming American. Throughout the country, pictures of Franklin adorned shop shelves. On snuff boxes, rings, medallions, plates, statues—everywhere was the image of Benjamin Franklin. His face had become, he joked, "as familiar as the Moon."[25]

"I FIND MYSELF HARNESSED AGAIN"

Franklin was able to secure an alliance with France, and French aid to the colonists was crucial in keeping the Continental army fighting. After the British were defeated, Franklin stayed in France to assist in hammering out the Treaty of Paris. On September 3, 1783, it was signed, granting America freedom and independence.

When Franklin at last returned to Philadelphia—to a free land that was no longer a British colony—he was tired. A bladder stone left him in constant discomfort, and age made him frail. Even so, he was recruited into service again in his hometown, this time as both a council member of the state's new legislature and a member of the Constitutional Convention. Although a part of him might have been flattered, Franklin seemed disgusted in a letter he wrote in 1785. "I find myself harnessed again in service for another year. They have eaten my flesh, and seem resolved to pick my bones."[26]

The greatest problem faced by the new nation was in getting the new states to work together. Each was acting more like a small independent nation than as a part of a whole. Franklin remained optimistic, but at times during the convention distrust and squabbling seemed to take over. Though the delegates eventually hammered out a plan for a federal government, few were happy with it; each delegate felt that somehow his state's interest had been sacrificed.

On the day the Constitution was to be ratified, Franklin asked to take the floor, a request he was by nature reluctant to make. Stoop-shouldered and pale, he stood and handed his written speech to a fellow delegate, who read it to the assembly. In the speech, Franklin urged them to put aside their egos and take the broader view. The document may not be perfect, he said, but it was as perfect as it could be with so many different viewpoints represented.

"On the whole," wrote Franklin, "I cannot help expressing a wish that every member of the convention who may still have objections to it would, with me, on this occasion doubt a little of his own infallibility, and, to make manifest our unanimity, put his name to the instrument."[27]

The words had their desired effect; the Constitution was accepted and signed. Best of all, Franklin knew he could finally go home.

WITHOUT BENJAMIN FRANKLIN

Benjamin Franklin lived for two years after the convention. He spent time with his grandchildren and wrote letters to old friends in Europe and America. He enjoyed reading newspaper accounts of current issues, especially engaged by the controversy over slavery. As his health and strength deteriorated, on April 17, 1790, Franklin lapsed into a coma and died.

Historian Carl Van Doren writes that the moment a great person dies, another story begins—that of "his continuing influence, his changing renown, the legend which takes the place of fact."[28]

Franklin's genius needs no exaggeration. But a simple list of his many accomplishments does not do justice to the value of Benjamin Franklin's life. He was more than the visible contributions he left behind. He was a statesman, a philosopher, a scientist, a writer, a public servant, a diplomat—in a world that would have respected him for excelling at any of these, he excelled at all of them.

Without him, say historians, the alliance with France that contributed to American independence would not have occurred. And without the alliance guaranteeing French support, the Continental army quite probably would have been defeated. In addition, his many discoveries and inventions were another legacy to future generations.

A Personal Tang

Some students of history maintain that Franklin's most important contribution was a model of a life well lived. "In any age, in any place," writes biographer Van Doren, "Franklin would have been great."[29] His ability to think outside the boundaries of his personal world, to remember that he was a member of a larger community, made him unselfish with his energy.

Franklin's time was rich in creative and innovative personalities. Within his circle of acquaintances alone are figures well known as patriots and strong leaders, such as George Washington, Thomas Jefferson, and John Adams. Yet in his style, Franklin stands alone.

He was more than a generation older than the other founding fathers, but it has been said that of all of them, Franklin is the only one whose name elicits a smile. He had what Van Doren calls a "personal tang," a spirit of constant optimism and humor that set the rules he lived by. Such a spirit allowed Benjamin Franklin to move through his many worlds with grace.

NOTES

1. Benjamin Franklin, *The Autobiography of Benjamin Franklin.* Notes by R. Jackson Wilson. New York: Modern Library, 1981.
2. Quoted in Ronald W. Clark, *Benjamin Franklin.* New York: Random House, 1983.
3. Franklin, *The Autobiography.*
4. Franklin, *The Autobiography.*
5. Franklin, *The Autobiography.*
6. Quoted in Clark, *Benjamin Franklin.*
7. Quoted in Clark, *Benjamin Franklin.*
8. Quoted in Catherine Drinker Bowen, *The Most Dangerous Man in America.* Boston: Little, Brown, 1974.
9. Quoted in Esmond Wright, *Franklin of Philadelphia.* Cambridge, MA: Harvard University Press, 1968.
10. Quoted in Carl Van Doren, *Benjamin Franklin.* New York: Viking Press, 1938.
11. Franklin, *The Autobiography.*
12. *Poor Richard's Almanack,* quoted in Wright, *Franklin of Philadelphia.*
13. Franklin, *The Autobiography.*
14. Letter to Peter Collinson, quoted in Milton Meltzer, *Benjamin Franklin: The New American.* New York: Franklin Watts, 1988.
15. *Pennsylvania Gazette,* May 9, 1751, quoted in Andrew Allison, ed., *The Real Benjamin Franklin.* Salt Lake City: Freeman Institute, 1982.
16. Letter to Richard Peters, May 14, 1757, quoted in Van Doren, *Benjamin Franklin.*
17. Letter to Mary Stevenson, March 25, 1763, quoted in Allison, *The Real Benjamin Franklin.*
18. Letter to John Hughes, August 8, 1765, quoted in Van Doren, *Benjamin Franklin.*
19. Letter to William Franklin, March 13, 1768, quoted in Van Doren, *Benjamin Franklin.*
20. Quoted in Alice Hall, "Philosopher of Dissent: Benjamin Franklin," *National Geographic,* July 1975.
21. Quoted in Bowen, *The Most Dangerous Man in America.*
22. Quoted in Frank Donovan, *The Benjamin Franklin Papers.* New York: Dodd, Mead, 1962.
23. Quoted in Frank Donovan, *The Many Worlds of Benjamin Franklin.* Mahwah, NJ: Troll, 1963.
24. Letter to Mrs. Thompson, February 8, 1777, quoted in Van Doren, *Benjamin Franklin.*

25. Letter to Jane Mecom, October 25, 1779, quoted in Van Doren, *Benjamin Franklin.*

26. Letter to Dr. and Mrs. John Bard, November 14, 1785, quoted in Van Doren, *Benjamin Franklin.*

27. Franklin, *The Autobiography.*

28. Van Doren, *Benjamin Franklin.*

29. Van Doren, *Benjamin Franklin.*

CHAPTER 1

Influences and Ideals

BENJAMIN FRANKLIN

Influences, Opportunities, and Rebellion: How Benjamin Franklin Got His Start

Claude-Anne Lopez and Eugenia W. Herbert

Like many early immigrants, Benjamin Franklin's father, Josiah, came to America searching for religious freedom. A pious man, Josiah Franklin had intended for his tenth and youngest son, Benjamin, to become a minister to the church. However, Josiah soon abandoned this plan and put Benjamin to work in his candle shop. Franklin historian, researcher, and former editor of Yale's Benjamin Franklin Papers, Claude-Anne Lopez along with Eugenia W. Herbert, the E. Nevius Rodman Professor of History Emeritus at Mount Holyoke College, suggest that Josiah did little to encourage his son's intellectual development, and that it was Josiah's brother, Benjamin, who had the greater influence on young Franklin's personal growth.

Benjamin hated working for Josiah. Much effort was given to find a new suitable occupation for young Benjamin, and he was eventually apprenticed to his brother James who ran a print shop in Boston. Although Benjamin would paint a negative picture of his brother as abusive, he did eventually regret this early opinion he held of his brother. After all, it was James's print shop where Benjamin's career began. Of course Benjamin was far from complacent, so, when the opportunity presented itself, Benjamin ran away to Philadelphia.

Josiah Franklin, Benjamin's father, had come to America in 1683 in search of religious freedom. A convert to nonconformism, he had left his native village of Ecton in Northamptonshire rather than submit to the beliefs and practices of the Church of England. Still in his twenties when he landed in Boston, Josiah quickly found that Massachusetts had little use for his skills as a silk dyer and turned to making candles and soap, for which there was considerably more demand. If he did not exactly prosper, at least he managed. His family grew fast, too fast. Three children had come over from England; two more were born soon after the arrival in America. Nowhere is the mother's name mentioned, nowhere except on her tombstone modestly tucked away to the side of that of her more durable successor. There lies "Ann Franclin, aged about 34 years.". . .

Five months after losing his wife, Josiah married again, this time a strong native girl hailing from Nantucket, Abiah Folger. She raised Ann's five surviving children, gave her husband ten more, and lived well into her eighties, never sick a day until her final illness. Of her own brood, four girls and six boys, the youngest son was Benjamin, born January 6, 1706 (to become January 17 after the calendar reform in mid-century).

BEN, THE YOUNGEST SON, IS A LEARNER AND A LEADER

Boston was seventy-six years old, Harvard College was seventy. The epic era of settling and struggling, of casting out the heretic, of hating and killing for the survival of soul and body, was over. No serious war had been fought with the Indians for the last thirty years. The witches' trials in Salem were receding into the past. A new century (which he would span almost in its entirety), the first stirrings of a more tolerant spirit, the first newspaper on the continent, those were the gifts around the cradle of Josiah Franklin's fifteenth child.

In a society where the privileges of seniority were firmly rooted, being the youngest son, the one who had to defer to the others, to obey, to pick whatever trade had not already been pre-empted, must have been galling to an eager and self-assertive boy. Luckily, he was not absolutely at the tail end of the family. Two brothers who immediately preceded him had died in infancy: one at three, the other . . . at the age of sixteen months. . . . Thus Benjamin was in effect the oldest child of the last cluster of three, made up of himself and two younger sisters who looked up to him and contributed to the self-confidence that was to be one of his prime assets.

The earliest stories he tells about himself are stories of proficiency. He was the one to whom his fellows turned in moments of crisis when they were out in their boats. He also was the one who led the others into scrapes, the one who organized the neighborhood boys into building a wharf out of stolen stones, with the result that most of them got soundly "corrected." The immediate moral of this anecdote, of course, is that one should not steal, as Josiah pointed out, not even for a useful purpose; but what Franklin is also saying is that at the age of ten he was already a leader of men.

He was a proud child, determined never to be made fun of twice for the same mistake. One day, he was given a little money to buy whatever he wished. On his way to the shop he met an older boy blowing a whistle. Charmed by this marvel, he bought it for all the coins in his pocket. When he got home and exasperated everybody with his shrill whistling, he was teased by one and all for having paid such an exorbitant price for a silly object, a lesson he never forgot. Spending your money unwisely not only makes you look foolish but it is wrong. The goods of this world, said the Puritan catechism, are a divine trust, to be administered to best advantage by human stewards. . . .

Even though several of the older siblings had already married and left home by the time Benjamin was growing up, the Franklin house on Union Street, at the sign of the Blue Ball, was crowded. Thirteen members of the family sat around the table in celebration when brother Josiah, a seaman, returned from the East Indies after an absence of nine years, only to go off again and disappear forever. The children were never allowed to take notice of what was served: Franklin professed to have found this culinary indifference a great asset in later life, but the number of recipes in his own hand found among his papers and the evident delight he took in French food belie that Spartan self-image. In order to have the young people benefit from intelligent conversation, his father would often invite some well-educated acquaintance to share their supper. As a man of recognized good sense, he in turn was frequently consulted by leading people on affairs of church and town. . . .

A RELIGIOUS FUTURE . . . UNTIL UNCLE BENJAMIN ARRIVES

A new wave of English immigration combined with natural increase to stimulate the rapid growth of Boston, from six thousand inhabitants in 1700 to twelve thousand some twenty years later. To many, the town's harsh living conditions seemed better than life in London with its inflationary prices and low wages, its cramped housing, its air full of soot, its chaotic traffic, its want of social mobility. Old Bostonians resented the recent settlers, fearing that new-fangled ideas might dilute and corrupt their own strict Puritanism. For all its sinfulness, they still considered Boston the closest thing to the New Jerusalem, the "city on the hill." Although churches of various denominations competed for the direction of souls, Congregationalism kept its hold on the civil as well as the religious life of the town.

The Franklin children were raised "piously in the Dissenting Way," [Franklin notes in the *Autobiography*] according to the very simple practices of the Congregational Church. An austere and egalitarian creed, without hierarchy, vestments, pomp, or ritual, Puritan Congregationalism recognized only two kinds of people: the "visible saints," who had received signs of their sanctity, thus earning admission into church membership—and everybody else. Even the "saints" could not be positively sure of salvation, but the others had a fairly certain prospect of damnation. Benjamin's father and mother became full-fledged members of the Old South Church soon after his birth, thereby joining the religious élite. They often opened up their house to prayer meetings, and Josiah's library was made up exclusively of works dealing with theology. These books would have been useful to Benjamin if his father had carried out his original intention of devoting his tenth son to the church as the tithe [the tenth portion, to be given to the church] of his male offspring. . . .

The most memorable event of Benjamin's childhood was the arrival from England of his Uncle Benjamin, who had lost his wife and decided to end his days in the New World. Josiah and Uncle Benjamin had been each other's favorite brother and had corresponded for over thirty years with little hope of meeting again. But when they were reunited and lived under the same roof, they found it hard to get along. By the time Uncle Benjamin arrived in 1715, he was too old to switch from silk dyeing to a new craft; he just hung around the house, spending his time in ways that were exasperating to his brother, delightful to his nephew. He had invented a short-hand system for taking down sermons, a pastime he much enjoyed, now justified by the necessity of storing up a large collection against the day when his namesake would become a minister. He told the younger Benjamin many family stories, especially the one about their ancestor who in the days of religious persecution had concealed a Protestant Bible by taping it under a stool, to be quickly turned over in cases of emergency. Pleasant as it was to have an old uncle around with so much time on his hands, Benjamin was to remember for the rest of his life his father's growing irritation. . . .

Annoyance with his brother's idleness may have provoked an anti-intellectual reaction in Josiah. Benjamin at eight had risen to the head of the class, yet his father withdrew him from grammar school after one year, declaring that in view of his large family a college education was more than he could afford for his son; many educated people never earned more than a "mean living" anyway. All thoughts of an ecclesiastical future were abandoned, and he was switched to a more down-to-earth type of school. He studied there for one year more, doing very well in writing, quite poorly in arithmetic. Those two years of formal education were the only ones he was ever to receive. At ten he was put to work in his father's shop, cutting wicks, dipping molds, running errands. He hated it. He wanted to go to sea, but his father would not hear of it.

A lucky man, Josiah. He played what looks like a dampening role in his son's life, saying no to just about everything, yet he has been portrayed for posterity in glowing colors. When Benjamin was doing well in school, his father took him out. When the boy, his distaste for candlemaking now obvious to all, was apprenticed to a cutler, his father called him home again rather than pay the fee. When Benjamin at thirteen composed verse and hawked his ballads on the streets with some success—another echo of his wool-gathering Uncle Benjamin?—his father told him bluntly that his poetry was awful. When Benjamin, at eighteen, tried to borrow some parental money to set himself up in business under the sponsorship of the governor of Pennsylvania, his father flatly refused to lend him a farthing.

ALTERED MEMORIES OF A FATHER AND A BROTHER

Nonpermissive, nonsupportive as he appears to modern eyes, this father shone in his son's memory as a wise and wonderful person. Was it because the son, in turn, was writing for his own son and wanted to establish that father knows best? Did he feel that his father had intended to toughen him for life? Franklin seems to look back on Josiah as a preview of himself—a stifled preview, to be sure, bogged down by near poverty and a huge family, but endowed with many of the qualities that would, in his own case, be allowed to soar. Well set and strong (so was Benjamin), ingenious (so was Benjamin), Josiah [as noted in the *Autobiography*] "could draw prettily, was skill'd a little in Music and had a clear and pleasing Voice, so that when he play'd Psalm Tunes on his Violin and sung withal as he sometimes did in an Evening after the Business of the Day was over, it was extremely agreeable to hear." In Benjamin's life, too, music would play its part. Josiah, furthermore, "had a mechanical Genius" and was very handy in the use of other tradesmen's tools, another proud bond between the generations. "Be encouraged to Diligence in thy Calling" reads the inscription composed for Josiah's tombstone. "Diligence in thy Calling" are the very words of Solomon that his father so often quoted: "Seest thou a Man diligent in his Calling, he shall stand before Kings, he shall not stand before mean Men" *(Proverbs 22:29)*. Benjamin turned this into prophecy: In the course of his life he would stand before four kings—George II and George III of England, Louis XV and Louis XVI of France—and sit down to dinner with a fifth, Christian VII of Denmark.

Having cast his father as a hero, Franklin quite unfairly cast his brother James as a villain. Nine years his senior, James had been away in England learning the printer's trade while Benjamin was growing up. He returned to Boston just when the family did not know what to do with Benjamin: The boy was not attracted to any of the trades proposed, not that of joiner, or bricklayer, or turner, or brazier. Josiah would have preferred each of his sons to embrace a different profession, but he finally yielded to this one's bookish inclinations and apprenticed him to James at the age of twelve.

The contract to which Benjamin reluctantly put his signature—he was still dreaming of the sea—was stringent but standard for the times. What, one wonders, was an apprentice allowed to do besides work and worship? He pledged to obey his master, keep his master's secrets, refrain from fornication or matrimony, stay away from cards and dice, never haunt alehouses, taverns, or playhouses, never absent himself day or night without leave. For all this, he was dressed and boarded, and received one good suit at the expiration of the contract.

James has gone down in history as the bully who beat his little brother out of jealousy over his greater gifts. He is depicted as the vindictive master who prevented his unhappy apprentice from finding any other employer in town, thus forcing him to flee his native city at seventeen. And when Benjamin, as "saucy and provoking" as only a younger sibling can be, reappeared in Boston after a seven-month absence, his pockets lined with silver, flaunting a new watch and . . . grandly buying his former fellow workers a drink, James is shown as sullen and resentful, silently staring at him, and then turning back to his work and telling their mother he would never forgive this last offense. Later, much later, Benjamin would admit that his behavior toward James had been his first great error. Eventually they were reconciled, and when James, still in his thirties, felt that his end was near, he asked Benjamin to raise his little son Jemmy. . . .

In truth, James was the powerful liberating force in his brother's life. It was he who opened up to Benjamin the world of words, of books, of ideas: not their father's books on divinity nor his ideas circumscribed by prudence, but London's ideas, those of the *Spectator* and the *Tatler,* witty and satirical, systematically in the opposition. James's tutelage brought Benjamin his first heady taste of challenging authority. The rebel in him which would one day defy the rule of the Penns [Pennsylvania's Founders], the sovereignty of the king, and the terror of lightning, had taken his initial steps in the brother's printing shop, not amid the father's candles.

EXCITEMENT SURROUNDS THE PRINTING PROFESSION, THE APPRENTICE RUNS AWAY

The printing shop was the meeting place of a lively group of young men seething with joyfully irreverent views. With their help James launched the *New England Courant* (1721), the fourth newspaper to be printed in America. More than a means of disseminating the news, he meant it to be a mouthpiece for those who presumed, without benefit of pulpit, to comment on the state of the commonweal and the foibles of their fellow citizens. The two Boston newspapers already publishing were anything but glad to see the advent of the *Courant*, especially since it denounced them as dull and dreary. . . . The clergy, the magistrates, the postmaster, Harvard, the rich and powerful, the whole Massachusetts establishment was considered fair game. . . .

For a sixteen year old in the process of shedding the beliefs of early childhood . . . all this irreverence and uproar was huge fun. Benjamin was dying to join the fray. He felt he had mastered the style of the *Courant's* writing staff. His arduous process of self-education was beginning to pay off. . . .

But James was soon in trouble himself. In June 1722, his paper insinuated that the Massachusetts authorities were not trying hard enough to capture a pirate vessel off the coast. This charge was considered a "high Affront" and James was sent to jail. Benjamin managed the paper efficiently in his absence. Some fifty years later he remembered with glee [recorded in his autobiography] that he had "made bold to give our Rulers some Rubs in it, which my Brother took very kindly, while others began to consider me . . . as a young Genius that had a Turn for Libelling and Satyr." Josiah and Abiah must have shuddered more than once at the boldness of these two, their youngest and brightest sons.

James, who seems to have been under some compulsion to get himself arrested and rearrested, was eventually forbidden to print or publish his paper, or any other paper or pamphlet, without previous authorization from the Secretary of the Province. To circumvent this difficulty, he made Benjamin the nominal publisher of the *Courant*—which implied, of course, a rescinding of the indenture contract. Benjamin knew very well this was only a ruse to fool the authorities, and, in fact, had secretly signed a new indenture to James for the rest of his term, but he wanted to take advantage of the subterfuge and win his freedom at once. He had tasted independence, he had savored leadership, he was seventeen and in full rebellion. . . .

Benjamin's rebellion was above all against the stifling atmosphere of Boston, where his "indiscrete Disputations about Religion" [he writes in his autobiography] had already begun to make him "pointed at with good people as an infidel or Atheist."

His lifelong fight against "arbitrary power" began right there. In defiance of father, brother, and contract, he ran away, all the way to Philadelphia. Here he landed in a state of exhaustion, dirty, disheveled, almost penniless, happy. Within a few hours, he had met his future wife. Within a few days, he had found work. Within a few weeks, the fugitive, forever anxious lest his shabby clothes, his hunger betray him to the town fathers, had become the prototype of the American boy whose chief asset is self-reliance.

Autobiography and Self-Knowledge in the Age of Enlightenment

Ormond Seavey

In this excerpt from his biography of Benjamin
Franklin, Ormond Seavey considers popular ideas
and writing conventions from the period known as
the Age of Enlightenment—also known as the Age of
Reason—in regard to Franklin and the genre of autobiography. One of the most important of these ideas
is the development and understanding of the self,
specifically in relation to the physical universe. The
original concept of "know thyself" heralds from ancient Greece and found a new audience during the
eighteenth-century Enlightenment, where it evolved
into a self-knowledge beyond the original self-
awareness found in the Greek version. This new idea
of knowing the self is deeply embedded in Franklin's
Autobiography.

Seavey, an American literature professor at George
Washington University, highlights the important role of
the writer during Franklin's time, noting that occasionally
the act of writing was more highly regarded than the content the writer produced. Franklin himself was first and
foremost a writer. He was, of course, many things, but
whatever he did he wrote about it, intent on sharing his
writing with others—another popular ideal of the Age of
Enlightenment.

Nowhere in the *Autobiography* does Franklin appear to be a
mystery to himself. Others are self-deceived or unaware of
their real interest, like his friend James Ralph, who fancied
himself a poet, or the Quakers, who could not square the
need for colonial defenses with their doctrinal prohibitions.
Franklin is only deceived by others, never by himself. . . .

Excerpted from "The Self-Made Man in the Enlightenment," in *Becoming Benjamin
Franklin: The Autobiography of His Life,* by Ormond Seavey. Copyright © 1988 The
Pennsylvania State University Press. Reprinted by permission of the author.

THE ENLIGHTENMENT PLACES SELF-KNOWLEDGE ABOVE SELF-AWARENESS

Just as Franklin felt he understood himself better than his associates understood themselves, the Enlightenment claimed to have made a breakthrough in the ancient effort [of the Greeks] to know ourselves. . . . Self-knowledge, as it appears in the eighteenth century, implies both a self greatly more knowable and also a more sustained period of knowing. Franklin's nature or fate is never suddenly revealed to him; his personality is known continuously over the uninterrupted course of his life. No moment of transcendent insight is ever called upon to clarify what has always been out in the open.

The two modes of self-consciousness [self-awareness and self-knowledge] differ importantly in the way they assess the differences that can be observed in the self over time. Personality as revealed by self-awareness is continually changing, but it could not be said to be developing and evolving in a series of stages. . . . Self-awareness readily accompanied an older theory of personality formation, according to which character is understandable in terms of certain ideal modes of behavior. In the Middle Ages and the Renaissance, qualities like courtesy, chastity, and courage manifested themselves, in life as in allegory, as personalities. Character was achieved through a process of imitation, by which a man conformed to a fixed and preexisting standard of conduct. . . .

It might be said that self-awareness is appropriate to souls, while self-knowledge applies to selves. The words are used in quite different contexts: a soul is given to one; a self is what one becomes. Unlike souls, selves are the products of their accumulated experiences. Franklin is not on the way to recognizing and accepting some preexisting identity; his identity is with him all along, and the act of writing the *Autobiography* affirms the continuity of his attitudes and responses. Self-knowledge involves embracing childhood as the first origins of the self; it assumes that personality is formed by development. In place of the dramatic possibilities made available by self-awareness, self-knowledge organized life narratively, in the manner of novels or autobiographies. The two modes, seemingly akin, are actually the reverse of each other. The instant of self-awareness separates one from society. One feels different from others, incomprehensible except to oneself. Self-consciousness, though, associates one with others in patterns of relationship consciously arrived at or recognized.

The two processes also relate to different stages of maturity. Self-awareness is the mark of freedom from adolescence, from the anxieties of dependence upon acceptance by others. Self-consciousness comes with the acceptance of ties with others, the acknowledgement that one can be simultaneously aware of oneself and of the social world. Along with its described evolution from poverty to affluence, Franklin's *Autobiography* depicts a progress from the isolated, self-assertive, doctrinaire young Franklin to an older Franklin who thrived on voluntary ties with others. The progression is like that described in [the English poet William] Wordsworth's *Tintern Abbey*, from the period of utter absorption in the sensations inspired by nature to the time when "the still, sad music of humanity" colors one's perceptions of the world.

The Enlightenment tended to believe that the self was not confused and disordered but complex and, finally, comprehensible. . . . Where the man of the Renaissance had seen inner confusion, the man of the Enlightenment saw an ordered complex not yet fully understood. The novel was credited as a breakthrough in depicting personal character. . . . When Franklin indicates his awareness of novelistic technique in the description of his Philadelphia journey [in the first part of the *Autobiography*], he is registering his awareness of how fully selves were known in his time.

SELF-MASTERY AS AN EXAMPLE TO SHARE WITH OTHERS

Where greater self-knowledge seemed possible, it might also be possible to bring the recalcitrant self under firmer control. Franklin perceived his own life as a successful exercise in self-mastery, and he wrote the *Autobiography* in part as a sort of textbook example. Further along he seems to have conceived of his life story as an adjunct to a practical treatise on the achievement of virtue, to be called the *Art of Virtue*. Self-mastery, as Franklin and his contemporaries saw it, required adaptation and flexibility; it was a matter of precept rather than rule, and his own successful instances of self-mastery were meant to be adapted by his readers to suit their own circumstances. The modern reader may see Franklin's recollected life as an adventure, in particular the journey from Boston to Philadelphia, but Franklin is clear that it was also part of a plan, a design for his life which he became gradually more successful at recognizing and implementing. The modern reader may enjoy the moments of confusion and wonderment in Franklin's experience. His contemporaries saw in such episodes a further and more subtle level of self-mastery, a readiness to submit all his experiences to his own detached analysis to make it all, his whole life, public. . . .

Franklin and his contemporaries valued this disposition toward self-mastery for more than the pleasure of self-consciousness that it afforded. One mastered oneself for the sake of engagement with society. Where self-awareness tended to detach one from social bonds, self-knowledge required the active awareness of others, including not just one's friends but society at large. Pure narcissism, the eighteenth century believed, could never be the source of anything but delusions. . . . Franklin was not going off into the wilderness when he left Boston, and he chooses not to describe his experiences of solitariness. He seems to be continually among people, and he judges them in large part for their capacity to adapt to and serve society. . . . In Philadelphia, Samuel Keimer, Franklin's employer, became the perfect negative example of self-centered, religiously fanatical unsociability—an unsociability directly linked in Franklin's mind to his lack of self-control.

Society as Franklin conceived of it was comprised of varied individuals bound by no predetermined pattern. It was not, as the older models of social organization would have suggested, an organism or any other systematic arrangement of human functions. In the market place it is every man for himself. Franklin does not conform his life to a traditional function, nor does he expect others to. There is thus an unavoidable uniqueness in the lives that surround him, and his readers are expected to be similarly distinctive. The eighteenth century valued uniqueness of personality. [The Scottish lawyer and writer James] Boswell cultivated and even amplified Dr. [Samuel] Johnson's singularity as a deliberate part of his biographical technique [in *The Life of Samuel Johnson*, about the prolific English writer]. But distinctiveness and singularity were supposed to be reconcilable with a disposition to participate fully in society, and society was supposed to be the richer for the harmonious variety of which it was comprised. A Bostonian in Philadelphia, an American in England, Franklin never describes himself as deeply accepting or accepted in the societies in which he took part, but he insists regardless that he had found a place.

Despite the uniqueness of these eighteenth-century lives, it was supposed to be possible for such lives to have meaning and coherence as a whole. Since character represented a summation of gradually accumulated experience, the autobiographies of the eighteenth century tended to insist that all experiences counted. They tried to reject nothing. Franklin's impulse to include all that he remembered made his narrative run slower and slower by the time he wrote the last sections, but no principle of exclusion permitted him to abridge. . . .

This, then, is the cultural ideal available to Franklin as he was assembling his own self-portrait. It is a being without unconscious or uncontrollable desires. The emotions of such a self are exercised but kept in check. His relations to others and to the state are a series of limited transactions calculated to secure mutual benefit to all parties. He is what he is because of his development from childhood, and he is developing eventually toward some final, completed stage of maturity. He is a model of self-regulation and social responsibility. Though Franklin did not meet this description, he measures himself and expects to be judged by that standard. . . .

In some important sense Franklin wrote in response to the needs of his time. If he began the project in a moment of special well-being, he pursued it out of a sense that posterity and his contemporaries needed it. And he was not alone in feeling that the autobiography of such a person as he had been would be required. The Enlightenment called upon the exemplars of its preferred modes of consciousness to testify on their own behalf, to demonstrate that such lives were possible and efficacious in the world. New sorts of autobiography appeared in the eighteenth century in response to the new self-consciousness. This body of self-referential writing was expected to show that life was now more fully understood.

WRITING HELPS CREATE THE SELF

Certainly self-expression became more important in the eighteenth century than it had been before. The feeling that one must write, that a record of one's experiences would be of use to others, and even that others need one's writing became a significant cultural phenomenon. For [the English poet Alexander] Pope the world was filled with people frantic to write or obsessed with the effects of writing. The observation seems to have been more than just an obsessed poet's perception. Even Franklin, surely no strong candidate for the muse's garland, had to be warned away from poetry by his father, and he records in his *Autobiography* a significant number of characters driven by the desire to write and publish. The urge to express oneself began early in life. Pope lisped in numbers, he claims in the *Epistle to Dr. Arbuthnot*—that is, his earliest childhood speech took the form of heroic couplets—and though he was at pains to show himself a person as well as a poet, his life was given over utterly to writing. The chance for self-expression could utterly transform one's life, as it did for [the Swiss-born French writer Jean Jacques] Rousseau. His life had been without direction until he chanced to read the Dijon Academy prize question. "The moment I read this, I beheld a new universe and became another man," [he writes in his Confessions]. Finding a fit occasion for writing, he was reborn. In a sense, the eighteenth century believed, writing *creates* the self. Certainly Boswell thought so. His fragmented energies found both a corrective and a display in his journal. He would fret on days when nothing exciting could be found for it, as if it led a surrogate existence more valuable than his own. So important did the act of writing become in the Enlightenment that it seemed to take a logical priority over life itself, so that [the great English satirist Jonathon] Swift could describe the aftermath of his own death in *Verses on the Death of Dr. Swift.*

"Knowing oneself" for the writers of the eighteenth century no longer meant the recognition of one's limitations in a world incomprehensibly better ordered than one can grasp. Self-knowledge had become a complex and exacting study, leading to knowledge as genuine as any that one could have about the physical world. Self-study was necessary in a situation where the self had cut itself loose from a belief in an assured place in a divine plan and floated in society guided only by its own navigation. Such a self must be sure that, in some way, its inner life counts in the world. Autobiography, in this broadened sense, thus enacts a kind of miraculous incarnation: a person's thoughts, feelings, and ambitions can be seen to interact with the large world of action.

Self-expression in the Enlightenment did not serve merely the function of revealing the author's inner state. One's own writings, and not just those that were overtly self-descriptive, served as a mirror, revealing oneself and one's surroundings. But the mirror image could be subtly altered. The writer's relationship to it was not the stunned fascination of Narcissus but the considered appraisal of the self-portraitist. In the case of Franklin a long series of pseudonyms and poses could serve the ultimate purpose of revealing himself to the world. In the case of Boswell the act of recording his experiences daily gave some coherence and continuity to a life otherwise chaotic. Johnson encouraged Boswell's plan of keeping a journal. "I told Mr. Johnson," Boswell records [in his journal: *Boswell's London Journal*], "that I put down all sorts of little incidents in it. 'Sir,' said he, 'there is nothing too little for so little a creature as man. It is by studying little things that we attain the great knowledge of having as little misery and as much happiness as possible.'" People in the eighteenth century showed an unprecedented concern for the preservation of the details of their own and others' lives. To hold such details in consciousness was in some way a means of control.

The Enlightenment took an increased interest in the writer himself and in writing as a manifestation of personality. There is something fairly new about this interest; in an earlier age the survival of a writer's works was not supposed to depend upon his own limited character and circumstances. Though he was an intimate friend of Shakespeare, Ben Jonson says nothing of personality in his dedicatory poem in the First Folio. A little later in the seventeenth century, John Aubry and Izaak Walton produced some short biographies of English writers, evidence of a new interest. By the later eighteenth century, literary biography would be important enough to command the talents of Dr. Johnson, the period's most important man of letters. The fame of authorship could even lure a young provincial like James Ralph from so distant a place as Philadelphia; Franklin recalls with dismay the effect of this mania on his friend. (He himself found more subtle and effective means to that end.) . . . Literary fame meant both the reputation of one's own work and the lingering echo therein of one's own personality.

THE DANGER OF DISSOCIATION PROMOTES HISTORICAL BIOGRAPHY

It would be a mistake to assume that the new emphasis on self-study and self-expression emerged simply out of the race's growing wisdom. The satisfactions of self-consciousness were considerable, but certain severe cultural problems emerged simultaneously. Young Franklin on his way to Philadelphia had cut himself loose from family, place, and religion, but he was therefore adrift and, as he later felt, in danger of capsizing in the sea of open possibilities. Under the older paradigm of selfhood that he was leaving behind, no one was truly intelligible by himself, but everyone could feel secure in his place in universal history and the cosmos. . . .

But in the process of this revision of history, the self's capacity for independence was in danger of being lost. . . . The central persisting problem of the Enlightenment was the relationship between the individual and the collective spheres of life. On one hand were the stars and planets, admirably moving according to the laws of gravity, and the immense movements of universal history, which followed yet undiscovered laws of their own. On the other hand was the self, proceeding about its business, trucking and bartering, examining and organizing its own life quite without regard to the larger order of things. Neither sphere seemed to relate to the other. At the level of personal experience the self appeared to be free, or at least rightfully free. The claims to personal distinctiveness made so forcefully by Franklin and others depended upon the sense of being free. But the universe was clearly oblivious to the efforts of such individual wills; it was in general perceived to be ordered and utterly stable. Both order and freedom offer considerable satisfactions, but the two are apparently contradictory as modes of describing how the parts of the universe relate to the whole. . . .

From the perspective of the universe and universal history, individual selves must look powerless and insignificant. History turns out to have no people in it, only vast forces and patterns. Historians themselves seemed to be leery of their own work's value. . . . Those who persisted in thinking on the universal level often found themselves driven to inhuman conclusions. Thus, a kind of history had to be defined in which individual selves could be found to be efficacious. Otherwise the only alternatives were a public world apparently inaccessible and immovable and a private world of free and virtuous impotence. Of what use was the new self-knowledge, to what point the expanded self-expression, if the self was imprisoned within the limits of private life?

Consequently, the most satisfying form of history was biography. It was biography that linked the great world and the small, public and private, historical and intimate. History, it was argued, would have to be the field for interminable and unresolvable debates; since its material was, ultimately, an invariable human nature, it had to view its subject from too great a height to see anything well. "The stratagems of war, and the intrigues of courts," wrote Dr. Johnson, "are, read by far the greater part of mankind with the same indifference as the adventures of fabled heroes, or the revolutions of a fairy region. Between falsehood and useless truth there is little difference." Histories and romances offered alternative defects; the one had no recognizable selves, and the other no believable societies. . . . So there was a great vogue for biography in the eighteenth century.

Since biography aimed at revealing character in the world, the subject of biography should speak, if possible, for himself. Thus, letters and passages of conversation were extensively incorporated into biographies. Biographers sought to be in reality what novelists like [Samuel] Richardson had pretended to be—the editors of papers and memorabilia entrusted to them. The inherent difficulty of biography was that its most basic subject, personality, was not really fully knowable by the biographer. Boswell began the *Life of Johnson* by lamenting, a little insincerely, that Johnson had not written his own life, and he offers as the defense for his own work the fact that it includes so great a quantity of Johnson's letters and conversation. The *Life of Johnson*, Boswell suggested, approached as closely as possible to being an autobiography of Johnson.

Autobiography might then be seen as the highest form of biography. Johnson himself had argued as much in *Idler 84*. "The writer of his own life," Johnson stated, "has at least the first qualification of an historian, the knowledge of the truth." As for the supposed impartiality of the biographer, Johnson suggested that he was no more likely to be without prejudice than the subject himself. "I must be conscious that no one is so well qualified as myself to describe the series of my thoughts and actions," wrote [English historian and member of Parliament Edward] Gibbon at the beginning of his autobiography. The two friends of Franklin who wrote encouraging him to continue his autobiography both use the same argument. "Considering your great age, the caution of your character, and your peculiar style of thinking" Benjamin Vaughan wrote, in a letter incorporated in the text of the *Autobiography,* "it is not likely that any one besides yourself can be sufficiently master of the facts of your life, or the intentions of your mind" (A, 139). The biographer might record accidental details about his subject's life; what the autobiographer sets down is the very essence of his experiences.

The eighteenth century assumed that a man might know himself in all his own essential features and tendencies. . . . Self-doubt existed in the eighteenth century as at any other time, but the age also offered a material number of significant figures who firmly claimed to know themselves. When Rousseau set out in his *Confessions* "to display to my kind a portrait in every way true to nature," he had no doubt of his perfect adequacy as portraitist. In the last days of his life [the Scottish philosopher and historian David] Hume wrote an autobiographical sketch ["My Own Life"], concluding with a summary assessment of his own personality. "I am, or rather was (for that is the style I must now use in speaking of myself, which emboldens me the more to speak my sentiments); I was, I say, a man of mild dispositions, of command of temper, of an open, social, and cheerful humour, capable of attachment, but little susceptible of enmity, and of great moderation in all my passions." The characterization goes on for a paragraph, detailing his sense of his own general relations to his friends, his work, and the literary public. In the present age of anxiety there is something rather breathtaking in this passage of Hume's, in the critical detachment that can put one's whole life into the past tense. It was in such a spirit of confident self-knowledge that Franklin went about the writing of his own autobiography.

As a Journalist, Franklin Learns Basic Role-Playing

James A. Sappenfield

University of Wisconsin English professor James A. Sappenfield examines the influence and development of the young Ben Franklin's approach to journalism, revealing Franklin as a careful observer—a highly regarded role for eighteenth-century Enlightenment scholars, who perceived "spectators" as rather superior beings, fully aware of others and themselves. Franklin's successful journalism is in part a product of his careful observations of the successes and failures of other newspapers and journals. Even more important, perhaps, is what Franklin learned about the presentation and use of personae and pseudonyms, which he found highly valuable when presenting challenging and/or potentially offensive ideas and commentaries. Not only was Franklin notorious for employing "masks" in his journalism, but he also relied on them for successful endeavors in the civic arena, especially when soliciting donations or spreading information, as he did in order to establish the first subscription library. What Franklin learned in his younger years as a journalist would prove invaluable for his future accomplishments, including his autobiographical masterpiece and his public service.

> If you would not be forgotten
> As soon as you are dead and rotten,
> Either write things worth reading,
> Or do things worth the writing.
> *Poor Richard,* 1738

Ernest Hemingway, as the critical cliché goes, learned his lean, muscular prose style as a reporter on the Kansas City *Star.* That other founder of literary modernism, Walt Whitman, is said to have developed his feeling for music and his heightened sensitivity to the American panorama from covering opera and politics for the Brooklyn *Eagle*, the *Freeman*, and the New Orleans *Crescent*. Among America's writers of the first and second ranks, a striking number were onetime, part-time, or full-time journalists: Philip Freneau, William Cullen Bryant, E.A. Poe, Mark Twain, William Dean Howells, Stephen Crane, as well as Whitman and Hemingway. The first and certainly most celebrated of America's journalist-authors was Benjamin Franklin. . . .

FRANKLIN'S *GAZETTE* COMBINES WIT AND RESEARCH

Franklin's practice as a journalist was a sort of amalgam of eighteenth-century journalism in the English-speaking world. The makeup of his own Philadelphia paper, the *Pennsylvania Gazette* was not significantly different from that of other colonial newspapers. It contained old foreign news, state papers, commercial intelligence, and some advertisements. Like some other colonial editors, Franklin made an attempt to cover local stories: fires, drownings, murders, and suicides. It was in the choice and presentation of local news that colonial journalists typically displayed such flair and wit as they could command. But to his wry accounts of bizarre accidents and domestic tragedies, Franklin occasionally added pieces of entertainment and instruction; and it is for this reason that students of American letters remember the *Gazette*. Franklin himself devised the formula for spicing his weekly with hoaxes and moral essays, but the formula owed much to James Franklin's journalistic experiment, the *New-England Courant*, and to Benjamin's experience as apprentice in James's Boston shop. . . .

The *Courant* was the first self-consciously literary periodical in America, and its failure was partially owing to a lack of wit and partially to the lack of a market. The English colonies were not ready for an American *Spectator*, but James Franklin had proved that there were readers who appreciated wit and sense. And his younger brother was not the only printer in the colonies to realize that literary materials might be introduced into the conventional colonial newspaper to enhance its commercial appeal. In 1727, shortly after the demise of James Franklin's *Courant*, another Boston printer by the name of Samuel Kneeland began the publication of the *New-England Weekly Journal*. Quite independently of each other Kneeland and Benjamin Franklin had derived the same lesson from the unlucky *New-England Courant.* Kneeland enlisted the pens of [the American Puritan theologian] Cotton Mather's nephew, the Reverend Mather Byles, the Reverend Thomas Prince of the Old South Church, and even of [New York and New Jersey] Governor [William] Burnet. . . . The *New-England Weekly Journal* blended news and features and survived until 1741 when its publishers bought the old *Boston Gazette* and combined the two papers into the *Boston Gazette and Weekly Journal.* Kneeland apparently could not write himself, and when his contributors' stocks of wit were exhausted after two or three years, he turned to reprinting English materials.

Benjamin Franklin was more fortunate. He was already a good writer and he loved writing. Philadelphia was deficient in learned divines. . . . Franklin himself was obliged to supply most of the pieces of entertainment and instruction for his publications, but he was equal to the task. The sort of writing that Franklin enjoyed most, that which he did for his own amusement, was the sort found in the *Spectator* and the other British literary periodicals. These publications were James Franklin's inspiration for the *Courant* as well, and Benjamin had cut his teeth on the *Spectator*-style letters of [Mrs.] Silence Dogood [which he had secretly] written for his brother's paper.

The elegant and successful *Spectator* was, of course, the work principally of two hands: Joseph Addison and Richard Steele. Its immediate predecessor, the *Tatler*, was Steele's project, though like the *Spectator* it had many and distinguished contributors. In the planning of the *Tatler* Steele was evidently conscious of several and varied antecedents to the periodical essay. Walter Graham [in his book, *English Literary Periodicals*] writes,

> Steele was a good journalist. He gave his readers what he knew they liked to read. It is reasonable to believe that before entering upon this new enterprise he made himself intimately acquainted with all the methods and devices of . . . [the journalist John] Dunton, [the English novelist and journalist Daniel] Defoe, and others of his more successful predecessors. Moreover, there could have been no uncertainty in his mind as to the tone of his publication or the kind of matter that should fill his columns. . . . In short, it may be said that everything in the evolution of the literary periodical in England leads up to the *Tatler.*

John Dunton's *Athenian Mercury* (originally the *Athenian Gazette, or Casuistical Mercury*), which first appeared in 1691, offered to answer queries from its readers. The work of three or four men, it pretended to be a publication of a populous club, the "Athenian Society"; and its writers addressed themselves to a range of questions, scientific and moral: "Whether or no fishes think? Which is greater, the

---

CENSORSHIP AND THE PRINTING PRESS

In his preface to Benjamin Franklin's An Apology for Printers, *Philip Wittenberg, the former Columbia University Lecturer in Law, recapitulates the rise of the printing press and its subsequent censoring. Free thinkers such as Franklin stood opposed to the statutes and laws that prohibited free speech, which led to the creation of the Constitution's First Amendment pertaining to free speech and a free press.*

At the age of sixteen Benjamin Franklin had already been seasoned as a printer who had experienced criticism and repression. His brother James had in 1720 or '21 begun to print a newspaper, the *"New England Courant,"* the fifth that had appeared in America.

As Franklin writes in his Autobiography:

> One of the pieces in our newspaper on some political point, which I have now forgotten, gave offense to the Assembly. He was taken up, censur'd and imprison'd for a month, by the speaker's warrant, I suppose, because he would not discover his author. I too was taken up and examin'd before the council; but, tho' I did not give them any satisfaction, they content'd themselves with admonishing me, and dismissed me, considering me, perhaps, as an apprentice, who was bound to keep his master's secrets.

His brother evaded the order by returning to Benjamin his indenture of apprenticeship thus making it possible for the paper to be printed under the name of Benjamin Franklin.

Franklin's experience was not novel, for up to that time the history of printing had run parallel with a story of suppression. Johann Gutenberg's invention of movable type in 1440 was followed shortly by the establishment in England of the first press by William Caxton. He had learned the art on the Continent and coming to Westminster had set up a press at "The Red Pail" in Almanary. A hundred years after the invention of the movable type we have the first repressive statute passed in 1553 under Henry VIII and by 1556 the Stationers Company was chartered by Philip and Mary . . . to prevent the

hurt or profit that cometh of love? . . . Steele frequently used letters from his readers in his issues of the *Spectator*, and he was not the first of the journalists accused "of first Writing Letters to themselves, and then answering them in Print" [as Defoe had noted in his *Review*.]. It is generally assumed that Benjamin Franklin wrote most of the letters addressed to the editor of the *Pennsylvania Gazette*, but this may not be true.

diffusion of literature attacking the Church and State. . . .

When the Star Chamber was abolished in 1640 by act of Parliament the House of Commons set up a licensing scheme to suppress the critical press, and in March of 1642 they enacted a law providing for a Committee for Examinations which had power to search "for presses that are kept and employed in the printing of scandalous and lying pamphlets.". . .

The remembrance of events by the Colonists led to the adoption in the Constitutions of the several states of guarantees of a free press. The First Amendment to the Constitution of the United States provided; "Congress shall make no law *** abridging freedom of speech or of the press." Many of the state Constitutions gave added force to the lesson of history by the use of the words "printing press" instead of "press," for the printing press itself had been deemed the enemy.

The passage of such constitutional clauses and of statutes to enforce and limit them has not brought freedom to the printer. Practically all of our states have laws limiting the press under one guise or another, whether such laws be aimed at what is called obscenity, libel or otherwise. In fact, although Massachusetts had passed its Constitution in 1780 establishing a free press, the record shows at least three convictions for libelous political attacks obtained between 1799 and 1803. The Constitution of Massachusetts, Declaration of Rights, Article 17 provides:

"The liberty of the press is essential to the security of freedom in a state; it ought not, therefore, to be restrained in this commonwealth."

Franklin and the other printers of the colonies had not fought in vain. Every prosecution of a printer brought forth protest. The Constitutions of the several states prove how effective that protest was. From the invention of movable type till today every age has had men like Franklin who keep alive the consciences of men and the right to the free diffusion of knowledge and opinion.

Preface in *An Apology for Printers* by Benjamin Franklin. New York: Book Craftsmen Associates, 1955.

In 1725, Charles Lillie issued, with Steele's permission, two
volumes of unused letters to the *Spectator*. In any event,
Dunton's *Athenian Mercury* provided two devices which survived to the heyday of the literary periodicals: authorship by
an imaginary club and correspondence between the editor
and his readers.

Edward Ward's *London Spy* (1698–1700) introduced the
motif of a peripatetic [mobile] observer of manners and
morals. Steele used it and passed it to Franklin, who employed it in the Busy-Body, and combined it with the device
of the imaginary correspondent in the Dogood Papers and
on numerous other occasions. The *Weekly Comedy* ("as it is
dayly acted at most coffee-houses in London") ran ten numbers between May and July of 1699. It may have been written by Ward also, and is memorable for the tag-names of its
dramatis personae: "Squabble, a lawyer; Whim, a projector;
Prim, a beau," among others. Ward's stock in trade was "filth
and ribaldry" [Graham notes] and the several variations of
the *Weekly Comedy* which appeared between 1699 and 1708
were all short lived. Daniel Defoe's *Weekly Review,* begun in
February 1704, drew upon Dunton's device of answers from
a group of writers: "Advice from the Scandal Club."

Steele invented a club of five men for the *Tatler.* Besides
the author and an anonymous bencher at the Trumpet in
Sheer-Lane, the group included Sir Geoffrey Notch, Major
Matchlock, and Dick Reptile. This circle of "heavy, honest
men" anticipated the circle of characters in the *Spectator*
which included Sir Roger de Coverley, Captain Sentry, Sir
Andrew Freeport, and Will Honeycomb. Benjamin Franklin
never employed the device of an imaginary coterie of characters, but he formed a real-life club for mutual entertainment and improvement, that is, the Junto of Philadelphia.

This is not to say that Franklin naively transferred fiction
into real life, as the lad who grew up to be the Great Gatsby
[of F. Scott Fitzgerald's book] tried to do. But it is interesting
that the creation of imaginary characters and correspondents was so congenial to Franklin's imagination. It was a
mode of writing ideally suited to prepare him for the com-
position of his masterpiece [The *Autobiography*], but for
Franklin it was more than that. Something in Benjamin
Franklin's nature embraced the device he found in the *Spectator* of inventing fanciful masks and voices. It was a clever
technique invented by journalists long before Steele, and

Franklin used it with great skill and sensitivity. But this device he did not confine to his journalism, nor even to his memoirs—the climax of his journalistic career. Franklin transferred the device to real life.

His greatest achievement in real-life masquerade was the image of fur-hatted American rusticity which he projected in the glittering French court during the American Revolution. Franklin's name was virtually a household word in France before he arrived. He was famous as the physicist whose lightning experiment had first been performed by French philosophers and as the author of *La Science du Bonhomme Richard* ["Father Abraham's Speech" or "The Way to Wealth" from *Poor Richard's Almanack*]. The French expected to find him the embodiment of natural reason, a kind of white noble savage, a homely "Quackeur" sage. Franklin was neither a Quaker nor a rustic, but he altered his cosmopolitan manners and dress to match French expectations, and they lionized him. Unquestionably the role that Franklin played in France was useful to him and to the American cause, but its utility was scarcely all that recommended it to him. It is clear that he played the role with great relish. As he himself observed [in the *Autobiography*], "So convenient a thing it is to be a *reasonable Creature,* since it enables one to find or make a Reason for every thing one has a mind to do."

FRANKLIN CONVENIENTLY DONS THE CONVENTIONAL MASK

In the *Autobiography* Franklin did rationalize his habit of public masquerade. The difficulty he encountered in soliciting funds for his first public project, the Philadelphia subscription library, made him "soon feel the Impropriety of presenting one's self as the Proposer of any useful Project that might be suppos'd to raise one's Reputation in the smallest degree above that of one's Neighbours, when one has need of their Assistance to accomplish that Project. I therefore put my self as much as I could out of sight, and stated it as a Scheme of a *Number of Friends,* who had requested me to go about and propose it to such as they thought Lovers of Reading. In this way my Affair went on more smoothly, and I ever after practis'd it on such Occasions; and from my frequent Successes, can heartily recommend it" (*Autobiography*). Again, describing his campaign to establish the Pennsylvania Academy, Franklin presented his proposals "not as an Act of mine, but of some *publick-spirited Gentlemen;* avoiding as much as

I could, according to my usual Rule, the presenting myself as the Author of any Scheme for the [public's] Benefit" (*Autobiography*). Franklin's "usual Rule" made him seem sinister and devious to those inclined to oppose his beneficient projects. In 1740, an attacker writing in a rival newspaper [Andrew Bradford of the *American Weekly Mercury*] complained that Franklin was "never at a Loss for something to say, nor for some Body to say it for you, when you don't care to appear yourself."

We need not arrive at a final moral judgment of Benjamin Franklin, nor for that matter a judgment about his psychic health. We need, however, to note this impulse of his to play roles—in his writings and in real life. The canny [*Moby Dick* author Herman] Melville recognized this tendency and in the novel *Israel Potter*, in which Franklin appears, Melville made his Franklin a character of several guises, protean [versatile like Proteus, the shape-shifting Greek sea god] in his shifts of voice and manner. For Franklin then, the popular journalistic device of employing masks or personae was a form which allowed him to indulge his natural bent. . . .

Whatever the particular application of a journalistic mask, the habitual use of them by Benjamin Franklin was the key to his development as a writer. We know that, whether consciously or not, every writer adopts a mask or pose or attitude when he begins to write. But Franklin was acutely conscious of the process. His impulse in writing, like his impulse in projecting, was to get his job of persuading done. As in the case of his projects, he usually decided to invent someone to speak for him rather than appearing himself. Franklin rationalized this journalistic device as well, writing an essay "On Literary Style" in 1729: "When the Writer conceals himself, he has the Advantage of hearing the Censure both of Friends and Enemies with more Impartiality." Doubtless he based this observation on his own experience in Boston with the anonymous Silence Dogood Papers. But unlike the strategy of projecting, the purpose of adopting a journalistic or literary mask was not always concealment.

The use of the journalistic mask was, after all, conventional; readers recognized that letters signed Alice Addertongue or Anthony Afterwit were likely to be the work of Benjamin Franklin, editor of the *Gazette*, just as they knew that Poor Richard Saunders was really the proprietor of the New Printing-Office. Yet, as a comic device, the journalistic mask functions to separate the actual author from his message. More often than not, Franklin's little sketches carried a serious message. Employing a persona accomplished precisely what hiding behind *"a Number of Friends"* did; that is, it relieved the reader of the unpleasant experience of taking advice from Benjamin Franklin. In addition, the persona might be tailored to the occasion and the circumstances. The mask could be male or female, old or young, poor or rich. . . . Franklin [used] all of these with great skill and sensitivity.

Newton Inadvertently Develops a New Scientific Approach

I. Bernard Cohen

I. Bernard Cohen, one of the founders of the modern study of the history of science and emeritus Victor S. Thomas Professor of the History of Science at Harvard University, illuminates the impact on Benjamin Franklin of the scientific method used by the great Sir Isaac Newton in the *Opticks.* As one of the preeminent figures from the Age of Reason, Newton revolutionized experimental philosophy by validating experiments for the collection of data as opposed to the traditional scientific method which typically required the use of complex mathematical equations and computations. This new method did not require calculations that only a mathematician could do but, rather, relied on experimentation and documentation of experiments. As such, the scope of scientific inquiry was widened to include experimental research—the kind Benjamin Franklin did. Cohen, whose previous work includes editing the 1941 addition of *Benjamin Franklin's Experiments: A New Edition of Franklin's Experiments and Observations on Electricity* as well as his book *Franklin and Newton,* succinctly demonstrates the direct correlation between Newton's work and Franklin's own early considerations of electricity.

Benjamin Franklin's preparation for a career of scientific research included a careful and profound study of the ideas and principles of investigation of Isaac Newton. It is, however, one of the paradoxes of Benjamin Franklin's career that his contemporaries considered him to be a foremost Newtonian scientist even though he did not have the skill or training to be able to read Newton's *Principia*. His Newtonian science was derived from the *Opticks*, which for eighteenth-century experimental scientists was a manual of the experimental art.

THE DIFFERENCE BETWEEN THE *PRINCIPIA* AND THE *OPTICKS*

In recent decades we have become aware that Newton's two great works—the *Principia* and the *Opticks*—became the foundations of very different and even distinct scientific traditions, derived from their subject matter, formal style, and mode of investigation and proof. The *Principia* was devoted to rational mechanics (a name introduced by Newton: "mechanica rationalis") and its elaboration in celestial dynamics and in the Newtonian "system of the world." This domain of science was traditionally developed mathematically, proposition by proposition, from an initial set of definitions and axioms, which in the *Principia* were the Newtonian laws of motion. It was befitting this rigorous and austere mathematical style that the *Principia* was written in traditional Latin.

The *Opticks* was a quite different sort of book and accordingly engendered a somewhat separate tradition in science. Written in a graceful English rather than in the severe Latin of the *Principia*, the *Opticks* was almost totally devoid of mathematics. That is, the *Opticks* did not develop its subject in a systematic manner by mathematical proofs (in the style of the *Principia*) but rather stated its propositions and then introduced "The Proof by Experiments." In actual fact, not once in the *Opticks* does Newton develop proofs or discussions in a complete sequence, using the recognized tools of mathematics, that is, equations, proportions, trigonometric identities, fluxions (or the calculus), and the like. Indeed, in book 2 Newton notes in passing that "all these things follow from the properties of Light by a mathematical way of reasoning," but "the truth of them may be manifested by Experiments."

In attempting to define the character of the *Opticks*, however, we must be careful not to confuse "mathematical" in this sense with "numerical" or "quantitative" or "exact." The *Opticks* is a quantitative work in that it is based on numerical results of measurements—for example, of the width of "Newton's rings" or various examples of refraction. Furthermore, the experiments lead to quantitative laws, such as the law of refraction, which are expressed in mathematical language (the sine of angles of incidence and of refraction). But such laws do not appear as consequences of a mathematical structure, as derivations from mathematical axioms, nor are they proved by the use of mathematical techniques. Nor, for that matter, does Newton in the *Opticks* go on to develop mathematically further propositions based upon such laws.

The result is that the *Opticks* was a work readily accessible to experimental scientists such as Benjamin Franklin, Stephen Hales, Joseph Black, and A.L. Lavoisier, who did not need to be trained in higher mathematics to understand its contents. That is, the *Opticks* did not demand of its readers a knowledge of the theory of proportions, the geometry of conic sections, the theory of limits, fluxions or the infinitesimal calculus, or skill in using infinite series, such as would be needed to follow the argument of the *Principia.*

I may note in passing that it was not Newton's original intent to develop this subject in a manner or style so different from that of the *Principia.* We have evidence aplenty . . . that Newton tried again and again to find a basis for producing a mathematical science of optics, but all of his efforts ended in failure. After years of hesitation and self-doubt, Newton agreed in 1704 to present to the world of science the results of his extensive and original experimental investigations in the domain of light and color. Thus he could guarantee his claims to priority in discovery. But the form of the *Opticks*— in English rather than in Latin and without mathematics— was, I believe, in a sense a confession of his failure. This is no doubt the reason why the title page of the *Opticks* does not bear the author's name. That this omission was the result of design and not of accident can be seen in the fact that in at least one copy of record, the name of the author has been inserted on a specially printed title page pasted onto the stub of the originally canceled or cut-off page.

THE "QUERIES" OF THE *OPTICKS* AND THE IMPORTANCE OF EXPERIMENT

The popular appeal of the *Opticks* was enhanced by the famous "Queries" which formed its conclusion. These dealt with a large variety of experimental and theoretical topics, including physical optics, vision, fire or combustion, radiant heat, electricity, magnetism, corpuscular or atomic physics, the phenomena and theory of waves, chemistry, the nature of matter, and even a possible cause of universal gravity. The first edition (1704) contained only sixteen Queries, which were rather short, but in later editions (Latin, 1706; revised English edition, 1717/1718) their number was successively increased to an eventual thirty-one, the later ones occupying many pages each. These Queries were not questions in the ordinary sense. All but one show their rhetorical nature by being in the negative. That is, Newton does not ask in a truly querulous [fretful] fashion whether flame may be "a vapour, fume or exhalation heated red hot"; rather, he insists (Query 10): "Is not Flame a Vapour, Fume or Exhalation heated red hot, that is, so hot as to shine?" That Newton knew the answer is evident at once in the ensuing discussion in which he presents the evidence to support his position. The form of query, in other words, was a rhetorical device so that Newton could freely set forth his ideas even on topics for which he had no mathematical proof or for which the experimental evidence was not overwhelmingly definitive. He introduced this section of the *Opticks* with the frank declaration that there were important subjects which he had hoped to pursue, but could no longer investigate. [As stated before the first query of book three,] he would, accordingly, conclude his treatise "with proposing only some Queries in order to [provoke] a farther search to be made by others."

Newtonians had no doubts concerning Newton's own beliefs in relation to each of the topics developed in the Queries. Stephen Hales, for one, said simply that in the latter part of the *Opticks* Newton had explained many things "by way of query." J.T. [Jean Théophile] Desaguliers, for another, particularly lauded the Newton of the Queries, which he said contain "an excellent body of philosophy." The form of question, he explained, had nothing to do with uncertainty about truth but arose merely from Newton's "modesty," since Newton would never assert as true any proposition that he "could not prove" by "mathematical demonstrations or experiments."

Sir Isaac Newton

In this sentiment Desaguliers was merely restating what Newton himself had said in the "Advertisement" to the second edition of the *Opticks*. In order "to shew that I do not take Gravity for an essential Property of Bodies," Newton wrote, "I have added one Question concerning its Cause." He had chosen "to propose it by way of a Question," he continued, "because I am not yet satisfied about it for want of Experiments."

In the Queries Newton had made an inventory of problems requiring experimental investigation and of areas to be explored by future investigators. Hence the Queries displayed a research program for those scientists of the eighteenth century who conceived that a major mode of advance in science lay in the use of experiments rather than mathematical derivations and mathematical solutions to problems. These scientists worked in such areas as optics, plant and animal physiology, heat, electricity, magnetism, and chemistry and the structure of matter.

A New Science Evolves from Newton's Experimental Philosophy

My own recognition of the significance of the *Opticks* in relation to the rise of the experimental science of the eighteenth century came about years ago during my reading of Benjamin Franklin's *Experiments and Observations in Electricity* and my attempts to understand [Franklin's long-time friend] Joseph Priestley's comparison of Franklin's "true principles of electricity" with Newton's "philosophy" and "the true system of nature in general" [which Priestly presented in his book *The History and Present State of Electricity*]. Eventually, I became aware of Hélène Metzger's writings, proposing the existence of a Newtonian tradition stemming from the *Opticks* rather than the *Principia*. Her works documented this influence of the *Opticks* in a chemical context; later I came upon a briefer suggestion of this thesis (again in a chemical context) by Pierre Duhem. At this time (1940–41), while I was preparing for the press my edition of Franklin's book on electricity, the nature and influence of Newton's *Opticks* became a subject of almost constant discussion between me and my fellow graduate student Henry Guerlac, who was then already deep in his studies of Lavoisier and his antecedents, a joyful complement to my own explorations of physics in that same era. As a result it would be well-nigh impossible for either of us to be absolutely certain how much came from the other, or how much we both derived from Hélène Metzger or from our common mentor Giorgio de Santillana.

A number of different kinds of evidence gave support to a difference in appeal of the *Principia* and the *Opticks* and, consequently, a different scientific tradition allied with these two works. For example, I discovered that John Locke [an English philosopher deeply involved with the Enlightenment and], a thoroughgoing Newtonian in philosophy, found the *Principia* wholly beyond his comprehension and appealed to [the Dutch mathematician and physicist] Christiaan Huygens to ascertain whether "all the mathematical *Propositions* in Sir Isaac's *Principia* were true." On "being told he might depend on their Certainty," J.T. Desaguliers reported, Locke "took them for granted and carefully examined the Reasonings and *Corollaries* drawn from them." Desaguliers contrasted Locke's approach to the *Principia* with the way in which "he read the *Opticks* with pleasure, acquainting himself with every thing in them that was not merely mathematical." The story of Locke's attempts to read the *Principia* had been told to Desaguliers "several times by Sir *Isaac Newton* himself" [which Desaguliers reports in *A Course of Experimental Philosophy*]. This general appeal of the *Opticks* can also be seen in the fact that Francesco Algarotti's popular book on Newtonianism (oft reprinted both in the original Italian and in translation) was devoted entirely to the *Opticks.* . . .

An example of the influence of the *Opticks* is afforded by Stephen Hales's *Vegetable Staticks* (1727), a work still ranked among the classics of experimental science. Hales was a pioneer in the application of quantitative methods to biology. In *Vegetable Staticks* he explored such topics of quantitative biological experiment as leaf growth, root pressure, and plant nutrition, and the quantitative study of gases. In a companion volume, *Haemastaticks,* Hales described the first measurements ever made of blood pressure in animals. The text of *Vegetable Staticks* contains seventeen mentions of Newton, of which fifteen are either quotations from or references to the *Opticks.* The other two are concerned, respectively, with Newton's method of calibrating thermometers and with his essay on acids. . . .

The principles of the Newtonian experimental philosophy were set forth in a series of first-rate nontechnical expositions—Henry Pemberton's *View of Sir Isaac Newton's Philosophy,* Herman Boerhaave's *New Method of Chemistry,* W.J. Gravesande's *Natural Philosophy,* J.T. Desaguliers's *Experimental Philosophy,* Hales's *Statical Essays,* and others. These works were read or studied by Franklin in the late 1730s and early 1740s, the years of self-education in the sciences and preparation for a career as a scientist. These books brought Franklin into contact with the experimental art and, in particular, with Newtonian atomism and the concept of a subtle and imponderable medium or fluid, manifested in heat, optical phenomena, and electrical effects—an aether or aetherial medium composed of particles that repel one another. This was a model for Franklin's concept of an electrical fluid. In Gravesande's book, for example, Franklin would have found a discussion of fire particles attracted by bodies, uniting to the corpuscles composing bodies, that—while contained in all bodies—do not enter into all bodies with equal facility.

Desaguliers wrote about magnetism in a way that could apply equally to electricity. . . . Like other Newtonians, Desaguliers introduced electricity in order to show that "attraction" actually occurs in nature. . . . The last five pages of Desaguliers's book on experimental Newtonian science (1734) were devoted to an exposition of electricity which may have been Franklin's first introduction to that subject. Here Desaguliers adapted and expanded Newton's fundamental concept of mutual particulate repulsion, that (Query 21) "aether (like our air) may contain particles which endeavour to recede from one another." This concept was basic to Desaguliers's thoughts on elasticity, Hales's on gases, Franklin's on the electric fluid, Lavoisier's on caloric, and—later—[John] Dalton's on atoms.

Not only did Desaguliers give a succinct summary of electrical experiments made in the 1720s and 1730s; he also included in the second volume an English version of his *Dissertation concerning Electricity* (1742), which had won the prize of the Academy of Bordeaux. He had been a younger member of Newton's circle and he was the author of a standard manual of Freemasonry, which Franklin published in an American edition. Desaguliers was, therefore, an especially important author for Franklin in the 1740s. Furthermore, Franklin knew Desaguliers's writings on stoves and chimneys and his English version of [Nicolas] Gauger's book on these topics. Accordingly it is significant that Desaguliers not only set forth principles of elastic imponderable fluids that formed a conceptual matrix for Franklin's idea of the electric fluid; he also—by including an essay on electricity in a treatise on Newtonian physics—declared that the nascent science of electricity was a legitimate topic of inquiry for the Newtonian experimental philosopher. . . .

FRANKLIN, THE NEW NEWTONIAN APPROACH, AND ELECTRICITY

From such works Franklin learned the Newtonian principles of particulate attraction and repulsion; he also became familiar with the concept of an elastic fluid. Above all he learned the Newtonian respect—stated explicitly in precepts by Gravesande, Desaguliers, and Hales—for carefully performed experiments that must be accurately reported.

Franklin's friend, the naturalist [George-Louis Leclerc] Buffon, once wrote that style is the man himself. Franklin is celebrated for a style of life and action and a style of prose. It is more for its style than its content that his autobiography is generally reckoned to be an American classic. In his report "Opinions and Conjectures," and in his other writings on electricity, and notably in his account of the experiment of the dissectible condenser (or capacitor), we may see Franklin as a master of expository prose. . . .

Franklin's style as a writer was matched by a style and skill in making experiments and drawing conclusions from them. The record of Franklin's initial electrical discoveries is contained in a series of epistolary reports sent by him to England on 25 May 1747, 28 July 1747, and 29 April 1749 (two letters), leading up to a formal presentation of the "Properties and Effects of the electrical Matter, arising from Experiments and Observations, made at Philadelphia, 1749." The heading of this paper was the source of the title given to his book.

In this 1749 summary Franklin shows the influence of ideas put forth by Newton in Queries 18–24 of the *Opticks*, concerning "a much subtiler Medium than Air," an "aethereal Medium." This aether, according to Newton, pervades and resides in the pores of bodies and varies in density from one body to another. We have seen that it is very "rare" (Query 21) and may ("like our Air") be composed of "Particles which endeavour to recede from one another." Because of this property or force of mutual repulsion, this "aether" constitutes an "elastick" fluid. The particles are characterized by an "exceeding smallness," so that it is by many orders of magnitude "more rare" than "our Air" and so can easily penetrate into ordinary bodies.

With some important alterations or modifications this is Franklin's electric fluid. From his postulates it is apparent that, like the aetherial medium whose properties Newton developed in the Queries of the *Opticks,* Franklin's electric fluid is subtle and particulate, composed of particles that repel one another. Postulate 1 reads: "The electrical matter consists of particles extremely subtile, since it can permeate common matter, even the densest metals, with such ease and freedom as not to receive any perceptible resistance." This primary statement is at once qualified by postulate 3, about the mutual repulsion of the particles: "Electrical matter differs from common matter in this, that the parts of the latter mutually attract, those of the former mutually repel each other."

At this point Franklin added a new and original additional property, expressed in postulate 4: that the particles of electrical matter "are strongly attracted by all other matter." These postulates accord with the general principle that all electrical phenomena are the result of a change in the distribution of the electrical matter in bodies or of some net change in the total quantity of electrical matter in individual bodies.

This principle is embodied in a more general principle which we know as "conservation of charge": that "electricity" is never created or destroyed in electrical phenomena, that electrical phenomena are caused by changes in either the distribution or the net quantity of electrical matter in bodies. In experiment after experiment, Franklin showed that the production of a positive charge in one body (a net gain in electrical fluid) is always accompanied by an equal and opposite negative charge (a net loss in electrical fluid) in one or more other bodies. Other experiments showed in a remarkable way how electrical effects may be produced by the temporary change in the normal condition (or equal distribution) of the electrical fluid in one or more bodies. We know this as electrostatic induction.

The doctrine of conservation had been a hallmark of Newtonian rational mechanics. The first "axiom" or "law of motion" in the *Principia* declared the property of inertia— the conservation of a body's state of motion or of rest. . . . In his first report on his research, Franklin explained how he and his fellow experimenters, Philip Syng and Thomas Hopkinson, had come to the conclusion "that the electrical fire was not created by friction, but collected, being really an element diffused among, and attracted by other matter, particularly by water and metals.". . .

The Franklinian explanation appears in the straightforward and clear unadorned prose that was the ideal of the Newtonian scientist. . . . The general significance of the new electrical theory was—as Franklin wrote in a letter to Cadwallader Colden in 1747—"that the Electrical Fire is a real Element, or Species of Matter, not *created* by the Friction, but *collected* only." Here was the first stage of the Franklinian revolution in electricity.

CHAPTER 2

The Legendary Ben Franklin

BENJAMIN FRANKLIN

Franklin, a Figurehead at the Framing of the Constitution

Martha J. Lamb

Noted historian, author, and editor of the nineteenth-century *Magazine of American History* (1883–1892) Martha J. Lamb takes a nostalgic look at some of the roles, revelations, and interactions that occurred during the 1787 Philadelphia convention in which the U.S. Constitution was established. Lamb's article was written in 1885 for the then-upcoming centennial anniversary of the establishment of the U.S. government. Lamb holds the framing of the Constitution in higher regard than the actual "adoption" of our government, and it is Franklin whom she notes assumes the father-figure role at the convention. In fact, Franklin was famous for cracking jokes and offering insights and solutions in order to assuage the various conflicts that arose. George Washington, an admirer of Franklin's, is also viewed in high regard by the convention, while the young Alexander Hamilton of New York presents a fresh challenge to Franklin. As always, Franklin contributes a memorable anecdote to sum up the conference.

The achievement . . . that preceded and was vastly more remarkable than its adoption, was the production of the Constitution. Such a form of government had hitherto been unknown to the science of politics. The structure was a special creation, and at a time when the future of the country was mapped only in the imagination. Its life-giving force was the pressure of a great necessity. The confederation was too weak to bear its own weight. It had no power over commerce. It could not even levy taxes or enforce the payment of duties. As a bond of union in a time of war it had been suffi-

Excerpted from "The Framers of the Constitution," by Martha J. Lamb, in the *Magazine of American History with Notes and Queries*, 8 (1885), pp. 313–45.

cient, but was totally inadequate as a system of permanent government. The wisdom of two continents predicted disaster unless vigorous remedies were applied. American thinkers were divided on the most important questions at issue, but of one opinion as to the imminence of the danger. Some were for kingly rule; and some were in chronic alarm lest an English or French prince should be placed on an American throne.

From Virginia finally emanated an invitation for a meeting of commissioners from the several States to meet in Annapolis [Maryland], for the purpose of discussing methods of regulating trade with foreign countries. . . . The meeting was held on the 14th of September, 1786. Nothing of importance was accomplished by it further than a recommendation to Congress that authority should be given for the holding of a general Convention, for the specific purpose of revising the "Articles of Confederation." But the feeble successor of that renowned Congress which had brought into existence the thirteen States, was averse to excluding itself from the right to inaugurate changes in the government, and did not comply with the request with alacrity. It questioned the constitutionality of a Convention, until thoroughly alarmed at the riotous condition of affairs in Massachusetts; and when it yielded, and advised the States to confer power upon a special assembly to convene in Philadelphia on the 14th of May, 1787, the act was not performed with special grace. Thus when the delegates had been appointed by their respective States, the situation was far from enviable. America fixed its critical eye upon them, and a general distrust of the policy of their undertaking prevailed. Their genius in government-making was yet to be displayed; and it was well known that the little which could be borrowed from experience was foreign in its character and irreducible to the exigencies [emergency situations] of affairs in the New World. . . .

They assembled in Philadelphia in the leafy months of May and June, 1787. They came from all points of the compass; some journeying in their own chariots drawn by four and six horses, others in springless stages, and not an insignificant few on horseback. Philadelphia was in hospitable humor, proud of being chosen as the place for the Convention, and her private citizens graciously entertained the distinguished statesmen as far as practicable. Pennsylvania provided eight delegates, the largest number of any of the

States, Virginia having only seven, although she initiated the movement. North Carolina, New Jersey, Maryland, and Delaware each sent five delegates. Massachusetts, South Carolina, and Georgia four; New York and Connecticut three; and New Hampshire two; Rhode Island was not represented. Each State acted its own pleasure in regard to the number of delegates chosen. New York struggled for five, but her inflexible Senate decreed there should be but three.

FRANKLIN AND WASHINGTON ARE RADIANT BEACON LIGHTS

Dr. Benjamin Franklin, President of Pennsylvania, was the leading delegate from that State; and he was the oldest man in the Convention. He had recently returned from his ten years' absence in Europe, crowned with glory, and had been welcomed home with addresses of congratulation, in which he was styled "the great philosopher," "the great politician," and "the illustrious and benevolent citizen of the world." He was quickly elected to the Presidency of Pennsylvania, an act which restored harmony to a community almost on the verge of civil war—and the day of his election was also the day of his inauguration. He resided in Market Street with his daughter [Sarah "Sally" (Franklin) Bache] and her seven beautiful children. His house was surrounded with pleasant and tastefully cultivated grounds. Prior to the meeting of the Convention he had added a new wing to his dwelling, in which he fashioned a commodious library, and contrived the "long arm" for taking books from high shelves, which he delighted in exhibiting to visitors. His public business not being arduous, he spent much time in his garden, and with his books, and in playing cribbage with his grandchildren. Writing to [his English friend] David Hartley of his domestic life at this period he said: "As to public amusements we have assemblies, balls and concerts, besides little parties at one another's houses, in which there is sometimes dancing, and frequently good music; so that we jog on in life as pleasantly as you do in England."

[George] Washington, the conspicuous leader of the Virginia delegation, was the first of the Framers to arrive in Philadelphia, and with characteristic promptness on the precise day appointed. He left Mount Vernon in the latter part of April, traveling with his own equipage [outfit]. At Chester, fifteen miles from the city, he was met by General [Thomas] Mifflin, Speaker of the Pennsylvania Assembly, and other gentlemen of distinction, and from Gray's Ferry was escorted by the city light-horse into Philadelphia—the bells ringing meanwhile—where public honors awaited him. His first act was to pay a visit of respect to Dr. Franklin.

The other delegates came slowly; day after day passed and still the majority of the States were not represented. In the mean time Washington was *fêted* [wined and dined] by the leading residents; and according to the newspapers of the day, he "went out one evening when the weather was very tempestuous, accompanied by a brilliant crowd of his friends of both sexes, and proceeded to the University to hear a lady deliver a lecture on the Power of Eloquence." He was also the guest of honor at a stately dinner-party given by Dr. Franklin, on which occasion a cask of porter fresh from London was broached, and its contents, wrote Franklin, "met with a most cordial reception and universal approbation."

Franklin was then eighty-one years of age, and Washington fifty-five. Franklin was of average height, stooping a little as he walked, full, broad physique, and benign, spectacled countenance. His intellect was never clearer, more acute, more active, more fruitful. Washington stood six feet and three inches in his slippers, as straight as an arrow, and was evenly developed. He had a long muscular arm, and a singularly large hand. His gravity and sublime self-poise were as notable as Dr. Franklin's wit, anecdotes and whimsicalities. Each of the two was gifted with worldly wisdom in liberal measure, and each had in his own line of the public service won world-wide fame. To a country groping in the dark for political guidance the successful soldier and the eminent diplomat were radiant beacon lights.

Franklin Offers Solutions and Advocates an Unimposing Government

The Convention was not formally organized until Friday, May 25, and then, as soon as the preliminary business was concluded, it adjourned until Monday. Pennsylvania gracefully proposed Washington as the President of the Assemblage, a ceremony that was to have been performed by Franklin in person, had not a severe rain storm prevented his attendance on the occasion. Robert Morris [also a Pennsylvania delegate] made the motion, which was promptly seconded by John Rutledge, of South Carolina, and Washington was placed in the chair. Franklin was in his seat on

Monday, and attended the Convention regularly, five hours every day afterwards for four months, his friends declaring that he grew in health and vigor under the daily exercise of going and returning from his house to Independence Hall. The Convention bound itself to secrecy and proceeded to its work with closed doors. . . . In the midst of this assembled greatness, Franklin in his well-fitting, picturesque costume was the observed of all observers—as he advocated a government unimposing, inexpensive. . . .

The first two months of the Convention were much occupied in discussing the terms upon which states as small as Delaware and Rhode Island could safely and justly enter a confederacy with such large states as Pennsylvania, Virginia and New York. The smaller were unwilling to be overshadowed or oppressed, and the larger declined to forego the importance due to their superior wealth and population. The small states demanded an equal representation in the national legislature, and the large states pronounced such a

At the Constitutional Convention in 1787, Franklin (center) was famous for using humor to help settle the conflicts that arose.

claim preposterous and unreasonable. They held it to be manifestly wrong that a state sixteen times as large as Delaware should have only the same number of votes. The debates were eloquent and earnest, then hot and acrimonious. Washington with lofty and severe dignity in the chair, and Franklin with contagious good humor on the floor, tried in vain to cool the heats of disputation.

Delaware, the smallest state represented, contended with the most spirit and persistence for an equality absolute and entire. No compromise would be considered for a moment. With the larger states the contest was for power, with the smaller states for existence. . . . It really seemed as if that one perverse rock was about to shipwreck the whole fleet. But Delaware carried her point in the end. Franklin came to the rescue with an amendment, or accommodation, to prevent the dissolution of the Convention, and after considerable wrangling, the simple, sensible and satisfactory settlement of the vexed controversy was that every state should have equal representation in the Senate without regard to size, and in the House every state should have a representation proportioned to its population—and no ill-feeling ever resulted therefrom. "Thus," writes [the English-born American biographer] James Parton, in his "Life of Franklin," "Rhode Island and Delaware, Pennsylvania and New York were made equal members of the same confederacy, without peril to the smaller and without injustice to the larger. Of all political expedients (in a great emergency) this was perhaps the happiest ever devised. Its success has been so perfect as scarcely to have excited remark. The nation is as unconscious of the working of the system as a healthy man is of the process of digestion.". . .

RESOLUTION DESPITE OPPOSITION AND FRANKLIN'S SUN METAPHOR

New York, the Empire state, conscious of her prospective importance, jealously resisted the national scheme. Of her three delegates Robert Yates and John Lansing were notably in favor of preserving the individual powers of the State. . . . Both Yates and Lansing vigorously opposed the Constitution, and when it was found impossible to patch up the Articles of Confederation to meet the emergency, they took the ground that the Convention was transcending its powers in attempting to construct a new instrument, and went home.

[Alexander] Hamilton, undaunted at being thus left alone
to represent so large and important a state, marshaled his
marvelous gifts and forces into full play. By the action of the
majority of her delegates New York had lost her vote in the
Convention, and little dreamed that the boldness, energy,
acute sense, and well-balanced intellect of her youthful
statesman, was to overbear by eloquence, interpret essential
needs by illustration, usurp powers with imperious will, and
then convince by argument a large proportion of her population that he was in the right, and compel in the end a public recognition and justification of his conduct. But such
were the facts. He was but thirty, and in size probably the
smallest man in the assemblage. Yet in certain respects he
was the greatest of them all. He unquestionably evinced
more remarkable maturity than was ever exhibited by any
other person at so early an age in the same department of
thought. His views, although held with great tenacity, were
also held in subordination to what was practicable. Franklin
opposed every proposition that tended towards arbitrary
government. He thought the Chief Magistrate should have
no salary and little power, and that the government should
be a simple and ingenious contrivance for executing the will
of the people. He said that ambition and avarice, the love of
power and the love of money were the two passions that
most influenced the affairs of men, and argued that the
struggle for posts of honor which were at the same time
places of profit, would perpetually divide the nation and dis-
tract its councils; and that the men who would thrust themselves into the arena of contention for preferment would not
be the wise and moderate, those fitted for high trusts, but the
bold, the selfish and the violent, and that in the bustle of ca-
bal [one party plotting to usurp power] and the mutual abuse
of parties the best of characters would be torn in pieces.

Hamilton went to the other extreme. He did not want a
monarchy, but he was for having a perpetual senate and a
perpetual governor. The great principle he cherished acknowledged the inalienable right of the individual state to
control absolutely its own domestic and internal affairs, because it was better able to do it intelligently than any outside
power, but which also recognized the desirability and necessity of a central government that should settle and determine national questions. To embody such a scheme, with all
its delicate details and shadings, in a written document, was

the puzzle of puzzles. The prudence of Franklin was one of the great influences that ruled the hour. His well-timed anecdotes and quaint observations created many a burst of genuine merriment, despite the serene grandeur and dignity of the presiding power. The day after Hamilton was deserted by his New York colleagues, Franklin, in a characteristic speech, attributed the "small progress made to the melancholy imperfection of the human understanding;" and urgently recommended that the sessions be opened every morning with prayer. . . .

Washington, Franklin, Hamilton and others accepted certain features they did not approve, because they believed it was the best government that the genius of America could frame, or that the nation could be induced to experiment upon. The finishing touches to the document were delegated to Gouverneur Morris [another Pennsylvania delegate], whose graceful pen gave to the substance its order and symmetry, and to the text its distinguishing elegance. Finally, as the delegations came forward in procession to sign the Constitution, Hamilton inscribed upon the great sheet of parchment the name of each state in its regular order. New York not being regarded as officially present the registry reads: "Mr. Hamilton from New York." During the performance of this ceremony [Virginia delegate James] Madison writes that the irrepressible humor of Franklin found expression in pointing to a sun painted upon the back of Washington's chair, remarking with a smile that painters had generally found it difficult in their art to distinguish a rising from a setting sun. "I have often and often," he continued, "in the course of the session, and the vicissitudes [fluctuations] of my hopes and fears as to its issue, looked at that sun behind the President without being able to tell whether it was rising or setting; but now I have the happiness to know that it is the rising sun."

Electrically Charmed

Thomas Fleming

Thomas Fleming, the highly respected historian and award-winning author of numerous fiction and non-fiction books, creates an exciting narrative of Franklin's famous 1752 kite-flying experiment, which allowed Franklin to prove that lightning and electricity are the same. Fleming, who is a contributor to National Public Radio (NPR) and a variety of television networks and shows such as The History Channel, PBS, and the Today Show, draws from the great amount of documentation Franklin left behind while taking note of the divergence from fact in some depictions of Franklin's world-famous experiment. Franklin's achievements in the study of electricity, Fleming explains, contributed to European perceptions of Franklin as superhuman. Furthermore, Fleming notes that Franklin freely offered to the public inventions that resulted from his various experiments such as the lightning rod and the "Pennsylvania fireplace," also called the "Franklin stove." Fleming's lively description exemplifies Franklin as a man who maintained his sense of humor and remained humble despite his renown.

From bright June sunshine, the sky above hot, muggy Philadelphia began changing to a sour gloomy gray. Soon there came glowering down upon the neat red-brick colonial metropolis a succession of huge black clouds. Windows slammed, tradesmen shut doors left open to relieve the stifling heat, mothers hastily called children indoors, and idlers vanished from street corners into the nearest tavern. The city was obviously about to endure that natural phenomenon known as a thunderstorm. People hoped it would bring some relief from the humid heat, which often made June in Philadelphia as unpleasant as equatorial Africa. But they also shivered with involuntary apprehension, as the first rumble of thunder surged over the city. Those black clouds carried in them deadly bolts of lightning.

FRANKLIN'S ELECTRICAL EXPERIMENTS ARE NOT MERE DABBLING

Only one man in Philadelphia greeted the oncoming storm with wholehearted delight. Benjamin Franklin had been waiting impatiently for weather like this for days. In his comfortable house on the southeast corner of Race and Second Streets, he called excitedly to his twenty-one-year-old son William. In a moment, Billy, as he was known in the family, appeared. He was a husky young man, over six feet tall, which gave him a two or three inch advantage over his father. He lacked the muscular, almost bear-like bulk of his father's chest and shoulders. But he carried himself with the confident, martial erectness of a soldier. Handsome was the only word to describe his rather narrow but fine-featured face. He shared his father's high forehead, and solid chin, but his mouth was not so relaxed or pleasant when it was in repose. Now it was pleasant enough, because William Franklin's face was aglow with excitement.

Franklin asked if everything was ready. William nodded. Quickly they slipped into loose cloth coats and hurried into the next room, where on a long table stood a variety of strange machines and apparatus. There were glass tubes and jars bound with strips of tin, glass globes on spindles, silk strings dangling from the ceiling. To anyone acquainted with eighteenth-century science, this apparatus, especially the tubes, and the peculiar tin encased jars with corks in their tops, through which a wire protruded, meant that this was the laboratory of a man interested in exploring the mysteries of electricity. For the last four years, this exploration had occupied almost all of Benjamin Franklin's days and nights. To find extra hours he had even resigned from his printing business [in 1748], sacrificing half his income, and moved to this house on the outskirts of Philadelphia where he was less accessible to his numerous friends.

When Franklin began his experiments electricity was a curiosity in the world of science. Experimenters created "electrical fire" by rubbing glass tubes with silk. They then stored the accumulated charges in the tin-lined bottles, called Leyden jars, in honor of the university where they were first invented [in the Netherlands]. But beyond the fact that electricity created magical effects—it could, for instance, animate a piece of twisted wire so that it looked like a living spider, or in a darkened room cause the gold border on an expensive book to glow—no one knew very much about it. In a series of classic experiments, Franklin had transformed electricity from a curiosity to a full-fledged branch of science. He had discovered the existence of plus and minus charges, and invented such terms as battery, conductor, and condenser. Now he was about to test his most daring hypothesis: that electricity and lightning were identical.

THE "PHILADELPHIA EXPERIMENT" OF 1752

As the first pattering of rain pelted the windows, William Franklin took from a dark corner of the laboratory a strange looking kite. It was made of a large thin silk kerchief. To the top of the vertical stick was fastened a pointed wire about fifteen or sixteen inches long. Benjamin Franklin took a Leyden jar and concealed it under his loose-fitting coat. Down the stairs and out the door went father and son. They hurried through the scattering raindrops to an open field not far from their house, part of the "commons" or grazing grounds of Philadelphia. On one side of the field was a shed, where citizens who grazed their cattle could take shelter from the rain or hot sun. While Franklin stood unobtrusively—he hoped—inside the shed, William raced across the empty pasture, and got the kite aloft in the tricky, gusty wind of the gathering storm. Then he too retreated under the shed.

William Franklin must have felt a little foolish, flying a kite in the rain. But he did not look nearly as ridiculous as his father would have looked, if someone had seen one of the leading citizens of Pennsylvania prancing across the commons on the same errand. There was the very large possibility that the hypothesis was wrong. If so, Benjamin Franklin did not want people guffawing at him in the streets, and maliciously asking him where he got his ridiculous idea about lightning. If his experiment turned out to be a dud, only William would know, and he could depend on his son to keep his mouth shut.

There was another reason why William was along. The experiment was dangerous. Franklin knew electricity could kill. He had killed animals with it, in his laboratory. Twice, by accident, he had knocked himself unconscious with it and, in another experiment, had prostrated [laid out] six grown men with a single charge. He also knew that lightning was far more powerful electricity than anything he had created in his laboratory. He had seen it reduce the metallic part of a roof, such as a drainspout, to molten jelly. This was not an experiment you could ask a friend to share. Only a son, who had already shared many lesser risks in the laboratory, could join Benjamin Franklin at this climactic moment.

In a few minutes, the kite was only a small dancing dot in the gloomy sky. William handed the kite string to his father. To the end of the twine was tied a strip of silk ribbon. Silk did not conduct electricity; it was an insulator. This was the only safeguard Franklin used against the deadly amount of electricity in the clouds above him. Contrary to the traditional [American lithographers Nathaniel] Currier and [James Merritt] Ives print, which shows Franklin and his son (pictured as a small boy) gleefully rejoicing when a bolt of lightning hit the kite, this was the last thing Franklin wanted to happen. The pointed wire at the top of his kite was designed to silently draw off some of the cloud's electric charge, just as a pointed conductor attracted electricity from a charged body in the laboratory. There was no need, much less a desire, for the massive and dangerous discharge of a lightning bolt. Where the twine and the silk joined, a small house key

Franklin's famous experiment with electricity is erroneously portrayed in this Currier and Ives print.

was fastened. This was where Franklin hoped the electricity would appear. Again and again, he touched the key with his knuckle. Nothing happened.

Over the city, the storm increased in fury. Thunder rumbled and lightning glinted. Then, William pointed excitedly toward a massive cloud moving downwind toward them. On it came, booming thunder while it passed right over their heads. The little kite danced and dived in the gusts of turbulence. Again, Benjamin Franklin touched the key with his knuckle. Surely now—

His face fell. The key was as cold and inert as it had been the day it was cast.

Now the sky was so black it was impossible to tell one cloud from another. More rain began to fall. The kite whirled and twisted and dived. Close to despair, Franklin gave up touching the key and stared disconsolately up at the murky sky. His mind raced back across the hundreds of experiments he had conducted, the studies he had made of the effects of lightning on houses and trees, trying to see where he had gone wrong. Then his eyes drifted toward the string in his hand. With an exclamation of triumph, he clapped his son on the back and pointed excitedly at the twine.

The loose threads were standing erect, separate from each other, just as if they had been electrified when suspended on a laboratory conductor. Cautiously Benjamin Franklin moved his knuckle toward the key. Through his hand and up his arm rushed that familiar tingling, shocking sensation which experimenters called an electric spark. . . . Now the rain began in earnest. As sheets of it swept across the field and thoroughly wet the string, Benjamin Franklin picked up the Leyden jar and touched its wire to the key. Electricity from the charged air within the cloud poured into it. This was the moment of maximum danger. If the kite had been struck by a lightning bolt at this point, most scientists agree that the charge would have leaped the strip of silk and both Franklins would have become charred corpses there on the Philadelphia common. But father and son were too enraptured by their discovery to worry about danger now. It was true! Electricity and lightning were one and the same. . . .

A few minutes later, the storm had passed. An exultant Franklin reeled in his kite and warned William to tell no one about their triumph. First he must communicate it to the scientific world. For the better part of the summer, father and son shared the momentous secret that was to catapult Benjamin Franklin into world fame.

It is difficult for the contemporary American to grasp why and how Benjamin Franklin's electrical achievements transformed an obscure Pennsylvania printer into the best-known American of his time. Today, most scientists are faceless figures, toiling anonymously in esoteric laboratories, their lives and works known only to fellow scientists. In the eighteenth century, scientists were celebrities whose writings were read by every educated man. When Franklin made his historic experiment with the kite in June of 1752, he had already written his masterwork, *Experiments and Observations on Electricity, Made at Philadelphia in America.* It was soon translated into Latin, French, German, and Italian. Scientists all over Europe attempted to prove or disprove his discoveries. . . .

In Franklin's report of his laboratory experiments, he had suggested another way to prove the identity of lightning and electricity. Erect a sentry box on a mountaintop or inside a church steeple, he said. The box should have a pointed iron rod in the roof, which would be connected to a Leyden jar inside. Because there was neither a church steeple nor a high mountain in the vicinity of Philadelphia, Franklin had not tried the experiment himself, and only later had the idea of a kite occurred to him. Now, before he had time to make his report to the world, letters from Europe informed him that a half dozen French and English scientists had successfully performed the "Philadelphia experiment," as it was soon called, using sentry boxes. Later, from Russia, came news that emphasized the danger of Franklin's experimental approach. A scientist in St. Petersburg had tried a variation on Franklin's sentry box idea, and put a rod on top of his house. He had failed to ground it properly and had been killed by a direct hit from a lightning bolt.

But the risk only made Franklin's triumph greater, in the eyes of an admiring world. The King of France [Louis XV] sent his personal congratulations across the ocean. The Royal Society, the elite of the English scientific world, elected Franklin a member by unanimous vote and bestowed upon him its highest accolade, the Copley Medal. Yale, then Harvard, gave him honorary degrees of Master of Arts and [the German] Immanuel Kant, the greatest philosopher of his time, called him the modern Prometheus [one of the Titans in Greek mythology], who had brought down the fire from Heaven.

Kant's words underscore the emotional explanation of Franklin's fame. In 1752, most men still believed that there was something divine about lightning. Emanating from the heavens, striking with such arbitrary yet devastating force, it was easily associated with the vengeance of an angry God. The man who tamed it readily acquired an awesome, almost superhuman image.

THE HERO DELIVERS TO THE PUBLIC

But instead of capitalizing on such a potentiality, Franklin avoided it. He announced the practical application of his discovery in an offhand, matter-of-fact way in a publication that had already gained him some modest fame in America—*Poor Richard's Almanack.*

> It has pleased God in his goodness to mankind at length to discover to them the means of securing their habitations and other buildings from mischief from thunder and lightning. The method is this: provide a small iron rod (it may be made of the rod-iron used by the nailers) but of such a length that one end being three or four feet in the moist ground, the other may be six or eight feet above the highest part of the building. To the upper end of the rod fasten about a foot of brass wire the size of a common knitting needle, sharpened to a fine point; the rod may be secured to the house by a few small staples. If the house or barn be long, there may be a rod and point at each end, and a middling wire along the ridge from one to the other. A house thus furnished will not be damaged by lightning, it being attracted by the points and passing through the metal into the ground without hurting anything. Vessels, also, having a sharp pointed rod fixed on the top of their masts, with a wire from the foot of the rod reaching down, round one of the shrouds, to the water, will not be hurt by lightning.

Although it would be difficult to patent an invention as simple as a lightning rod, it was typical of Franklin to give his idea away. When he invented a stove in 1742 which heated a room instead of allowing most of the warm air to go up the chimney, the Governor of Pennsylvania proposed to give him a monopoly patent. Franklin not only refused the favor, he published a pamphlet in which he completely described the construction and operation of the stove, so that any good blacksmith could make one. He redesigned the street lights of his time, discarding the globe shape and substituting "four flat panes with a funnel above to draw up the smoke." This meant that the lamp did not grow dark in a few hours, but remained bright until morning. When one of his older brothers became afflicted with a bladder disorder, Franklin invented the rubber catheter which is still in use today. When his eyes began troubling him, he invented bifocals, which enabled him to get along with only a single set of glasses. All of these ideas he donated to the world, free of charge. "As we enjoy great advantages from the inventions of others," he said, "we should be glad of an opportunity to serve others by any inventions of ours."

Gradually, cities around the world—Philadelphia, Boston, London, Paris—began to sprout these small sharp pointed spires, called lightning rods. Inevitably, there was some opposition from those who made it a business to superintend the relationship between men and God. When an earthquake struck Boston in 1755, one preacher assured his congregation that it was a warning from on high, because so many in the city were defying the divine will by resorting to those works of the devil, lightning rods.

FRANKLIN IS HUMBLE, HUMOROUS, AND CHARMED

In Europe, what made Franklin's name even more famous was the last part of the title of his historic essay on electricity. That such discoveries could be made by a man from "Philadelphia in America" was doubly amazing to Europeans who had become accustomed to thinking of the New World as a region inhabited largely by savages and frontiersmen with little more brains than it took to swing an ax, plow a furrow, and fire a gun. To his fellow Americans, who knew him better, Franklin was amazing in still another way. Here was a man who had astonished the civilized world, yet his formal education had ended in the second grade. He had arrived in Philadelphia at the age of sixteen, with a Dutch dollar and a few pennies in his pocket, a dirty, hungry, runaway printer's apprentice from his native Boston. At the age of 42, he had made enough money from his newspaper, *The Pennsylvania Gazette,* and from *Poor Richard's Almanack,* to retire from business and devote himself to science.

Yet with all his fame, Benjamin Franklin remained the same charming, genial man his friends had always known. Commenting on the congratulations from the King of France, he told one of his New England correspondents that his feelings reminded him of the story of a young girl who suddenly began prancing about in a proud and haughty manner. No one could figure out why "till it came to be known she had got on a pair of silk garters." Although his honors were not covered by petticoats, Franklin decided he had "not so much reason to be proud as the girl had; for a feather in the cap is not so useful a thing, or so serviceable to the wearer, as a pair of good silk garters."

At home, Franklin delighted in entertaining his friends and acquaintances with electrical showmanship. He placed a lightning rod on his chimney and connected it to two bells on his staircase. Between the bells was a little brass ball suspended by a silk thread. When the wire was charged, the ball would dance back and forth, striking the bells and announcing that the house was electrified. Often the bells rang when there was neither lightning nor thunder, making visiting ladies squeal with alarm. One night so much electricity rushed down the rod that Franklin was able to see it "in a continued dense white stream seemingly as large as my finger" between the bells. The whole staircase was "inlightened as with sunshine," he said, "so that one might see to pick up a pen."

In his laboratory, Franklin let the ladies feel the tingle of gentle shocks, he created miniature bolts of lightning, he made metals glow and wires dance. Once, on the banks of the Schuylkill [river in Philadelphia], he ignited some rum by sending an electric charge from one side of the river to the other. It was during one of these laboratory demonstrations that Franklin almost killed himself. He was showing how electricity could kill a turkey, using a charge from two specially constructed Leyden jars which contained as much power as forty of the ordinary size. The spectators were talking to Franklin and to one another. The conversation distracted him, and he accidentally touched the top wires of the jars while his other hand held the chain which was connected to the outside of both jars. There was an enormous flash and a crack as loud as a pistol. Franklin's body vibrated like a man in an epileptic convulsion. He described the impact as "an universal blow from head to foot throughout the body." Although he did not fall, for a few moments he blacked out completely. Lucky as usual, he escaped with nothing more serious than a soreness in his chest, "as if it had been bruised."

One day a crowd of gawkers gathered in front of Franklin's

house, hoping to catch a glimpse of an electrical miracle, or of the electrician himself. Franklin got rid of them with a humorous demonstration of his powers. He sent a healthy charge surging through the iron fence around the front of his house. The galvanized curiosity seekers vanished in a cloud of dust, convinced that the Devil himself was inside them.

This was the Franklin that Philadelphia loved—a man who somehow managed to combine laughter with everything, even the pursuit of scientific truth. Already his close friends in Philadelphia treasured gems of his wry humor. Once a neighbor came to him and asked how he could stop thieves from tapping a keg of beer he had in his backyard.

"Put a cask of Madeira [wine] beside it," was Franklin's answer.

Creating a Public Image

R. Jackson Wilson

The numerous memorable portraits and popular depictions of Benjamin Franklin are no accident. As Smith College's Parsons Professor of History R. Jackson Wilson explains, Franklin was quite adept in creating a popular public image, whether by expertly choosing appropriate attire for portraits and engravings or through his careful organization and artistry in composing his autobiography. In effect, Franklin was nothing less than an eighteenth-century publicist and above all else a writer who skillfully marketed himself and the ideas he supported. Wilson, who has been a Woodrow Wilson Fellow and who has held several fellowships in addition to teaching throughout the country and south Australia, offers keen insight into the historical importance of Franklin's marketing technique, specifically its political implications overseas as well as the resounding influences for generations to come.

In the winter of 1776–77, Benjamin Franklin sat for a portrait. It was a rush job, only a drawing to be used for an engraving [to be done by Augustin de Saint Aubin] to be put on sale later in the year. Its purposes were political. Franklin was in France as commissioner for the rebellious American Colonies. And the engraving, like the Franklin medallions that appeared in France at about the same time, was part of a publicity campaign to cultivate French support for the cause of American independence.

A PUBLICITY EXPERT, FRANKLIN MARKETS HIMSELF

Like any good publicist—and he was surely one of the world's best—Franklin arranged things carefully. The artist,

Charles Nicolas Cochin, was an experienced man of sixty-
one, politically uncontroversial, by and large unimaginative,
and thoroughly professional: in short, exactly the sort of
man needed for the task. The sitter was seventy, the agent of
a government born in the extreme controversies of revolution and war, a man of tireless imagination, and thoroughly
professional: in short, perfectly suited to his role. He chose
his clothes carefully. He wore a plain brown coat of the kind
French aristocrats liked to associate with the "Quaker" faith
Franklin let them suppose he held to. At his neck was a simple bit of marvelously white linen. But his master stroke was
a large, limp cap of marten fur. It was exactly the detail that
might most effectively foster a public image of Franklin as
the simple man of virtue from the New World. He wore it for
the portrait despite the fact that the first purchase he had
made in France, a few weeks before, was wigs—of the
smaller French fashion, to replace the larger and heavier
English wigs he had worn in London. And he let some long
strands of gray hair fall from under the fur cap, to empha-
size the fact that he might not wear a wig even if he were
hatless. (During much of the winter and spring, he took to
wearing the fur hat even at receptions indoors, as though it
were part of him and not just a garment; later, when the
French alliance had been successfully made, he stopped using the hat altogether.)

The plain suit and simple linen scarf, and particularly
that fur hat, were just the things to wear for a man whose
collected works had been republished in France in 1773 with
a little poem on the frontispiece that said he was the man
who "*Fait fleurir les Arts en des Climats sauvages*" [suc-
ceeded intellectually in a "primitive society" as America was
then considered]. But more than "Climats sauvages" were
involved. Franklin's simple costume was not merely the costume of an American. Aggressively simple clothes were becoming the fashion for intellectuals in France, and wearing
them was subtle testimony to his reputation as a learned
man. Even the fur hat had been adopted a decade earlier by
[Swiss-born French writer and philosopher] Jean-Jacques
Rousseau. Franklin understood his problem very well. He
had to convince the French not only that he was a figure of
New World innocence and simplicity, but also that he was a
man of profound learning, an authentic philosopher. In a
portrait made ten years earlier, by the British painter David

Martin, Franklin had posed in an ornate blue coat, with elaborate braid and gold buttons. He had worn a full-scale English wig. And he had been very much the philosopher, deeply absorbed in his books and writing, working intently under a bust of no less distinguished a colleague and model than Isaac Newton [the English mathematician and physicist]. Now, for the French, Franklin had put off the gentleman's bright colors, the braid and buttons and the wig. But he decided, for the second and almost the last time in his life, to use one prop that did effectively suggest his philosophical achievements: his glasses, the bifocals he himself had invented, and that had been such an important feature of the Martin portrait of the complete philosopher.

The result was a masterpiece—of posing if not of art. The picture held in balance two potentially contradictory assertions of personality. It was the portrait of an American, a plain man of simple virtues, in touch with wilderness, a naif. But it was also the portrait of a philosopher and savant, and this sagacious man also knew how to frame his mouth in a way that suggested shrewdness and perhaps even irony. . . .

Even the simplest portrait is a contrived affair—usually the product of the artist's efforts more than the subject's. But Franklin's 1777 effort went far beyond the ordinary limits of poses and props. It managed ingeniously not merely to suggest but to insist on certain definite messages. Its most immediate content was of course political. But the politics of revolution and war shaded over into larger ideological claims about the relationships among knowledge, virtue, and natural innocence. And to these ideological messages was joined another claim—the most elusive but perhaps the most insistent of all—that here was a truly extraordinary man, not a typical American at all, nor even just a man of earnest virtue and learning, but a man of remarkable vision and insight, a celebrity worthy of the boast that saluted him everywhere in France, that he had ripped the lightning from the sky and the scepter from the tyrant.

FRANKLIN APPLIES PR SKILLS TO HIS AUTOBIOGRAPHICAL COMPOSITION

In 1771, about halfway between the time of David Martin's philosopher portrait and Cochin's fur hat drawing, Franklin went to work on another portrait of himself, a manuscript that eventually became known as his autobiography. He described growing up in Boston, being an apprentice in his brother's newspaper office, then running away to make a new start. He told of how he had gone first to New York, looking for work as a printer. There was no work there, so he headed on south, for Philadelphia. Here Franklin paused in his narrative to take a quick inventory: "near 300 miles from home, a Boy of but 17, without the least Recommendation to or Knowledge of any Person in the Place, and with very little Money in my Pocket." Then he began to be "more particular" in his description of his trip. He was setting the stage for what is probably the most artful paragraph in his autobiography, a sketch of himself that would become nearly a folk image for generations of readers. He wrote with care and economy, and with a fine eye for detail, of the seventeen-year-old boy's first morning in Philadelphia. He has only a Dutch dollar and about a shilling in copper coins, and he gives the copper away. He is hungry. The trip down from New York has been a hard one. He has spent a miserable and wet night on an old boat in a storm. Another boat on which he traveled, just the night before, was lost for a time in the darkness. He has had a fever. He knows no one, and even his companions on the boat are headed farther down the Delaware. He has committed a serious crime by violating his indenture to his brother, so now he is incognito. For the moment, he has only the somewhat ragged working clothes on his back, plus a spare shirt and stockings stuffed incompletely into his pockets. He has some difficulty getting food because he does not know the names and prices of bread in this strange place. He tries to ask for "bisket," and gets nowhere; then for a "threepenny Loaf," with the same result. Finally, he asks the baker for three pennies' worth of anything, and is surprised at being given "three great Puffy Rolls." He tucks one under each arm and starts munching on the third while he walks up the streets away from the Delaware River. He can eat only one of the rolls, so he turns back toward the Delaware, where he drinks from the river. Then he gives the other two rolls away, to a woman he had been on the boat with, as though to divest himself of every remaining bit of surplus. He wanders into a Quaker meeting. He looks from face to face, but no one speaks, and he falls into a sleep so deep that he has to be roused when the meeting is ended.

The story may be true, even in its details—just as it is true that Franklin really owned a fur hat in 1777. But, true or not, it is a piece of writing as cunning and effective as his decision to wear that hat for the Cochin drawing. In one paragraph, Franklin created a classic picture of a lad poised between a past he has escaped and a future he has not yet begun to have. He is caught in midair, without resources and hindrances, simultaneously lost and free, hungry and broke but content with bread and water, alert and watchful but able to sleep innocently in that silent meetinghouse. He is on his own, without family, property, or job. He is pure possibility.

But Franklin's skill was even greater. He managed to build into his sketch another, quite different figure, a sage and celebrated old man, who was, after all, managing the whole scene. He began his paragraph by intrusively pointing out the contrast between the boy he was about to describe and the man he had become. "I have been the more particular in this Description of my Journey, and shall be so of my first Entry into that City, that you may in your Mind compare such unlikely Beginnings with the Figure I have since made there." He ended the paragraph with a wry sentence about the meetinghouse: "This was therefore the first House I was in or slept in, in Philadelphia"—a quick reminder that he would not only sleep in but eventually own a number of others. And at almost exactly the midpoint of the paragraph, he inserted another even more pointed reminder of the man that boy would become. "Thus I went up Market Street as far as fourth Street, passing by the Door of Mr. Read, my future Wife's Father, when she standing at the Door saw me, and thought I made as I certainly did a most awkward ridiculous Appearance."

The effect of these three sentences is the same as the effect of wearing his bifocals in the 1777 drawing. The risk that earnest and innocent youth might be taken as permanent awkwardness and rusticity is offset by an insistence on "the Figure I have since made." The gratuitous agreement with Miss Read's later report that the boy looked "ridiculous"—"I certainly did"—is an equally emphatic reminder that the man writing this paragraph is a man of fame, reputation, and learning. The boy may be perfectly naive, but the writer visibly hovers over him, wearing a sophisticated look that blends affection with canny assessment. . . .

EXAMINATION OF THE AUTOBIOGRAPHY REVEALS ARTIFICE

The technique Franklin put to work in this famous paragraph was one he used over and over in the book he called his "History." It was a writing stratagem that enabled him to generate a figure of himself that was simultaneously that of an earnest young tradesman and a wily old celebrity. He was writing a book that could be read in two distinct ways, by two different kinds of readers. An innocent reader—Franklin obviously had in mind aspiring young men of the type he had once been—could read it deadpan, as an improving and inspiring set of lessons on life. Thousands of young men would eventually read it that way. But Franklin could expect a more sophisticated reader to have quite a different sense of him and his book. In the early pages, gently and without insisting overmuch on the point, he made it very clear that he had mastered the essential books of the eighteenth century. In the course of arguing that modern Romance languages should be learned before Latin, he unobtrusively made it clear that he was, linguistically, a very learned gentleman. He even toyed with improvements on some lines of [famed eighteenth-century English poet and literary genius] Alexander Pope. The reader who absorbed the import of such passages would neither admire a tradesman's struggle for success, nor mock the pious moralism of a provincial burgher [an upright citizen of the middle class]. Such a reader would see beyond the surface of things. In fact, if Franklin could expect a cultivated reader to admire anything, it would be neither his youthful character nor his middle-aged achievements; it would be his mature capacity to control scenes and passages in which irony was gently superimposed on earnestness, to the damage of neither. For such a reader, this was the awareness that would rescue Franklin from the main nightmare of the self-made man: that he might appear ridiculous to people of refinement and cultivated taste. Franklin was the very model of the bourgeois-become-gentleman. But he knew he spoke prose, and an artful prose it was, for those who could read it.

It is a bit indiscreet to attribute artful stratagems to the writer of a personal history. Autobiographies are normally meant to be taken as faithful reportings, with no textual space for a cunning narrator. And Franklin's is seemingly one of the most plain and honest of autobiographies. It was written in straightforward English prose. There is no pretension in either its content or its language. Readers may have admired Franklin; they may have chuckled with him; or they may have become indignant at his moralizing and apparent small-mindedness. But whatever Franklin's huge audiences have felt about his book, they have almost always agreed on one point: that the man they have met in the book *is* Franklin, plain and unadorned. The man seems to be so fully and honestly in his book that generations of readers have responded to the story as if it *were* the man.

In ordinary men and woman, plainspokenness may be a mere habit. But in a writer it is something else. It is a device designed to disarm and invite the reader onto the author's ground. Franklin's autobiography, especially in the part he wrote in England about his youth in Boston, Philadelphia, and London, is a very seductive book. It involves the reader so gently, so imperceptibly, in the story that it is difficult to see the writer at work. Even the beginning, with its return address ("Twyford, at the Bishop of St. Asaph's 1771"), its conventional salutation ("Dear Son"), and its stiff opening sentence ("I have ever had a Pleasure in obtaining any little Anecdotes of my Ancestors"), was a bit of framing whose obvious purpose was to create the impression that the reader was looking over Franklin's shoulder, eavesdropping on a man writing, not a writer. Franklin's most stunning artistic achievement in his autobiography was, in fact, to generate an atmosphere of artlessness. And this, in turn, has led most of his readers to make an almost perfect confusion between the tale and its teller.

FIRST AND FOREMOST, FRANKLIN WAS A WRITER

But Franklin was above all a teller, a writer. He did many things, but he almost never did anything without writing about it. He invented a new kind of stove—then wrote about it. He devised electrical experiments that may have been the most important scientific work of the century—then wrote about them. He wrote early and often: poems, broadsides, essays, letters, almanacs, speeches, projects and by-laws, metaphysical essays, parodies, epitaphs, and even prayers. By the time he set to work on his autobiography, he was in fact a very famous author. A fourth edition of his *Experiments and Observations on Electricity* had just been published in England. The next year, he would be made a foreign associate of the Académie des Sciences [French Academy of Sciences]. Two years later, in 1773, the French edition of his various writings was published. He had already been called by [eighteenth-century Scottish philoso-

pher and historian] David Hume the first man of letters
America had produced. In August 1772, he boasted that
"Learned and ingenious foreigners that come to England, almost all make a point of visiting me." And he understood
perfectly well that "a principal Means" behind all this fame
was his ability as a prose writer.

Franklin knew the popular rhyme "The man of words and
not of deeds/is like a garden full of weeds." But for him, language and action were so inextricably blended that he could
frame a hilarious alternative: "A man of deeds and not of
words/Is like a garden full of . . ." He was a writer with more
than enough wit and skill to write for two audiences at once,
to write a sketch that skillfully juxtaposed youth and age, innocence and irony. He had more than enough talent and experience to write a whole book with such method. The autobiography was not a series of barely connected spurts of
prose, each with its own logic. A governing set of authorial
purposes and writing techniques gave the whole book a definite shape, consistency, and subtlety.

Was Benjamin Franklin a British Spy?

Cecil B. Currey

*In this historical interpretation by Cecil B. Currey,
professor emeritus of history at the University of
South Florida, an alternate image of Benjamin
Franklin emerges. The evidence Currey presents in
this excerpt from his book* Code Number 72/Ben
Franklin: Patriot or Spy? *is drawn from a variety of
sources such as British archives, peer opinions of
Franklin (usually voiced in letters), and even some
of Franklin's own letters. Currey, an expert in U.S.
military history, takes a look at these documents to
piece together his theory that Franklin was a British
spy, a theory enhanced by seemingly odd circumstances pertaining to many of Franklin's papers.*

There seems to be a general agreement among historians on
the fact that Franklin considerably aided the American cause
[as Diplomat to France]. And yet there is reason to suspect
that this was not his primary purpose on his mission to
France [1776–1785]. Those who have made him central in the
drama which culminated in the delivery of French aid to
America have heavily glossed over the background of European power politics and continental intrigue within which he
operated. To be sure, Franklin did emerge from the war years
as an American hero, but those who have praised his life in
France could do so only by winking at bits and pieces of evidence which simply do not fit into the usual Franklin mold.
Writers have been able to uphold Franklin as a paragon of
moderation, wisdom, and virtue only by suppressing or ignoring comments by his peers which were often bitter,
pointed, and possibly quite close to the mark. Franklin repu-
diated and dismissed as sheer madness critical descriptions
of himself by those who best knew him, and through the

Excerpted from "Envoy in Paris," in *Code Number 72/Ben Franklin: Patriot or Spy?* by
Cecil B. Currey (Englewood Cliffs, NJ: Prentice-Hall). Copyright © 1972 by Cecil B.
Currey. Reprinted by permission.

years the voices of his critics have been muted while Franklin's own voice still booms forth. Ben's defenders have carefully steered away from detailed analysis of several projects in which he involved himself while in France.

POPULAR PERCEPTIONS OF FRANKLIN CONTRADICT MANY PEER OPINIONS

The popular picture of Franklin as a hero remains uncorrected only because so few have been interested in examining the frame in which it hangs. As one author [Thomas Perkins Abernethy] has suggested:

> So great is the reputation of [Franklin] that almost no modern writer has undertaken to question the uprightness of his actions or failed to accept his testimony at face value, while the evidence given by [others] so far as it relates to Franklin, though supported in many instances by . . . other reliable authorities, has been thrown out of court without serious consideration. Such historical practice is, of course, not justifiable. A discarding of hero worship and a careful weighing of all contemporary evidence would produce a conclusion quite different from that which has been reached.

Past authors have not always checked Franklin's words against contemporary descriptions of his activities made by his peers. Some have been unwilling to give an honest hearing to Franklin's critics. When these things are done, the results are startling. The shadowy phase of Franklin's life that emerges here does not fit easily into the accepted view of Benjamin Franklin. To be sure, there remain large gaps which have had to be bridged by speculations and suppositions. Where such speculations are interposed upon the available records, their speculative nature is explicitly acknowledged rather than carefully hidden, as is too often the case in other works on Franklin.

Getting at the truth about Benjamin Franklin is no easy matter. One modern interpreter [Malcolm R. Eiselen] has suggested that at times Franklin resembled a chameleon. A chameleon blends with its background as a defense, hiding itself from careful investigation and known dangers. The allusion to Franklin is apt. His adulators tend to make us forget that Franklin was not always praised. A contemporary [Edward Thornton] described him as a man of "talents without virtue." His old enemy Alexander Wedderburn thought of him as the most "hypocritical, abandoned old rascal that ever existed—a man who, if ever one goes to Hell, he will." George

Chalmers, a Tory historian, wrote of Franklin that he was "trained in the hardy school of private treachery, stained with the honourable blood of injured friendship, he thought he was qualified to be a public traitor—and he did not err. Unhappy man! His ambitious villainy is stopt for want of space."

These comments, however, should not be counted very heavily, for they were uttered by men with whom Franklin had only limited contacts. His colleagues, those with whom he worked closely while in France, should have known him better, and we should expect that their evaluations would be of more worth. John Adams worked side by side with Franklin for months. An admittedly testy person, Adams soon came to view Franklin darkly and held to this conviction all his days. He described Franklin as "secretive" and said that his "practical cunning united with his theoretick Ignorance render him one of the most curious Characters in History. After Yorktown, as tentative peace negotiations with Britain began in earnest, Adams warned that in those delicate maneuverings, "Franklin's cunning will be to divide us; to this end he will provoke, he will insinuate, he will intrigue, he will manoeuvre."

The opinion of Arthur Lee, who had known and worked under and with Franklin for years, is also interesting in this respect. Lee was a proud, cantankerous, difficult man at best, and later writers have sometimes described him as nearly paranoid in his relations with others. The charge originated with Franklin who felt that Lee had unwarrantedly crossed him, but it has remained to darken the worthwhile accomplishments of that cranky man from Virginia. For several years after their first acquaintance, Lee could speak of Franklin's "wisdom and industry" and his "firmness and equanimity which conscious integrity alone can inspire"; these were qualities which, Lee observed, "must endear him" to Americans. Further association with Franklin and observation of him brought Lee to change his mind, however. By 1778 he was convinced that Franklin was "dangerous" and "capable of any wickedness." It would be necessary to watch Franklin circumspectly in order to gather information leading to his "detection and punishment.". . .

WAS FRANKLIN AN EIGHTEENTH-CENTURY JAMES BOND?

In these ways was the Philadelphian assessed by two men— one of whom is dismissed as utterly unreliable by the bulk of historiography, while the other was destined to become the second President of the United States. Both were highly suspicious of Franklin, and their suspicions appear to have been abundantly true. But the full truth was even worse than anything these men even dared to suggest, although Arthur Lee seems to have hinted at the possibility. A cell of British Intelligence was located in Franklin's headquarters in France, and Benjamin Franklin—covertly perhaps, tacitly at least, possibly deliberately—cooperated with and protected this spy cell operating out of his home in France from shortly after his arrival in that country until the end of the war. Willingly or not, he made himself a party to treason toward his own country while serving as its representative abroad. British Intelligence referred to him in its codes as "72," "Moses," and perhaps in other ways.

One author [Richard Deacon] has put the issue in a straightforward way. His words are so pungent that they bear reproducing in full.

> ... it was when Benjamin Franklin was at the American Embassy in Paris that the British Secret Service achieved its most conspicuous success. . . . Not only did Britain learn all the American secrets but many items of French intelligence as well, for the French trusted Franklin and gave him a great deal of information. The kindest deduction one could make from all this was that Franklin was duped by his assistant [Bancroft] and, from a security point of view, was utterly incompetent. But a close examination of the facts by no means suggests that this was the case. Franklin was widely travelled, an efficient administrator, a man of the world, fully cognisant of intrigues and highly intelligent. It is unthinkable that he did not know something of what was going on. And when Arthur Lee confronted him with the charge that [Edward] Bancroft was a spy in the service of the British and actually gave proof of this, showing how Bancroft's links with the British Secret Service had been uncovered and how when he visited London he was in touch with the Privy Council, Franklin stubbornly refused to accept the evidence. Franklin countered by denouncing Lee and insisted that Bancroft's visits to London produced worthwhile intelligence for America. The truth was that all Bancroft brought back from these trips was false information provided by the British.

If Benjamin Franklin was innocent of complicity in the British spying operations, then the information leakage from his embassy is incomprehensible. Those security leaks could be explained if Franklin was duped or himself somehow involved with the British Secret Service.

Consider other items regarding Franklin's career in France.

The French Foreign Ministry and other Americans in Paris complained that the British ambassador knew their every move.

Copies of many of Franklin's reports to the Congress as well as the reports of others ended up in the British archives.

Franklin vehemently rejected charges of espionage made against Bancroft, refusing to investigate these legitimate denunciations. Instead, he reviled those who had made the charges and continued to use Bancroft in positions of trust and responsibility. So employed, Bancroft had access to major American state secrets and all of the commission papers. . . .

A MYSTERIOUS PAPER TRAIL: EVIDENCE FOR SPYING

The following account of Franklin's activities in France has been pieced together using very few of his own manuscripts. His surviving papers have had to be supplemented in almost every case with material drawn from records of his contemporaries. Part of this difficulty has been caused by time's natural attrition of old manuscripts. Perhaps thousands of Benjamin Franklin's papers have been destroyed. His correspondence for a period of twenty years, including material which would have been helpful in reconstructing the early years covered in this study, were left in the hands of a longtime friend, Joseph Galloway, when Franklin sailed for France in the fall of 1776. Galloway's home was later ransacked and many of Franklin's records were destroyed. After Ben's death in 1790, others of his papers from the war years were stored in a barn and later given away to those interested in them. Of these many never have been recovered, and of those not dispersed in this way, many deteriorated badly from the conditions under which they had been stored.

William Temple Franklin later took still others of his grandfather's manuscripts to London. He planned to use many of them for a printed edition of Benjamin Franklin's works. After he had used those which he wanted, the remaining ones were discarded, and after his death no one claimed those manuscripts still in his possession. Some years later a London tailor was found using those grand old quarto sheets for cutting dress patterns. Thus the years have taken their toll.

Other factors have reduced the total number of available documents. Caught up in clandestine diplomatic and political affairs, it is entirely possible that Franklin deliberately got rid of those papers which might compromise his position. We know that this was, upon occasion, the case. Franklin once wrote to [his American comrade Silas] Deane urging that a record be "buried in oblivion." "I earnestly desire," wrote Franklin, "that you would put that paper immediately in the fire on receipt of this, without taking or suffering to be taken any copy of it, or communicating its contents." At another time his grandnephew, Jonathan Williams, Jr., who was deeply involved with Franklin in profiteering and, perhaps, spying, wrote his uncle to say that he had immediately destroyed the old doctor's letter after reading it. What we have a record of in two cases after 190 years may be supposed to have happened on other occasions. We know that Franklin was an assiduous paper-saver and record keeper—a veritable "pack rat." He retained as many as possible of the documents that crossed his desk. Why would he frantically urge Deane to destroy a memorandum? Why should Williams have destroyed a message immediately after reading it? The most obvious answer is that those papers, held in the wrong hands, might well be used to hurt Franklin's career and the pursuits in which he was engaged.

What things were done on verbal orders only that were never committed to paper? This has always been the most common way in which intelligence agents have operated. [An authority on Franklin's diplomatic career in France] Samuel Flagg Bemis has put the matter well. "It lies," he has written, "in the very nature of his trade that the international spy should, whenever he can, obliterate the traces of his work; nevertheless, despite his efforts, his story will sometimes leave material for the sober historian. . . ." It is not only the spy who is interested in obliterating the record of his passing. From time to time involved governments also have suppressed or restricted public printing of such "traces." Such publications might damage future official policies or might picture past ones in unfavorable ways. If activities like these were publicly aired and the public at large learned about participation in clandestine programs, governmental office holders might find their reputations lessened. Governments also have exerted themselves in efforts to protect agents who have been directly involved in the field, so long as hurt might come to the principals concerned or to their immediate relatives by such publications.

Not too long after the close of the war, rumors appeared that the British government was indeed trying to keep some of Benjamin Franklin's writings from being published. In the introduction to an early collection of his printed papers, the editor charged that the English administration had bribed William Temple Franklin to keep him from issuing a long awaited edition of his grandfather's works. Temple, the editor wrote, "had found a bidder . . . in some emissary of government, whose object was to withhold the manuscripts from the world." Such charges had earlier been made in the *Edinburgh Review,* the *American Citizen,* and the *National Intelligencer.* One such story appeared in *The Argos or London Review in Paris,* 28 March 1807. Three days later Temple made a rebuttal in the paper in which he denied the allegation. Whatever the reasons for Temple's delay in issuing his grandfather's papers (and a major factor may well have been his preoccupation with the very profitable land agency in which he was working), twenty-eight years passed between Benjamin Franklin's death and Temple's publication of his works in 1818.

The policies of Britain in those years have long since passed into dust. The archives of England and of France have for generations been open to the researcher. In these records, says Bemis, "may be found two principle classes of sources . . . : reports of operatives and spies to their superior officers, which in turn were digested and summarized for perusal by higher executives, and petitions and memorials for reward for past services rendered." Such materials are available. Those two-hundred-year-old papers tell in their always archaic, often dry, sometimes quaint style the devious involvements of Franklin in Paris.

In addition, many of Franklin's papers have survived and have been used in this story. Of the records which he kept, many were retained simply because to him they did not seem compromising. He did not know that one day someone would lay them side-by-side with other records, fitting the whole into a revealing pattern. From such a procedure there emerges an unrecognized, or at least unexpressed, view that differs considerably from earlier descriptions of Franklin, his friends, his work. It can now be seen that many of the things Franklin said, used by earlier historians as evidence for his moderation, his industry, or his talents, were set forth to conceal himself from danger. Still other statements he made were camouflage for his real ambitions, desires, and activities.

The characters involved in this strange situation were numerous and varied. . . . The story of their activities and of Franklin's part in them does not begin when their paths first crossed during the American Revolution. The roots are elsewhere, in the character of Benjamin Franklin and in his career during the prewar years.

Ben Franklin's Highly Experimental Practice of Medicine

Whitfield J. Bell Jr.

Medical historian Whitfield J. Bell Jr. spent seven years as an associate editor of the papers of Benjamin Franklin. Franklin, as Bell notes in this article, was always interested in public welfare and consequently sought to share medical information with the public by publicizing his research as well as the findings of others. Whether sharing information about smallpox inoculations, promoting general healthcare and preventive medicine, or experimenting with alternative treatments utilizing electricity, Franklin's motivation was always benevolent. Bell himself was the recipient in 1996 of the Lifetime Achievement Award from the American Association for the History of Medicine.

Medicine was a branch of knowledge with which almost every educated man in the eighteenth century had some acquaintance. Laymen discussed medical principles as they did eclipses, humming birds, and Greek forms of government. They bought, read, and annotated medical texts, treated illnesses in their own households, sometimes even attended anatomical lectures. It is not surprising that in such an atmosphere Benjamin Franklin too should have been interested in medical science, or that he should have made discerning comments on health and disease and even prescribed remedies for the sick.

SCIENCE, PUBLIC WELFARE, AND INOCULATION FOR SMALLPOX

In Franklin's case the general climate of the age was reinforced by his special scientific interest. Among the books and gadgets and electrical apparatus in his library, for ex-

Excerpted from "Benjamin Franklin and the Practice of Medicine," in *The Colonial Physician and Other Essays,* by Whitfield J. Bell Jr. Copyright © 1975 by Science History Publications. Reprinted by permission.

ample, a visitor in 1787 saw a "glass machine for exhibiting the circulation of the blood in the arteries and veins of the human body." Because physicians had had formal scientific training and were likely as well to be rationalists with warm humanitarian sympathies, Franklin found them congenial, and he was closely associated with a number of them in both his experimental work and in his public career. . . .

Throughout his life Franklin was a willing publicist of medical information. He had definite theories of disease and therapy and, as was the case when he believed his ideas would benefit men, he urged them strongly and constantly in his publications and in private letters. He reprinted John Tennent's *Every Man His Own Physician,* recommending it to the public but warning that as Pennsylvania ipecac [a medicinal root] was stronger than the Virginia variety, the prescribed dosages should be modified accordingly. Franklin spread abroad other men's medical ideas as well. No sooner had he returned to England from a visit to Paris, for example, than he sent his friend [French physician and botanist] Jacques Barbeu-Dubourg a copy of Thomas Dimsdale on smallpox inoculation which they had been discussing; and his parting gift to the Royal Society of Medicine in Paris was a copy of [the preliminary work by England's John] Haygarth on smallpox.

Smallpox was something about which he was deeply concerned through more than sixty years. It was a great killer, terrible and swift; as a result laymen as well as physicians devoted a good deal of thought and energy to measures of prevention and treatment. Franklin was an early advocate of inoculation, and never wavered in his support of it. His brother James' newspaper, the *New England Courant,* it is true, had attacked inoculation, but that was because [the American clergyman and author] Cotton Mather endorsed it; and the Franklins were anti-clerical. In Philadelphia, where such rivalries did not prevail, the younger Franklin supported the new preventive measures and at every opportunity spread knowledge of improved methods of preparing the patient and administering the disease. . . .

Repeatedly as the years passed Franklin collected statistics from towns where smallpox was epidemic. All the figures showed that taking smallpox by inoculation was many times safer than to receiving "in the natural way"; and Franklin spread the figures and his conclusion as widely as he could in private letters to physicians and others. In 1759 he presented statistics from a recent Boston epidemic, with the arguments based on them, as a preface to Dr. William Heberden's *Some Account of the Success of Inoculation for the Small-Pox*. Skilful, humane, and successful, Heberden was convinced that inoculation was so safe and desirable that it might and should be practiced by intelligent laymen; his pamphlet presented plain instructions, expressed, at Franklin's suggestion, in simple language, to enable any person to perform the operation and conduct the patient through the disease and convalescence. Franklin sent 1500 copies to America for free distribution by physicians and leading citizens. . . .

A PROGRESSIVE ATTITUDE TOWARD HEALTH MAINTENANCE

Franklin never tired of propagandizing his conviction that fresh air, exercise, and temperance are essential to prevent disease and preserve health. "Wouldst thou enjoy a long Life, a healthy Body, and a vigorous Mind?" *Poor Richard* [a character Franklin created to author his almanac] asked in 1742; then "bring thy Appetite into Subjection to Reason." Here was Franklin's basic principle of healthful living. Though he did not always practice it, he never forgot it; and whenever illness overtook him, he resumed his rational regimen, putting more reliance on moderation in food and drink, fresh air and gentle exercise than on the doctors' powders and potions. . . .

As a youth Franklin had come upon a copy of Thomas Tryon's seventeenth century *Way to Health, Long Life and Happiness*. Convinced by Tryon's arguments, but partly, it must be admitted, for economy's sake, young Franklin had become a vegetarian; and, though he resumed meat-eating, he often returned to the vegetarian diet for brief periods for reasons of health. "In general," he wrote, "mankind, since the improvement of cooking, eats about twice as much as nature requires. Suppers are not bad, if we have not dined, but restless nights naturally follow hearty suppers after full dinners. . . . Nothing is more common in newspapers than instances of people who, after eating a hearty supper, are found dead abed in the morning."

Franklin believed in exercise as stoutly as in temperate diet, and for the same reason—that medical treatment was uncertain. Exercise, he advised his son, was "of the greatest importance to prevent diseases, since the cure of them by physic is so very precarious." He advocated swimming as "one of the most healthy and agreeable" exercises, and he himself swam when he was 70 years old; recommended that people walk when they could not swim, and swing dumbbells in their rooms when they could not walk—as he did daily at 82. . . .

Franklin was the great advocate of fresh air. The lack of it, he pointed out to English physicians, was a cause of high mortality in the manufacturing towns. "Our Physicians," he wrote in 1773, "have begun to discover that fresh Air is good for People in the Small-Pox and other Fevers. I hope in time they will find out that it does no harm to People in Health;" and he derided English fears of fresh air. "Many London

FRANZ MESMER'S MAGNETISM IS SCRUTINIZED BY FRANKLIN AND OTHERS

Although Franklin certainly advocated a variety of progressive medical treatments, not all alternative therapies gained his support. As a University of Houston mechanical engineering and history professor John H. Lienhard explains, Franklin chaired the committee that sought to determine the validity of Franz Mesmer's theory of "animal magnetism." After extensive testing, the committee could not rationalize Mesmer's use of magnets to treat illness. However, Lienhard, an expert in thermal sciences and cultural history, concludes that the future holds in store endless possibilities when it comes to magnets and healing.

It's 1784 in Paris. A Royal Commission submits its report on Mesmerism. The report is a masterpiece of clean, rational, scientific analysis. But then, look who wrote it!

The Chairman of the committee is our ambassador to France, Ben Franklin. He's the reigning expert on electricity. Here's the French chemist, Antoine Lavoisier. He first isolated oxygen. Ten years later he'll lose his head on the guillotine. The guillotine's inventor, Dr. Guillotin, is also on the committee.

For six years, Franz Mesmer has swept Parisian society with his magnetic and hypnotic cures. He's formed a theory of "animal magnetism." Illness occurs when the flow of our natural electromagnetic force becomes blocked. The wealthy flock to Mesmer's salon to be cured by magnetic fluxes. . . .

Now these rationalists put Mesmer under their lens. Stephen Jay Gould [Harvard paleontologist and science writer] tells us families go out once a day to take the air," he remarked; "three or four persons in a coach, one perhaps sick; these three go three or four miles, or as many turns in Hyde Park, with the glasses both up close, all breathing over again the same air they brought out of town with them in the coach with the least change possible, and render'd worse and worse every moment. And this they call *taking the Air*." John Adams [the second U.S. president] has left an amusing account of Franklin's fervid advocacy of fresh air. Travelling together to New York, the two men shared a small room at an inn at New Brunswick, N.J. The window was open when they entered the room; Adams shut it tight at once. "Oh," said Franklin, "don't shut the window; we shall be suffocated." Adams declared he was afraid of the night air. "The

they know they can't look at animal magnetism directly. Mesmer claims it has no material properties.

Nor can they study Mesmer's cures. No doubt he cured many people just by keeping them out of 18th-century doctors' hands. What they can do is look for the effects of animal magnetism.

So they replicate Mesmer's sessions—over and over. Franklin, Lavoisier, and the rest sit for 2½ hours at a time around a container filled with magnetized rods. Like Mesmer, they play eerie music on a glass harmonica. The glass harmonica, ironically enough, was something that Franklin had developed.

Still, this strict and sober adherence to the ritual fails to cure Franklin's gout—or any other illness in the committee.

Mesmer also made his cures available to the public. He claimed to've magnetized certain trees in Paris. You can cure yourself by hugging them. So they take a Mesmer disciple to five such trees at Franklin's home. He embraces one at a time. At the fourth he falls in a swoon. But they've tricked him. They've applied magnets only to the last tree, the one the man never reached.

These rationalists finally did Mesmer in. Yet they didn't end the belief that drove the fad. How could they? We know perfectly well there's more to healing than rational science can tell us.

Who on that committee could've foreseen the magnetic dimension of modern scanners? What modern doctor knows the dimensions, yet unseen, of future healing? In the end, we catch a glimpse of Mesmer's ghost—riding in laser beams, X-rays, and ultra-sound.

Ben Franklin and Franz Mesmer, February 2001, www.uh.edu/engines/epi710htm.

air within this chamber will soon be, and indeed is now, worse than that without doors," Franklin replied firmly. "Come, open the window and come to bed, and I will convince you. I believe you are not acquainted with my theory of colds." And with that Franklin threw up the window. Poor Adams leaped into bed, and the Doctor, Adams recorded, "then began a harangue upon air and cold, and respiration and perspiration," which soon put Adams to sleep and, he believed, put Franklin to sleep as well, for the last words Adams remembered hearing from his companion were pronounced in a faraway drone as though Franklin were already losing consciousness.

Franklin's advocacy of cold air baths was widely known in the eighteenth century, and perhaps as widely marvelled at. He thought them less a shock to the system than cold water. "I rise almost every morning," he wrote, "and sit in my chamber without any clothes whatever, half an hour or an hour, according to the season, whether reading or writing. This practice is not in the least painful, but, on the contrary, agreeable." After all, he told Dr. Rush, people do not *catch* cold from being cold or wet; but because of poor ventilation, too rich a diet, and too little exercise. One of the unwritten medical classics is Franklin's treatise on colds; only an outline of it—a very full outline, be it said—survives; but like the great work he contemplated on the "Art of Virtue," it was never finished. So famous, indeed, was Dr. Franklin's air bath that some hygienists believed it should have a local habitation as well as a name: at least a German magazine in 1798 published a picture of Franklin's *Luftbad:* an attractive Chinese pavilion suited to a quiet corner of a romantic garden. . . .

ELECTRICITY OFFERS HOPE; FRANKLIN RECOMMENDS SHOCK TREATMENT

But it was, as one might expect, as an electrician that Franklin played his most active and intimate role as a practitioner of medicine. He was the first electrician in the world; and electricity—"the pure physic of the skies"—was believed by many to be the most powerful, because it was the most nearly divine, of all medicines. Certainly it seemed at first to offer benefit in cases of nervous disorders. The press in the late 1740s and early 1750s was filled with accounts of spectacular cures: the blind saw, the deaf heard, paralytics walked home after submitting to shocks from the miraculous fluid. Franklin did not fail to note that most of these "cures" took place in remote Italian, German or Russian villages, and were unsubstantiated; and he considered that even in less backward places some persons were "too premature in publishing their imaginations and expectations for real experiments." But patients given up as incurable grasped at any hope; soon they began to appeal to Franklin. He could not refuse, nor did he. . . .

Too often, of course, the results were negative, as Franklin knew they would be; and not all the improvements which patients made could properly be ascribed to the electrical treatment. To Sir John Pringle in 1757 Franklin summarized his experience in measured terms. He first observed "an immediately greater sensible Warmth in the lame Limbs that had receiv'd the Stroke"; the next morning the patients usually reported a pricking sensation in the paralyzed limbs during the night; and the limbs themselves seemed to have recovered strength and to be more capable of movement. Sometimes this improvement continued for five days, "but I do not remember that I ever saw any Amendment after the fifth Day." Seeing that improvement did not continue, the patients became restless and discouraged; most went home and relapsed; "so that I never knew any Advantage from Electricity in Palsies that was permanent. And how far the apparent temporary advantage might arise from the exercise in the patient's journey, and coming daily to my home, or from the spirits given by the hope of success, enabling them to exert more strength in moving their limbs, I will not pretend to say."

Yet confidence in the powers of electricity continued little abated, especially in rural areas and among quacks like the notorious James Graham, and even in London. Not long after Franklin reached England in 1757 Sir John Pringle begged him to electrise the epileptic daughter of the Duke of Ancaster; and a young Border squire, who had lost his hearing after an attack of smallpox, proposed coming to London to be electrised, if Franklin thought it would help. Similar expressions of confidence in electricity and Franklin greeted the old man when he reached France as an American agent in 1777. Some, who wanted his endorsement, claimed striking successes, like DeThourry of Caen, who told Franklin that of 60 patients treated electrically, only one had been harmed and only two or three had remained unaffected, all the rest—the qualification did not escape Franklin—"who persevered in treatment and whose malady was not of long standing, being cured or almost cured." Others asked only for information, and instruction, like Père Guinchard, a country priest who had bought an electrical machine to bring relief and cures to his beloved parishioners.

If faith in medical electricity was slow dying, it was partly because the philosophers kept observing new phenomena and unnoticed qualities which might have therapeutic value. Franklin's friend Dr. Jan Ingenhousz, physician to the Austrian Court, accidentally received a very severe shock. When he recovered, he told Franklin, he "felt the most lively joye in finding as I thought at the time, my judgment infinitely more acute. . . . What did formerly seem to me difficult to comprehend, was now become of an easy Solution. I found moreover a liveliness in my whole frame, which I never had observed before." This accident, together with two similar ones that had happened to Franklin, induced Ingenhousz to suggest to "the London mad-Doctors" that similar shocks should be administered to the insane at Bedlam. . . . Ingenhousz had been unable to persuade either the "mad-Doctors" or anyone else to his view; but Franklin, as Ingenhousz asked, recommended electric shock treatment to the physician appointed by the British government to treat epileptic and insane persons. . . .

What there remains to say—or to say again—is that in all Franklin did both as a publicist and a practitioner of medicine he revealed the inquiring intelligence and easy competence which distinguish every facet of his many-sided genius. He thought clearly and constructively about health and disease, developed some sound theories and proposed sensible practices, and was ever mindful who it is that medicine is meant to serve. No more in medicine than in statecraft did Franklin view things narrowly or discuss them dogmatically. He knew too much for that, was too widely experienced, too tolerant. This comprehension and sound sense, this conviction that was always open to new knowledge breathe through a private comment on mesmerism, that exceedingly popular French doctrine from which, like electricity in its youth, all things were expected. None of the cures said to have been effected by mesmerism, Franklin pointed out, had come under his observation, and so he could express no opinion; but there being so many Disorders which cure themselves, and such a Disposition in Mankind to deceive themselves and one another on these Occasions; and the living long having given me frequent Opportunities of seeing certain Remedies cry'd up as curing every thing and yet soon after totally laid aside as useless, I cannot but fear that the Expectation of great Advantage from this new Method of treating Diseases, will prove a Delusion. That Delusion may however in some cases be of use while it lasts. There are in every great rich City, a Number of Persons who are never in health, because they are fond of Medicines and always taking them, whereby they derange the natural Functions, and hurt their Constitutions. If these People can be persuaded to forbear their Drugs in Expectation of being cured by only the Physicians' Finger or an Iron Rod pointing at them, they may possibly find good Effects tho' they mistake the Cause.

CHAPTER 3

The Political Career of an Eighteenth-Century Activist

PEOPLE
WHO MADE
HISTORY

BENJAMIN FRANKLIN

From Publishing to Politics: Franklin Expands His Influence

William S. Hanna

William S. Hanna, professor emeritus of history at
the University of Oregon, explains how Franklin
made the transition into politics. Franklin was already a public figure within his own community: He
had established organizations and improved living
conditions in the city, and he was the leading printer
in Philadelphia. As Hanna points out, Franklin's out-
going personality was a key asset that allowed
Franklin to transcend boundaries of class and religion. It was, however, a need for military defenses
that offered Franklin a chance to prove his political
savvy and demonstrate his problem-solving skills.
Hanna, an expert on colonial American history,
notes that Franklin placated both the Quaker Assembly and the English government officials who were
at a standstill regarding Pennsylvania defenses when
he proposed, publicized, assembled, and even raised
funds for a voluntary militia.

The first half of his life was not without indications of his future; yet Philadelphians had no reason to be awed by him or
to imagine that they lived in the Age of Franklin. Nor could
they guess that the future would regard them chiefly as
props and scenery for the unfolding epic of his career. To his
contemporaries, he was a successful and prosperous tradesman, a popular and respected member of society, undoubtedly talented and ingenious, and certainly a genial friend
and associate. He was also one of the best-known men in the
City—but a popular writer with his own press, newspaper,
almanac, and bookstore was likely to be well known in any
case. He was recognized as a public figure busily engaged in

civic good works, a joiner and organizer full of interesting ideas and projects. As a token of their recognition and esteem, his fellow Philadelphians urged him to run for public office. When Franklin decided to run, neither he nor his fellow citizens suspected that his almost casual election to the Assembly in 1751 was the beginning of an extraordinary political career and an exceedingly turbulent period in Pennsylvania history. For politics did become his chief occupation, propelling him to the top in the Assembly, sending him to England for most of the years between 1757 and 1775, and then making him, in succession, an Imperial statesman, a Revolutionary, and a Founding Father. . . .

FRANKLIN'S POLITICAL APPRENTICESHIP

Both his business and his political careers began with a period of apprenticeship. It is significant that although he wrote a great deal about his efforts to be a successful printer, he virtually ignored his beginnings in politics. Before 1751 he had carefully remained outside the political order, letting others have the power and the responsibility of managing provincial affairs. Yet Franklin was Pennsylvania's most socially engaged citizen, its chief instrument of public progress, a preacher and practitioner of public virtue and service to society. How could he have ignored for over twenty years the most obvious instruments of influence and leadership? This paradox is not resolved by searching for Franklin's theories of government in his writings from the 1730's and 1740's. They reveal no serious speculation about political matters or problems of government and no analysis of or suggestions for improving local conditions. It was almost as if the institutions of government and the political structure had not existed. Even when he took a place as Clerk of the Assembly— a position he assumed in 1736 and held for 15 years—he gave no sign of interest in legislative proceedings. Despite the opportunity for a first-hand education, the only legacy Franklin left from the experience was his famous "magic squares"— the doodlings of boredom designed to pass the time while he sat in the House. Franklin's untypical reaction to something that occupied a fair amount of his time cannot be dismissed as a simple lack of interest or a dislike for the Byzantine character of local politics, for he was a politician even if he denied both the fact and the interest.

Whether it prepared him for a political career or not,

Franklin's experience in Philadelphia before 1751 gave him a number of attitudes—almost theories—about his role in society, together with some personal objectives, techniques, and resources that he came to use habitually. These were, however, developed outside of the political order, and, in a way, expressed his criticism of government and of the squabbling, time-consuming proclivities and scanty accomplishments of the politicians. Franklin thought he had better ways of doing things, and spent more than twenty years perfecting alternatives to direct political action. Consequently, he was an outsider, a maverick, little understood by the leading politicians and later causing them considerable puzzlement and alarm.

When Franklin arrived in Philadelphia, he was a poor printer from Boston without influential connections. His first task was to establish himself, in his trade; then he would develop a printing business and a newspaper. The highly vulnerable nature of his trade made his task far from easy. Successful printing and, above all, publishing required wide public acceptance, and it was easy to make enemies if the product served political interests. Franklin needed no reminder of the hazards of business. Political partisanship had nearly ruined his brother's paper in Boston, and politics was taken just as seriously in Philadelphia. Franklin quickly realized that any political activity on his part might incur the wrath of the Quaker or the proprietary leaders. Unable to afford to engage in local feuds or to identfy [sic] with any faction, he maintained a policy of strict neutrality in issues that might touch the sensitivity of the leaders. When he felt compelled to express his true feelings in his newspaper, he concealed his identity with a pseudonym. The reward for such wise behavior was just what he wanted: the bipartisan friendship of the gentlemen and their patronage for himself and his business. In 1736, the Assembly and its Quaker leaders thought well enough of him to reward him with the colony's printing and the Clerkship of the House.

FRANKLIN'S TACTICS CONSIST OF A PLEASING PERSONALITY AND GOOD PLANNING

Avoidance of issues and concealment behind a pseudonym may not have been examples of editorial courage, but the strategy was prudent and it suited Franklin's first objective, the achievement of financial security as a prerequisite for his larger ambitions. In the 1730's, Franklin was unable and unwilling to compete with the gentlemen who ruled the City. These men did not welcome a challenge to their prerogatives and were quite capable of punishing an upstart.

FRANKLIN'S MILITIA

With a booming printing business and numerous "partnerships" he had made with young printers, Franklin had more time to focus on improving the community. In this excerpt from his autobiography, he describes his role in establishing the association for the defense of Pennsylvania.

I had on the whole abundant Reason to be satisfied with my being established in Pennsylvania. There were however two things that I regretted: There being no Provision for Defence, nor for a compleat Education of Youth. No Militia nor any College. I therefore in 1743, drew up a Proposal for establishing an Academy; & at that time thinking the Rev^d Mr Peters, who was out of Employ, a fit Person to superintend such an Institution, I communicated the Project to him. But he having more profitable Views in the Service of the Proprietor, which succeeded, declin'd the Undertaking. And not knowing another at that time suitable for such a Trust, I let the Scheme lie a while dormant.—I succeeded better the next Year, 1744, in proposing and establishing a Philosophical Society. The Paper I wrote for that purpose will be found among my Writings when collected.—

With respect to Defence, Spain having been several Years at War against Britain, and being at length join'd by France, which brought us into greater Danger; and the laboured & long-continued Endeavours of our Governor Thomas to prevail with our Quaker Assembly to pass a Militia Law, & make other Provisions for the Security of the Province having proved abortive, I determined to try what might be done by a voluntary Association of the People. To promote this I first wrote & published a Pamphlet, intitled, PLAIN TRUTH, in which I stated our defenceless Situation in strong Lights, with the Necessity of Union & Discipline for our Defence, and promis'd to propose in a few Days an Association to be generally signed for that purpose. The Pamphlet had a sudden & surprizing Effect. I was call'd upon for the Instrument of Association: And having settled the Draft of it with a few Friends, I appointed a Meeting of the Citizens in the large Building before mentioned. The House was pretty full. I had prepared a Number of printed Copies, and provided Pens and Ink dispers'd all over the Room. I harangu'd them a little on the Subject, read

Because he could not risk direct action, he was forced to devise other ways of exerting his influence and accomplishing his social objectives. These substitutes for public position and power were remarkably successful. Beginning with the

the Paper & explain'd it, and then distributed the Copies which were eagerly signed, not the least Objection being made. When the Company separated, & the Papers were collected we found above Twelve hundred Hands; and other Copies being dispers'd in the Country the Subscribers amounted at length to upwards of Ten Thousand. These all furnish'd themselves as soon as they could with Arms; form'd themselves into Companies, and Regiments, chose their own Officers, & met every Week to be instructed in the manual Exercise, and other Parts of military Discipline. The Women, by Subscriptions among themselves, provided Silk Colours, which they presented to the Companies, painted with different Devices and Motto's which I supplied. The Officers of the Companies composing the Philadelphia Regiment, being met, chose me for their Colonel; but conceiving myself unfit, I declin'd that Station, & recommended Mr Lawrence, a fine Person and Man of Influence, who was accordingly appointed. I then propos'd a Lottery to defray the Expence of Building a Battery below the Town, and furnishing it with Cannon. It filled expeditiously and the Battery was soon erected, the Merlons being fram'd of Logs & fill'd with Earth. We bought some old Cannon from Boston, but these not being sufficient, we wrote to England for more, soliciting at the same Time our Proprietaries for some Assistance, tho' without much Expectation of obtaining it. Mean while Colonel Lawrence, William Allen, Abraham Taylor, Esquires, and myself were sent to New York by the Associators, commission'd to borrow some Cannon of Governor Clinton. He at first refus'd us peremptorily: but at a Dinner with his Council where there was great Drinking of Madeira Wine, as the Custom at that Place then was, he soften'd by degrees, and said he would lend us Six. After a few more Bumpers he advanc'd to Ten. And at length he very good-naturedly conceded Eighteen. They were fine Cannon, 18 pounders, with their Carriages, which we soon transported and mounted on our Battery, where the Associators kept a nightly Guard while the War lasted: And among the rest I regularly took my Turn of Duty there as a common Soldier.

The Autobiography in *Benjamin Franklin: Writings*. Ed. J.A. Leo Lemay. New York: Literary Classics of the United States, 1987.

Junto Club in the 1730's and extending to the Association [for the defense of Pennsylvania: a militia] of 1747, Franklin managed a personal system of power that operated outside the structure, permitting him to do what he wanted without bothering much with political factions or issues.

One of Franklin's most valuable tools was a pleasing personality. He has left full accounts of his self-examination and of the deliberate effort he made to correct or disguise what he thought were flaws in his personality and to strengthen his strong points. He worked hard to fashion an influential personal instrument especially suited to the small, intimate society of Philadelphia in the 1730's. The physical size of the City and the small number of men who counted in its life made it a congenial place for one who practiced social leadership by personal charm. He took great pleasure in deliberately applying the most suitable personal technique to gain a particular objective. Especially anxious to win the approval and favor of the leading gentlemen, he carefully cultivated a reputation for thrift and industry, and to impress the learned and powerful James Logan [a Quaker statesman and agent for Pennsylvania founders, the Penns] he asked to borrow books from that great man's library. By applying such appropriate psychology, Franklin soon ingratiated himself with the Logans, Pembertons, Hamiltons, and other influential Philadelphians.

From a strong base of personal relationships and friendships Franklin sought to increase his effectiveness by developing special organizations designed to extend his influence and gain support for his projects. He formed or belonged to a proliferation of organizations, which enlisted virtually every man in the City with the time, talent, or money to contribute. The extent of his participation in such enterprises was greater than that of any other man in Philadelphia and concentrated a unique power in the hands of one man. By acting alone or as a member of a group, he achieved by mid-century a virtual monopoly of public and private welfare projects in the City. Indeed, some claimed that almost no public undertaking of this sort could be considered without his advice and support. . . .

FRANKLIN CANNOT BE LABELED; HE SEES A BIGGER PICTURE

In a society defined by a clear though not rigid class structure, he was virtually a classless man. Middle-class in origin

and trade and lacking a formal education and an advantageous marriage, he nevertheless came to possess the advantages of a member of the upper class—fortune, prestige, public acclaim, influence, high-placed connections, and power. Good works, political neutrality, and the capacity to make friends permitted him to move across class lines in his private and public associations. To some of his contemporaries in 1748 he was a gentleman; to others he was still a printer with an apron and ink-stained hands.

His freedom to move easily in the middle and upper levels of Philadelphia society was paralleled by his relationship with various religious denominations. Religious association provided an important measure of a man's place in Pennsylvania, giving the communicant a social, ethnic, and often a political—as well as a doctrinal—identification. Franklin accepted religion's utility as a moral, stabilizing force in society and encouraged its general principles, but rejected what he considered sectarian excesses and prejudices. Heterodox, rational, and inclining to deism, he found little of value in interdenominational disputes and the fine points of theological differences, which preoccupied so many Pennsylvanians. While members of the several denominations might despair of the ultimate safety of his soul, they could find little cause to fear that he would give partisan aid to a rival sect. This was an advantage. But Franklin's freedom from identification with traditional orthodoxies and their particular interests also meant that he did not share their particular aspirations.

While politics was an intense, inward-turning concern in Pennsylvania, Franklin's attention turned increasingly outward, to other colonies and to England and Europe. This had begun early in his career. Printing and publishing not only provided an income and a means of influencing his fellow citizens but gave him an unequaled access to information. Through his print shop and bookstore passed the news and ideas that comprised the recorded culture of the contemporary Atlantic civilization, and his mind absorbed something from everything that came to his notice. This constant supply of information was quite as much a part of his trade as ink and type.

He was educated by his trade to look beyond his city, and especially in the direction of England and Europe. It is significant that his *Pennsylvania Gazette* contained more news about Philadelphia, England, Europe, and other colonies

than about the rest of Pennsylvania. Because of this, Franklin was undoubtedly better informed about affairs in London or in Boston than he was about those fifty miles west of Philadelphia. Publishing gave him an eastern orientation and correspondingly less knowledge of or interest in the interior of the province. Always a Philadelphian and later a man of the world, he was not as thoroughly a Pennsylvanian. . . .

FRANKLIN TESTS HIS POLITICAL STRATEGIES, CREATING A VOLUNTARY MILITIA

Just before Franklin retired from active business, he got an opportunity to test his political theories and techniques in the colonial defense crisis that arose during "King George's War" (War of the Austrian Succession). In an atmosphere of passion and deadlock, he undertook to interpose himself between the feuding politicians with a brilliantly conceived solution to a problem that had hitherto been all but insoluble. With the publication of *Plain Truth* and the formation of the Association in 1747, he abandoned his political aloofness and stepped into the rivalries and issues of politics.

The deadlock between the Quaker-controlled Assembly and the proprietary executive over providing defense had virtually paralyzed the government and brought down English censure on the colony. Pennsylvania was defenseless and was making little contribution to the larger war effort. This alarming political and military situation suggested to Franklin the possibilities for a rational compromise. In *Plain Truth* he proposed a voluntary association of citizens in a militia to defend the colony. Impartially criticizing the stubbornness of the two major parties, he appealed to all public-spirited men for assistance and urged the leaders of the political factions to give up their political or religious objections for the common welfare. Franklin offered them inducements to join in his scheme. By making the Association voluntary, he permitted the Quakers to remain outside if they chose. The Governor got some sort of a military force, even if it was not quite legal, and a sufficient defense effort to answer English criticism.

The popular response to Franklin's proposal was enthusiastic. Some contributed money; others enlisted in the militia. Swept along by the force of Franklin's campaign, the political leaders who had hitherto been cool to the proposal now supported it. (Some, especially the Quakers, did so unofficially.) For his part, Franklin helped to organize and enlist

companies of men and select the officers. In addition he petitioned the Proprietor for cannon and directed the plans to fortify the City. Since the Assembly would not appropriate money for defense, he promoted a lottery. The whole undertaking quickly became a triumph for Franklin's peculiar methods. It was a perfect expression of his ability to arrive at a reasoned solution to a difficult problem.

Behind his glittering success lay certain other problems. . . . Could any government permit the vital military power, which belonged under executive control, to be gathered into the hands of an extralegal, independent body? No matter how obvious the need for action, was it not destructive of the powers of government, and did it not tend further to disturb the balance between the executive and the legislature? Franklin had turned from the established agencies of government and appealed to the people. If he believed this necessary, then he must also believe that there was a fundamental weakness in Pennsylvania's government. . . .

On the other hand, proprietary leaders were pleased that a way had been found to circumvent the Quaker refusal to let the Assembly pass legislation for a militia. And they found further consolation in the fact that the Association had soon come under the control of the regular leaders of the colony. Although proprietary men were worried about Franklin's unorthodox methods—he might be something of a "tribune of the people"—they also saw that he favored defense. Should the same dispute break out again, he might prove a valuable friend of the government.

Franklin had not considered the theoretical implications of his action or attributed the political impasse that had brought about the crisis to any basic defects in the government. In order to force the leaders to act, he had deliberately avoided the real issues and resorted to compromise, massive application of his personal influence, and an adroit appeal to the people. While some of the politicians might grumble at his solution, he had put enough in his plan to attract both sides. In the process he had nonetheless subverted Quaker pacifism and ignored the proper prerogatives of the executive.

For Franklin the Association was a significant test. His ideas and methods had been put to work in a crisis and had proved sound. Could he not repeat this triumph in other areas? Now retired and provided with a sufficient income to support him in whatever he chose to do, he could afford to

consider taking public office. He had a number of worthwhile projects in mind, and a public position might be very
useful in winning support for them. He was bound by no fac-
tional ties, and he had just demonstrated his freedom to ar-
bitrate between contending parts of the government. Acting
as an independent force in politics, he could support the reasonable and the useful on his own terms. If politics should
prove a burden, he could always withdraw.

The Influence of Native American Ideas on Benjamin Franklin

Bruce E. Johansen

In this excerpt from Bruce E. Johansen's ground-breaking book, *Forgotten Founders: Benjamin Franklin, the Iroquois, and the Rationale for the American Revolution*, Franklin's connection to Native Americans is examined. According to Johansen, this contact had a tremendous influence on Franklin and the development of his political ideas, evident in the Albany Plan of Union. Johansen, who is a professor of communication and Native American studies at the University of Nebraska, explains that Franklin first became acquainted with the Native American treaties by publishing accounts of them. Franklin became particularly interested in the 1744 Lancaster treaty, which contained transcriptions of speeches from Canassatego, the eloquent spokesman for the great council. Soon after, Franklin became an advocate for Native American concerns; he continued to promote similar ideas when he was appointed commissioner for trade negotiations on behalf of the Pennsylvania colony.

By 1744, his thirty-eighth year, Franklin had a thriving printing business that published one of the largest newspapers in the colonies, the *Pennsylvania Gazette,* as well as *Poor Richard's Almanack,* which appeared annually. As the province's official printer, Franklin ran off his press all of Pennsylvania's paper money, state documents and laws, as well as job printing. As the postmaster, he had free access to the mails to distribute his publications. If a family, especially a Pennsylvania family, kept printed matter other than the Bible in the house, it was very likely that whatever it was—newspaper, almanac or legal documents—bore Franklin's imprint. . . .

THE AMBITIOUS PRINTER PUBLISHES NATIVE AMERICAN TREATIES

Like any publisher of ambition, Franklin always kept a sharp eye out for salable properties. During 1736, he had started printing small books containing the proceedings of Indian treaty councils. The treaties, one of the first distinctive forms of indigenous American literature, sold quite well, which pleased Franklin. Filling the seemingly insatiable appetite for information about the Indians and the lands in which they lived that existed at the time on both sides of the Atlantic, Franklin's press turned out treaty accounts until 1762 when, journeying to England to represent Pennsylvania in the royal court, he found several English publishers in competition with him.

One warm summer day in 1744, Franklin was balancing the books of his printing operation when Conrad Weiser, the Indian interpreter and envoy [a government representative] to the Iroquois, appeared at his door with a new treaty manuscript—the official transcript of the recently completed meeting between envoys from Pennsylvania, Virginia, Maryland, and the sachems [North American Indian chiefs] of the Six Nations confederacy at nearby Lancaster. Weiser, an old friend of Franklin's, explained that this was probably the most interesting and noteworthy treaty account he had ever brought in for publication. At last, said Weiser, the Iroquois had made a definite commitment toward the Anglo-Iroquois alliance that Pennsylvania and other Colonial governments had been seeking for more than ten years.

The Iroquois, explained Weiser, were being careful. If they were to ally with the English, they wanted the colonials to unify their management of the Indian trade, and to do something about the crazy patchwork of diplomacy that resulted when each colony handled its own affairs with the Iroquois.

Taking the handwritten manuscript from Weiser, Franklin sat at his desk and quickly thumbed through it, reading a few passages, bringing to life in his mind the atmosphere of the frontier council. The treaty had two main purposes, Franklin surmised. The first was to deal with a recurring problem: Indian complaints that Englishmen, mostly Scotch-Irish frontiersmen, were moving onto Indian land without permission, disrupting hunting and social life. The second, and more important, objective was to polish the covenant chain, to secure the alliance against the French. . . .

IMPRESSED BY NATIVE AMERICAN IDEAS, FRANKLIN PROMOTES THEM

The 1744 treaty, one of the more dramatic during this period, impressed Franklin when the interpreter's record was delivered to him a few weeks later. He printed 200 extra copies and sent them to England. Within three years after he printed the proceedings of the 1744 treaty, with Canassatego's advice on Colonial union, Franklin became involved with Cadwallader Colden [a Crown official botanist, and expert on Native American history] on the same subject. A new edition of Colden's *History of the Five Indian Nations Depending on the Province of New York in America*, first published in 1727, was issued during 1747. Franklin was a frequent correspondent with Colden at this time; both had similar interests in politics, natural science, and Deism. . . .

Shortly after its publication in 1747, Franklin asked Colden for a copy of his new edition, and read and appraised it for its author. Franklin then, began his own fervent campaign for a federal union of the British colonies, a cause he did not forsake until the United States was formed a quarter-century later.

Franklin requested a copy of Colden's book at a time when alliance with the Iroquois was assuming a new urgency for Pennsylvania. During 1747, French and Dutch privateers had raided along the Delaware River, threatening Philadelphia itself for a time. In response, Franklin organized a volunteer militia that elected its own officers (a distinctly Iroquoian custom). The militia grew year by year, repeatedly electing Franklin its colonel until the British, worried about the growth of indigenous armed forces in the colonies, ordered it disbanded in 1756.

Franklin thought enough of Colden's history to ask for fifty copies to sell through his own outlets. . . . Franklin was concerned that one bookseller, by the name of Read, was not giving Colden's work sufficient advertising in Philadelphia. "In our last two Papers he has advertis'd generally that he has a parcel of books to sell, Greek, Latin, French and English, but makes no particular mention of the Indian History; it is therefore no wonder that he has sold none of them, as he told me a few days since." Franklin complained that no one in Philadelphia except himself had read the book, and he thought it "well wrote, entertaining and instructive" and "useful to all those colonies who have anything to do with Indian Affairs."

FRANKLIN SUPPORTS A COLONIAL CONFEDERATION

As early as 1750, Franklin recognized that the economic and political interests of the British colonies were diverging from those of the mother country. About the same time, he began to think of forms of political confederation that might suit a dozen distinct, often mutually suspicious, political entities. A federal structure such as the Iroquois Confederacy, which left each state in the union to manage its own internal affairs and charged the confederate government with prosecuting common, external matters, must have served as an expedient, as well as appealing, example. As Franklin began to express his thoughts on political and military union of the colonies, he was already attempting to tie them together culturally, through the establishment of a postal system and the American Philosophical Society, which drew to Philadelphia the premier Euro-American scholars of his day.

During 1751, Franklin read a pamphlet written by Archibald Kennedy titled "The Importance of Gaining and Preserving the Friendship of the Indians to the British Interest Considered." Kennedy, collector of customs and receiver general for the province of New York at the time that he wrote the brochure, maintained that alliance with the Iroquois was "of no small importance to the trade of Great Britain, as to the peace and prosperity of the colonies." Indian traders, called "a tribe of harpies" by Kennedy, "have so abused, defrauded and deceived those poor, innocent, well-meaning people." Kennedy asserted that fraud in the Indian trade could be reduced if that trade were regulated through a single Indian commissioner, instead of a different one for each colony, which was the existing system. As with Kennedy, so also with the Iroquois; they too much resented the behavior of the traders. Canassatego had told the Colonial commissioners at Lancaster in 1744 that the Indians would be poor "as long as there are too many Indian traders among us." Resolution of this problem was the key to maintaining the Anglo-Iroquois alliance in Kennedy's opinion. The appointment of a single Indian commissioner would also be a small step along the road to Colonial confederation for mutual defense. The Iroquois had been advocating a unified Colonial military command for at least seven years—since Canassatego's speech to the 1744 Lancaster treaty. Under Kennedy's scheme, each colony would have contributed men and money to the common military force in proportion to its population.

PLANS FOR A UNION INCLUDE REGULATING NATIVE AMERICAN TRADE

Franklin was sent Kennedy's brochure by James Parker, his New York City printing partner, from whose press it had been issued. Following the reading of the brochure, Franklin cultivated Kennedy's friendship; the two men consulted together on the Albany Plan of Union (which included Kennedy's single-Indian agent idea). At the Albany congress itself, Franklin called Kennedy "a gentleman of great knowledge in Public Affairs."

After he read Kennedy's brochure, Franklin wrote to Parker that "I am of the opinion, with the public-spirited author, that securing the Friendship of the Indians is of the greatest consequence for these Colonies." To Franklin, "the surest means of doing it are to regulate the Indian Trade, so as to convince them [the Indians] that they may have the best and cheapest Goods, and the fairest dealings, with the English." Franklin also thought, in agreement with Kennedy, that the colonists should accept the Iroquois' advice to form a union in common defense under a common, federal government:

> And to unite the several Governments as to form a strength that the Indians may depend on in the case of a Rupture with the French, or apprehend great Danger from, if they break with us. This union of the colonies, I apprehend, is not to be brought about by the means that have heretofore been used for that purpose.

Franklin then asked why the colonists found it so difficult to unite in common defense, around common interests, when the Iroquois had done so long ago. In context, his use of the term "ignorant savages" seems almost like a backhanded slap at the colonists, who may have thought themselves superior to the Indians but who, in Franklin's opinion, could learn something from the Six Nations about political unity:

> It would be a very strange thing if Six Nations of Ignorant Savages should be capable of forming a Scheme for such an

Union and be able to execute it in such a manner, as that it has subsisted Ages, and appears indissoluble, and yet a like union should be impracticable for ten or a dozen English colonies.

Within a year of reading Kennedy's brochure, Franklin, whose role in Pennsylvania's Indian affairs was growing, prepared a report on the expenses of the province's Indian agents. Part of the report was sharply critical of Indian traders:

> Some very unfit Persons are at present employed in that business [the Indian trade]. We hope that the Governor will enjoin the justices of the County Courts to be more careful in the future whom they recommend for Licenses; and whatever is thought further necessary to enforce the Laws now being, for regulating the Indian Trade and Traders, may be considered by the ensuing Assembly. . . .

Recognizing that the Indians' complaints about the conduct of English traders had to be addressed if the Anglo-Iroquois alliance was to be maintained, Franklin took a major step in his personal life. During 1753 Franklin, who had heretofore only printed Indian treaties, accepted an appointment by the Pennsylvania government as one of the colony's commissioners at a meeting with the Six Nations planned for later that year in Carlisle. . . .

FRANKLIN'S INVOLVEMENT IN NATIVE AMERICAN AFFAIRS AND THE CARLISLE TREATY

During the year before Franklin attended his first treaty council in an official capacity, the possibility of conflict with the French was accentuated by a French advance into the Ohio Valley. During June 1752, French troops attacked the Indian town of Pickawillany. . . . [Governor] James Hamilton's proclamation appointing Franklin, Richard Peters, and Issac Norris to treat with the Indians at Carlisle specifically mentioned the alliance with the Twightwees, allies of the Iroquois who lived in the Ohio Valley, and who had been attacked by the French during 1752. The treaty, which started Franklin's distinguished diplomatic career, began November 1, 1753. An account of the treaty was printed and sold by Franklin's press. The major subject of the Carlisle treaty was mutual defense against the French. The Indians also brought up the behavior of traders, especially regarding their distribution of rum among Indians. The chiefs said they wanted such practices stopped. Scarrooyady, an Iroquois who had assumed a leadership role following the death of Canassatego during 1750, told the commissioners:

Your traders now bring us scarce any Thing but Rum and
Flour. They bring us little Powder and Lead, or other valuable
Goods. The rum ruins us. We beg you would prevent its coming in such Quantities, by regulating the Traders. . . . We desire it be forbidden, and none sold in the Indian Country.

"Those wicked Whiskey Sellers, when they have once got
the Indians in Liquor, make them sell their very Clothes
from their Backs," Scarrooyady emphasized. Concluding
their report to the provincial government on the treaty council, Franklin, Peters, and Norris advised that the sachem's
advice be taken. "That the traders are under no Bonds . . .
and by their own Intemperance, unfair Dealings and Irregu-
larities will, it is to be feared, entirely estrange the affections
of the Indians from the English." Franklin's opposition to the
liquor trade was strengthened the night following the formal
conclusion of the treaty council, when many of the Indians
there became very drunk and disorderly, yielding to the ad-
dictive qualities of the liquids that their chiefs had deplored
only a few days earlier.

Two stated desires of the Iroquois leadership—that the
Indian trade be regulated along with the illegal movement of
settlers into the interior, and that the colonies form a federal
union—figured importantly in Franklin's plans for the Albany congress of 1754. Plans for this, the most important intercolonial conference in the years before the last North
American war with France, were being made at the time of
the Carlisle treaty conference. The London Board of Trade
wrote to the New York provincial government September 18,
1753, directing all the colonies that had dealings with the
Iroquois to join in "one general Treaty to be made in his
Majesty's name." It was a move that began, in effect, to bring
about the unified management of Indian affairs that Colden,
Kennedy, Franklin, and the Iroquois had requested. Similar
letters were sent to all colonies that shared frontiers with the
Iroquois and their Indian allies, from Virginia northward.
Franklin was appointed to represent Pennsylvania at the Al-
bany congress. . . .

THE ALBANY PLAN OF UNION TAKES FORM

The Albany congress met for two interconnected reasons: to
cement the alliance with the Iroquois against the French and
to formulate and ratify a plan of union for the colonies.
Franklin, well known among the Indians and a fervent ad-

vocate of Colonial union, was probably the most influential individual at the congress. . . .

Debates over the plan had taken more than two weeks. On June 24, [1754], the Colonial delegates voted without dissent in support of Colonial union that, said the motion voted on, "[is] absolutely necessary for their [the colonies'] security and defense." A committee was appointed to "prepare and receive Plans or Schemes for the Union of the Colonies." Franklin was a member of that committee. Thomas Hutchinson, a delegate from Massachusetts who also served on the committee, later pointed to Franklin as the major contributor to the plan of union that emerged from the deliberations of the committee: "The former [the Albany plan] was the projection of Dr. F[ranklin] and prepared in part before he had any consultation with Mr. H[utchinson], probably brought with him from Philadelphia.". . .

On July 9, the Iroquois having left town, Franklin was asked to draw up a plan of union based on the previous two weeks' discussions. Franklin's final draft was commissioned two weeks to the day after his *Pennsylvania Gazette* published the "Join or Die" cartoon, one of the first graphic editorials to appear in an American newspaper, and a forceful statement in favor of Colonial union. . . .

The plan of union that emerged from Franklin's pen was a skillful diplomatic melding of concepts that took into consideration the Crown's demands for control, the colonists' desires for autonomy in a loose union, and the Iroquois' stated advocacy of a Colonial union similar to theirs in structure and function. For the Crown, the plan provided administration by a president-general, to be appointed and supported by the Crown. The individual colonies were promised that they could retain their own constitutions "except in the particulars wherein a change may be directed by the said Act [the plan of union] as hereafter follows."

FRANKLIN'S PLAN HAS THE IROQUOIS IN MIND

The retention of internal sovereignty within the individual colonies, politically necessary because of their diversity, geographical separation, and mutual suspicion, closely resembled the Iroquoian system. The colonies' distrust of one another and the fear of the smaller that they might be dominated by the larger in a confederation may have made necessary the adoption of another Iroquoian device: one colony could veto the action of the rest of the body. As in the Iroquois Confederacy, all "states" had to agree on a course of action before it could be taken. Like the Iroquois Great Council, the "Grand Council" (the name was Franklin's) of the colonies under the Albany Plan of Union would have been allowed to choose its own speaker. The Grand Council, like the Iroquois Council, was to be unicameral, unlike the two-house British system. Franklin favored one-house legislatures during and later at the Constitutional Convention, and opposed the imposition of a bicameral system on the United States.

Franklin's Albany Plan of Union provided for a different number of representatives from each colony (from seven for Virginia and Massachusetts Bay to two for New Hampshire and Rhode Island) as the Iroquois system provided for differing numbers from each of its five nations. This division of seats was based, however, in rough proportion to population and contributions to a common military force, while the Iroquois system was based more on tradition. But the number of delegates to the proposed Colonial Grand Council (forty-eight) closely resembled that of the Iroquois Council (fifty). There is no documentary evidence, however, that Franklin intended such a slavish imitation.

The legislature under the Albany plan was empowered to "raise and pay Soldiers, and build Forts for the Defence of any of the Colonies, and equip vessels of Force to guard the Coasts and protect the Trade on the Oceans, Lakes and Great Rivers," but it was not allowed to "impress men in any Colonies without the consent of its Legislature." This clause strikes a middle ground between the involuntary conscription often practiced in Europe at the time and the traditional reliance of the Iroquois and many other American Indian nations on voluntary military service.

The Albany plan also contained the long-sought unified regulation of the Indian trade advocated by the Iroquois, Kennedy, Colden, and Franklin:

> That the President General with the advice of the Grand Council hold and direct all Indian Treaties in which the general interest or welfare of the Colonys may be concerned; and make peace or declare war with the Indian Nations. That they make such laws as they judge necessary for regulating Indian Trade. That they make all purchases from the Indians for the Crown. . . . That they make new settlements on such purchases by granting lands. . . .

The last part of this section aimed to stop, or at least slow, the pellmell expansion of the frontier that resulted in settlers' occupation of lands unceded by the Indian nations. Such poaching was a constant irritant to the Iroquois; the subject of land seizures had come up at every treaty council for at least two decades before the Albany plan was proposed. Like the traders' self-interested profiteering, the illegal taking of land by frontiersmen was seen by Anglo-American leaders as a threat to the Anglo-Iroquois alliance at a time when worsening diplomatic relations with France made alliance with the Iroquois more vital.

FRANKLIN'S NOTABLE PLAN IS REJECTED

The Albany Plan of Union gained Franklin general recognition in the colonies as an advocate of Colonial union. The plan also earned Franklin a position among the originators of the federalist system of government that came to characterize the United States political system. . . . While the Iroquois and Franklin were ready for a Colonial union, the legislatures of the colonies were not. Following its passage by the Albany congress on July 10, 1754, Franklin's plan died in the Colonial legislatures. The individual colonies' governing bodies were not ready to yield even to the limited Colonial government that Franklin proposed within his definition of federalism: "Independence of each other, and separate interests, tho' among a people united by common manners, language and, I may say, religion . . ." Franklin showed his dismay at the inability of the colonies to act together when he said that "the councils of the savages proceeded with better order than the British Parliament."

Franklin believed, at the time that his plan failed to win the approval of the colonies, that its defeat would cost the British their alliance with the Iroquois. "In my opinion, no assistance from them [the Six Nations] is to be expected in any dispute with the French 'till by a Compleat Union among our selves we are able to support them in case they should be attacked," Franklin wrote, before the Iroquois' willingness to maintain the alliance proved him wrong. Although he was wrong in this regard, Franklin's statement illustrates how important the Iroquois' prodding was in his advocacy of a federal union for the colonies.

Franklin's plan was also rejected by the Crown, but for reasons different from those of the Colonial legislatures. To the British, the plan was too democratic. It gave the colonists too much freedom at a time when the British were already sending across the ocean spies who reported that far too many colonists were giving entirely too much thought to possible independence from Britain. Franklin already was under watch as a potential troublemaker (hadn't he raised his own militia?).

The separate Colonial governments and the Crown had, in effect, vetoed the plan of the Albany commissioners—a veto beyond which there could be no appeal. Nonetheless, the work of the congress was not in vain.

Franklin's Political Ideals

Paul W. Conner

The late Paul W. Conner, whose experience included teaching political science at George Washington University and Princeton University as well as social science at Pace University, takes a close look at Benjamin Franklin's social ideals. These ideals, as Conner points out, were dominant in Franklin's political concepts of a New Order, inspired by the great American territorial expanse and all its potential, and a Virtuous Order, which contained Franklin's ideal of benevolence—that by helping others one helps oneself. Conner notes that Franklin did not initially advocate American independence from England. However, through his fifteen-year residency in England (from 1757 to 1762 and from 1764 to 1775) and that country's actions toward her colonies, it became apparent to Franklin that England would not work toward America's best interest. Franklin's realization finally led him to advocate American separation from England as he still hoped to fulfill his vision of the New Order. Conner also briefly considers the paradox of government which concerned Franklin. Although Franklin recognized the need for some governmental authority, he advocated the least amount of intervention.

The image of Franklin as a narrow, unimaginative *petit bourgeois* [small tradesman], perched on a hard stool and squinting at his ledgers, recedes into caricature when one glimpses the grand conceptions of political integration which he envisioned from 1747 onward. . . . After institutionalizing Philadelphia street-sweeping, fire-extinguishing, and book-reading, he moved into a larger political sphere with plans for structuring Pennsylvania's defenses, integrating the colonies, keeping the British Empire together, and—when the latter failed—unifying first America and then Europe.

UNITY THROUGH A VIRTUOUS ORDER

In a way, it was odd that Franklin should become infatuated with vast and airy schemes. An essential feature of his Virtuous Order was republican simplicity—a concept which bespoke independent family units and minimal government. Would not unification mean added layers of office-holders—an encrustation of parasites to feed on the fruits of the laborious? Perhaps, but there were two more important considerations. The ideal of benevolence [an aspect of the Virtuous Order], for one, implied interdependence. As a free trade theorist [George Whately] had said in a pamphlet [Principles of Trade] which Franklin annotated approvingly,

> It is a vain Imagination that we exist only for ourselves, or our particular Country. The al-wise Creator has ordain'd that a mutual Dependence shal run thro' all his Works. . . .

It was logical that this "mutual Dependence" be expressed politically as well as economically, and in Franklin's mind the ideas of beneficent commercial intercourse and political union were intermingled in such schemes as the Albany Plan and his proposal for the "United Colonies of North America." His desire for unity was not motivated entirely by concern for benevolence. In his mind lingered a larger consideration: the fear that his social ideal would evolve too rapidly for orderly, harmonious growth, and would lose all its virtue—benevolence included—in the confusion. The paradox of government, in Franklin's eyes, was its double role of encouraging and expediting social evolution while, at the same time, channeling and controlling it. Political unity was a step toward both the constructive liberation of social energy and the effective exercise of a directing authority.

Authority, of course, could become excessive, impeding rather than aiding the evolutionary process; and in such a case it might become necessary to dissolve that unity upon which an overweening power had developed. Not just any sort of unity would do; it had to be suited to the goals of the New Order [how Franklin perceived political reform in America] and sensitive to its needs. A unified Pennsylvania administration, for example, would enable the colony to flourish within its protected frontiers, and intercolonial

FRANKLIN IS A DELEGATE TO THE ALBANY CONGRESS OF 1754

The threat of French invasion of the colonies prompted the convening of what was considered the most important "Indian conference" of the time. As the late Franklin biographer Catherine Drinker Bowen explains, Franklin was a natural choice as one of the delegates, based on his expertise, but Franklin himself had greater hopes for the conference than strictly an alliance with the Iroquois. In this excerpt from her last book, The Most Dangerous Man in America: Scenes from the Life of Benjamin Franklin, *which was the culminating effort of a lifelong interest she had in Franklin, Bowen emphasizes the importance of the historical event at hand, especially Franklin's significant role.*

The projected conference at Albany was to be the most important and to boast the most distinguished membership. No previous Indian conference had been ordered from England, all others being locally inspired by needs of the moment. This time the need was greater, the French threat more pressing. That powerful body called the Board of Trade and Plantations, sitting in London, had invited to the conference all the colonies north of the Potomac—nine of them. Governor Hamilton had chosen the Pennsylvania delegates: two from his Council (John Penn and Richard Peters), representing the Proprietors of the Province; two from the Assembly (Isaac Norris and Benjamin Franklin), representing the popular side of government—and Conrad Weiser, Indian agent and provincial interpreter.

The choice of Franklin as delegate was natural enough. Not only had he a hand deep in the political business of the Province, but he showed a very real interest in Indian affairs, having traveled out to Carlisle, Pennsylvania, for an Indian conference only the previous year. His scientific reputation in England and Europe, his honorary degrees and fame as a philosopher, would be of help at Albany; the colonists needed prestige in dealing with the London Board of Trade. That Franklin could turn so abruptly from electrical experimentation to the problem of Indians and colonial union shows a singular flexibility that was part of his nature—the ability to move from one activity to another without frustration or loss of balance. A few years previously, Cadwallader Colden had announced that he was done forever with New York politics, having retired in favor of botany and natural philosophy. "I wish you all the Satisfaction that Ease and Retirement from Publick Business can possibly give you," Franklin had replied under the date of October, 1750. "But let not your Love of Philosophical Amusements have more than its due weight with you. Had Newton been Pilot but of a single Ship, the finest of his Discoveries would scarce have excus'd, or atton'd for his abandoning the Helm one Hour in Time of Danger; how much less if she had carried the Fate of the Commonwealth."

High-sounding words, that somehow do not carry the authentic Franklin ring. Indeed, it would be hard to credit their sincerity did we not know that Franklin had followed these same precepts himself . . . as in the year 1747 when, in all the climax and excitement of electrical work, he had stopped to write and print two thousand copies of a pamphlet, "Plain Truth," warning against the very real menace of French privateers on the Delaware River. "Plain Truth" had urged an association of voluntary militia for Pennsylvania's defense—and achieved it, thereby angering Thomas Penn, who denounced such actions as too "independent of Government." Franklin was a dangerous man, Penn told Richard Peters at the time, "of a very uneasy spirit and I should be very glad if he inhabited any other Country."

That had been seven years ago. At Albany in this summer of 1754, Franklin would for the first time move far beyond the local Pennsylvania scene. More than half the North American colonies were included in his plans for union, with a possibility of even wider involvement. As for the Six Nations, everyone north of the Carolinas knew that they comprised the powerful Iroquois confederacy of Mohawks, Senecas, Oneidas, Onondagas, Cayugas, and later the Tuscaroras, who lived along the lakes below Canada and whose Indian empire, with its tributary tribes, reached from the St. Lawrence to the James River and from the Hudson almost to the Mississippi.

Between Iroquois and English the covenant chain had indeed become dangerously corroded. Should the French succeed in seducing away the Iroquois—and the French were masters of such seduction—not only the Hudson and St. Lawrence river forts which controlled the fur trade would fall, but the Ohio region with them.

Catherine Drinker Bowen, *The Most Dangerous Man in America: Scenes from the Life of Benjamin Franklin.* Boston: Little, Brown, 1974.

unity would prepare the way for orderly expansion westward. Anglo-American unity, on the other hand, though it could shield North America from alien incursions, was managed by a distant and insensitive center which proved itself to Franklin to be incapable of directing without smothering. The creation of a unified framework within which the New Order could evolve harmoniously was an essential part of Franklin's quest.

He could hardly reframe the world (though he tried) and was therefore confined to America in working out his designs. The American continent was to be the home of the New Order and, hence, required unification sufficient to its purposes. The Philadelphia Franklin, that unifying spirit in Pennsylvania and intercolonial politics, who promoted road building, quickened inter-city mail deliveries, reprimanded Connecticut for enacting a "selfish" tariff, served on committees of the Pennsylvania Assembly dealing with the unification of Indian policy and colonial defense, solicited intercolonial unity schemes from his correspondents, represented Pennsylvania at the Albany Congress, and who was convinced that "Obstructions of the general Interest from particular Disputes in the Colonies show more and more the Necessity of . . . Union," was a man bent upon giving British America a chance to grow. Unity—both within and among the colonies—would ensure, first, protection, and second, expansion. . . .

THE ALBANY PLAN OF UNION AND BRITISH RESISTANCE

Franklin rested his hopes for intercolonial unity upon the Albany Congress of 1754. The colonies north of the Potomac [River] were instructed by the Board of Trade in London to meet for the purpose of wooing the Five [eventually "six"] Nations [of Native American tribes], but Franklin arrived in Albany with more on his mind than Iroquois or Frenchmen. When Massachusetts showed an interest in discussing colonial union, he took up the opportunity and proposed that the colonies unite for a more comprehensive purpose than defense. Unity for defense was a well-worn proposal. His old mentor James Logan had argued for a single colonial command to resist the Indian threat over twenty years earlier, but Franklin was now prepared to go a step farther. His Albany Plan of Union would have made the separate American governments partners in western land development—an imaginative conception, but offensive to colonies such as Massachusetts, Connecticut, and Virginia, which, with their English collaborators, possessed equally imaginative trans-Appalachian [mountains] aspirations for themselves. Franklin's Pennsylvania, where a pacifically inclined Quaker majority in the Assembly was showing little interest even in frontier defenses, seemed unlikely to share in the opening of the West; his proposal, therefore, would have had the dual virtue of promoting unity and Pennsylvania.

He [Franklin] appears to have engineered the Plan's passage with few alterations and was naturally grieved when neither Britain nor the colonial legislatures saw fit to ratify it. The defeat was important in the development of Franklin's political thought, for it caused him to re-evaluate the role of the British government in American politics. Previously, he had felt that

> A voluntary Union entered into by the Colonies themselves ... would be preferable to one impos'd by Parliament; for it would be perhaps not much more difficult to procure, and more easy to alter and improve, as Circumstances should require, and Experience direct.

Shortly before the 1754 Congress, however, it appeared to at least one of his correspondents that mutual jealousies would prevent a colonial federation, unless London stepped in. Franklin himself also came to this opinion, and suggested that the Albany Plan "be sent home, and an Act of Parliament obtain'd for establishing it." Six months after the Congress he was convinced that "if there be an Union it must be form'd at home by the Ministry and Parliament." He added cheerily, "I doubt not but that they will make a good one, and I wish it may be done this winter."

The fact that they did not, after Franklin placed his hopes in their hands, was a disappointment and served him with an early warning of England's incapacity or unwillingness to facilitate American expansion. Not even the French menace could favorably dispose the home government toward colonial unification. By 1760, after reacclimating himself to the mood in London, he came to understand the dread that many in Britain felt when they contemplated the growing colonies. Sensing their uneasiness, he quieted it with assurances that fierce intercolonial rivalry made "the union of the whole ... impossible ... without the most grievous tyranny and oppression." In private, however, his conviction grew that the Britons, not the Americans, were to blame for colonial division. He read with close attention a 1765 essay [by William Knox] describing how Parliament had passed colonial laws "restraining their commerce; prohibiting the carriage or exportation of their manufactures from one colony to another; [and] taxing the productions of one colony when brought into another." For all this, Franklin had one word. "Wicked," he scratched in the margin.

FRANKLIN MOVES TO ADVOCATE THE ANGLO-AMERICAN SPLIT

However much it must have pained him to admit that Americans were seriously divided, it probably distressed him even more to admit to himself that the bonds of empire were, in reality, strangling all hopes of intercolonial unity. He had once found comfort in that majestic edifice, the British colonial system. Its center of gravity would move westward across the Atlantic, and it would rise to new splendor, all the while remaining ever British and ever united. . . . The New Order would encompass all North America, span the Atlantic to include the British Isles, and no doubt have its capital, conveniently, in Philadelphia—the successor-city to Athens, Rome, and London. America would be the fountain of virtue whose waters would cleanse a soiled England and purify the Empire. If America were not permitted to expand in size, however, how could she grow in virtue? And if her virtue were restricted, wherewith would the English be purified?

Franklin's fifteen-year stay in England before the revolution was an important transitional period in his thinking on Anglo-American relations, for he became convinced that Parliament was antagonistic not only to colonial evolution but to the very concept of the Virtuous Order. . . . Gradually, therefore, he despaired of promoting a transoceanic New Order. . . . Increasingly, he turned during his final years in England to his old interest, the unity of the American colonies. Though his lengthy stay in London and his friendships there rendered the thought of total separation an unpleasant one, there were aspects of his experience as colonial agent which only served to heighten his awareness of his American identity and stimulate his interest in American unity. He was the representative of four colonies, not just one, and the English public often compounded the American governments and spoke of them as a single entity. . . .

In this rather undiscriminating atmosphere, the tendency was also to ascribe to Franklin the role of American spokesman. He found himself eventually defending not only Pennsylvania but all the colonies, signing articles in the London newspapers "A New Englandman," "The Colonist's Advocate," and "An American." He counseled the colonists to hold fast in their non-importation agreements, predicted that American strength would make her too dangerous an adversary for England to mistreat, and set down a point-by-point refutation of the arguments advanced by the pamphleteer, Matthew Wheelock, who questioned the ability of the colonies to hold together if set adrift:

WHEELOCK: The inhabitants of Nova Scotia and Florida could hardly attend a centrally-located American parliament.

FRANKLIN: Very easily. Tis but a Weeks Voyage from the Extremes to the Central Colonies.

WHEELOCK: The provinces differ in products and interests.

FRANKLIN: Strange, that differing in Productions should be a Reason of their not being capable of agreeing in Government.

WHEELOCK: Quarrels would develop, and the losing side would call in French or Spanish assistance.

FRANKLIN: Silly enough!

WHEELOCK: Without Great Britain as umpire, the colonies would war with one another and decide disputes by the sword.

FRANKLIN: Why not by Mediation, by Arbitration, or by considerate and prudent Agreement?

Only one point did Franklin concede. "Their divisions into provinces at present makes every colony a little state of itself," wrote Wheelock in 1770, and Franklin agreed, "There you hit it. And they will always (probably) continue so." It was with relief and approval, therefore, that he greeted such manifestations of American unity as the Massachusetts remonstrances and the Continental Congress. After 1774, he could ridicule the British expectation of imminent American fission as "A Groundless Supposition."

FRANKLIN'S VIRTUOUS ORDER AND THE AMERICAN REVOLUTION

When he returned to America [in 1775], he pitched into the task of American unification by lending his services to Congress, drafting a scheme for the "United Colonies of North America," and chairing Pennsylvania's Constitutional Convention and Committee of Public Safety, in the latter capacity corresponding with New Yorkers in order to co-ordinate defense of the middle states. Although Franklin's concern for American unity in the years leading up to the revolution was related to military considerations, it was also prompted by his vision of American virtue. It was necessary that the Virtuous Order be unified so that it might protect itself against the alien ethic, as represented by Britain.

After the revolution was under way and Franklin settled in France, his tendency to view political unity as a concomitant [a natural complement] of social virtue increased. In France, he could see that his identification of American independence with virtue had been correct. Everyone confirmed his view.

> All Europe is on our Side of the question, as far as applause and good Wishes can carry them. Those who live under arbitrary Power do nevertheless approve of Liberty, and wish for it; they almost despair of recovering it in Europe; they read the Translations of our separate Colony Constitutions with Rapture; and there are such Numbers everywhere, who talk of Removing to America, with their Families and Fortunes, as soon as Peace and our Independence shall be established, that 'tis generally believed we shall have a prodigious Addition of Strength, Wealth, and Arts. . . . Hence 'tis a Common Observation here, that our Cause is *the Cause of all Mankind,* and that we are fighting for their Liberty in defending our own. 'Tis a glorious task assign'd us by Providence; which has, I trust, given us Spirit and Virtue equal to it, and will at last crown it with success.

The revolution was nothing less than a rite of rebirth, whereby a redeemed America severed all connections with English iniquity [sinfulness] and, purged, entered into a blessedness which the entire world could vicariously share. The unification and victory of America, its innocence regained, would mean the consolidation and triumph of virtue.

This was an awesome responsibility, and whether or not America lived up to it, Franklin hoped she would keep up appearances. Like a tradesman, who must marshal his energies and discipline his will in order to impart an impression of diligence to his potential customers, so too America, just entering nationhood, should consolidate her resources and authority so that she might create an image of virtue. The idea of each state's pursuing its own foreign policy hardly suggested that unity of resolve, which agreement upon moral fundamentals should engender; nor did the sight of an impecunious [poor] nation soliciting Europe for handouts to support her armies and schools suggest the frugal diligence, bounty, and liberality in sponsorship of learning which one expected of a virtuous society. Franklin let Congress know that his situation was an awkward one, recommended a united front in foreign affairs, and expressed relief when he learned that the financial requisitions of Congress were finally being heeded by the states. For good measure, he added his own strokes to the portrait of America as united in righteousness with his *Information to Those Who Would Remove to America* (1782?), which pictured the New World Arcadia as a moral unity—industrious, egalitarian, and upright.

With the post-revolutionary period came a subtle change in Franklin's thought. He seems to have shifted perspective and superimposed the ideal upon the actual. Granted, his increasing idealization of American society may be dismissed as propaganda intended to counteract the insinuations of British journalists that the American china vase was about to shatter, and his public actions and private letters occasionally revealed his awareness that all was not harmonious in America. Yet one senses that Franklin had convinced himself with his own propaganda that his quest was at an end, and the millennium at hand. Before leaving France [in 1785], he assured his acquaintances that Americans were not disunited, were favored with an exemplary constitution, were uniformly content, and were better governed than any other people on earth. Once in Philadelphia, Franklin announced to the world that he had returned to America and, not surprisingly, found it virtuous, evolving, and harmonious.

Franklin Departs England and Returns Home to War

David Schoenbrun

In March of 1775, after nearly twenty years of service abroad in England, Franklin set sail for his home in Philadelphia. Franklin had been working to ease tensions between the colonies and the British monarch, King George III, but his efforts had backfired, resulting in his dismissal as Postmaster General of America. Moreover, although Franklin had negotiated the replacement of the hated Royal Governor of the Massachusetts Bay Colony, the new governor, General Thomas Gage, was even more unpopular with colonists than his predecessor, Thomas Hutchinson. David Schoenbrun, the distinguished reporter, worked as a CBS News correspondent for nearly twenty years and was a lecturer at Columbia University.

The packet bound for Pennsylvania, four sails billowing in a fresh wind, glided out of Portsmouth Harbour under fair skies—rare weather for England on the day that the calendar, but rarely nature, proclaims the first day of spring. Ever the scientist, Benjamin Franklin had brought some simple instruments aboard, so that he could chart the Gulf Stream and observe its particularities. Expecting never to cross the ocean again—he was sixty-nine, in the winter of his life in an era when many men died in their forties—Franklin believed this was his last chance to conclude his maritime observations for a monograph on the subject during the days of rest ahead back home. Full of enthusiasm, the old man rose at dawn, and for hours at a time, until nightfall, he leaned over the ship's rail, dipping his thermometer, at the end of a long rope, into the Gulf Stream waters. He was among the

Pages 3–21 from *Triumph in Paris: The Exploits of Benjamin Franklin*, by David Schoenbrun. Copyright © 1976 by David Schoenbrun. Reprinted by permission of HarperCollins Publishers, Inc.

first, perhaps the very first, to note, during night vigils, that those waters are not phosphorescent.

Franklin kept careful records of the temperature of the air as well as of the sea. He discovered, on crossing out of the Stream, a sharp drop in water temperature. From this he inferred the tropical source of the flow, and deduced its cause: the trade winds. He was one of the first to make this discovery, too.

He noted that the Gulf Stream had not only a flow, but a color, of its own, different from that of the surrounding ocean, and he observed a greater density of Gulf weed. He sighted a whale in the Atlantic but none in the Gulf Stream. He thought that, perhaps, the Stream could be considered a kind of river running through the ocean and that if it were so studied, it might be better understood. . . .

IN BETWEEN COUNTRIES, FRANKLIN STANDS HIS GROUND

It was this pride that kept him working diligently every waking hour on that voyage in 1775, despite the aches and pains of old age. He suffered from boils, a skin rash that itched maddeningly, and the agony of the gout, but he kept up his studies of the sea by day and then, in the ship's common room, by the poor light of candles, worked until dawn on a long letter to his son William, Royal Governor of New Jersey, a passionate servant of the King. He wanted William to know what had happened in England, that his own career had ended and that he was coming home brokenhearted, fearing that war would inevitably break out between the colonies and the motherland. Later, in an outline for his autobiography, he entitled the letter "Negotiation to Prevent the War." It runs to more than fifty finely printed pages. In his introduction to Franklin's *Autobiographical Writings*, historian Carl Van Doren asserts that with this "masterpiece in the literature of diplomacy," "American diplomatic literature may be said to begin."

The negotiations that Franklin wrote about had been prompted by a series of events beginning in London in the fall of 1773. Franklin, America's principal representative there—he was commercial and political agent of the Massachusetts Bay Colony, New Jersey, Pennsylvania and Georgia—was caught in a cross-fire of conflicts. His mission was to represent the colonies in their commercial relations with London and also to be the advocate in their grievances against unfair laws and edicts of the Parliament and the royal government.

Franklin was profoundly American in his manners, his dress, his love for and faith in his native land. He was just as loyal and patriotic an Englishman and was, in addition, a royal servant, since he held a Crown commission as Postmaster General for the colonies. He had a dream, that he wrote of often and advocated at every opportunity, of a giant British Empire, girdling the globe, based upon a commonwealth of free nations, each with its own laws, its own government and freedoms, but bound together by a compact with the Crown for mutual benefit, mutual defense and the propagation of English freedoms.

Because of his love for America, he had all along advised members of Parliament and the King's Cabinet not to impose onerous taxes upon the Americans unless they were granted the right to representation in the Parliament. He had warned London constantly that Americans had founded a new land, built a society against great odds, and were capable, and determined, to govern themselves. For this, Franklin was denounced as a radical revolutionary, disloyal to his King. Because of his love for England and his vision of an Empire, with America as the greatest jewel in its crown, he just as constantly had counseled Americans not to resist violently, but to be patient and to allow him to negotiate in good faith. He kept writing home to report on the many good friends and freedom-loving Englishmen who were working to correct the grievances, men like Edmund Burke and Lord Chatham, William Pitt the Elder. Because of that, he was denounced by American radicals as a Tory, a valet of the King and disloyal to America.

A friend in London had given Franklin letters from the Royal Governor of the Massachusetts Bay Colony, Thomas Hutchinson—a haughty, arrogant man, much hated in Boston—who had written to London demanding police and army reinforcements to help him put down demonstrations in the colony. Franklin had sent the copies to Boston to prove to his friends there that it was not the Crown, but their very own Governor, who was oppressing them. Franklin begged his correspondents to keep the letters secret, to use them only to prove to the Boston radicals that there was still hope of redress from the Crown. He had miscalculated badly. Sam Adams, one of the leaders of the Sons of Liberty, saw the letters, read them at public meetings and led new demonstrations. He also accused Franklin of trying to save face for the King. But George III felt Franklin had betrayed his trust as Postmaster General by making the letters public and instructed the Solicitor-General to take action against him. Once again, Franklin, the would-be peacemaker, was caught in the middle between warring factions.

THE "COCKPIT": AN AMERICAN AGENT, THE OBJECT OF HOSTILITY

The colonial leaders in Boston sent Franklin instructions to petition the removal from office of the hated Governor Hutchinson. Franklin had begun lobbying among his friends, telling them that Hutchinson was now the target of such odium that he could no longer govern efficiently. Hearings on the petition were set for January 1774.

On January 28, the eve of the hearing before the Privy Council, tea ships returning from Boston brought London news of the infamous Tea Party. Agent of rebellious Massachusetts, the most prominent American at hand, Franklin was the target for all the wrath of the realm.

The hearing was held in the "Cockpit," so called because cockfights had once been staged there. It began quietly enough, he later wrote his Boston friend Thomas Cushing, with Franklin's counsel, Dunning, reading a copy of the Massachusetts petition and resolves, including the demand to remove both Hutchinson and Lieutenant Governor Andrew Oliver from office. But the proceedings flared as Alexander Wedderburn, the fiery and ambitious Solicitor-General, stepped up to the table and launched into a violent attack upon the Massachusetts Assembly. The assemblymen were incorrigible dissidents, he charged. The governors were excellent men with a ten-year record of colonial administration without a single charge of misconduct. The Bostonians simply disliked them and had no real case against them.

Then Wedderburn sailed into his main target, not the petitions or resolves, but Franklin himself:

"They [the governors] owe, therefore, all the ill will which has been raised against them, and the loss of that confidence which the Assembly themselves acknowledge they had hitherto enjoyed, to Dr. Franklin's good offices in sending back these letters to Boston." Wedderburn warmed to the attack.

"Nothing then will acquit Dr. Franklin of the charge of obtaining them [the letters] by fraudulent or corrupt means, for the most malignant of purposes; unless he stole them from the person who stole them. This argument is irrefragable."

Wedderburn looked directly at Franklin, and pointing an accusing finger at his victim, shouted: "I hope, my lords, you will mark and brand this man, for the honor of this country, of Europe, and of mankind." Wedderburn, waxing melodramatic, pounded the table and, raising his voice, declaimed: "He has forfeited all the respect of societies and of men. Into what companies will he hereafter go with an unembarrassed face or the honest intrepidity of virtue? Men will watch him with a jealous eye; they will hide their papers from him and lock up their escritoires [writing tables]."

Many of the lords and spectators, particularly those who hated and envied Franklin, laughed, cheered and rapped the table as Wedderburn conducted his scandalous attack on one of the most respected men in the world. Not all, however, joined in. Edmund Burke frowned and grimaced. As he came out of the hearing room, he told friends that the attack was "beyond all bounds and measure." Dr. Joseph Priestley turned his back upon Wedderburn, who had come forward to speak to him, and walked away coldly furious. Ralph Izard, of South Carolina, stated that if he had been so insulted he would have struck back.

Franklin did not strike back.

He sat there, through the entire tirade, never interrupting, never frowning, his head high, immovable, his eyes fixed on the distance, unblinking. . . .

THE AMERICAN AGENT PLAYS A POLITICAL "CHESS GAME"

The ax fell on Franklin the very next day, as he had known it would. He was summarily fired from his position as Postmaster General for America. At first he wanted to pack up and go home. But he could not bring himself to leave London in disgrace after almost two decades of service as agent. He had a host of friends to whom he wished to make his farewells and he hoped that, perhaps, after all, one last chance might offer itself to him to prevent the calamity of war, to redeem himself so that he might leave London in triumph, his laurels in bloom.

In the course of his long service to America in London, Franklin had relaxed at the many London clubs of which he was a member. There were dozens of clubs for men of all tastes and backgrounds: for merchants and traders, for wits and for gamblers; for men of letters and of the arts; for men of science and of medicine. Franklin qualified for almost all of them and all of them wanted Franklin as a member. He often appeared at the Royal Society Club, as a guest of the leading host of famous men of the day, Dr. John Pringle, with whom he enjoyed a quiet evening of chess. It was a conversation in that club and his passion for chess that brought him, quite unexpectedly, the chance he had waited for through the long months of humiliation following upon his dismissal as postmaster.

One of the members approached Franklin, early in November 1774, and said that "there was a certain lady who had a desire of playing with me at chess, fancying she could beat me, and had requested him to bring me to her; it was, he said, a lady with whose acquaintance he was sure I should be pleased, as sister of Lord Howe's, and he hoped I would not refuse the challenge."

Franklin would certainly not refuse so charming a challenge. He loved both chess and ladies. By the end of the month, he had cleared some time, setting the rendezvous for Friday morning, December 2.

"I . . . played a few games with the lady, whom I found of a very sensible conversation and pleasing behaviour, which induced me to agree most readily to another meeting a few days after; though I had not the least apprehension that any political business could have any connection with this new acquaintance."

His last remark could only have been tongue-in-cheek. One of the lady's brothers was General Sir William Howe, who had fought at Quebec, and was rumored to be getting a new command in America. The other, even more important, was Rear Admiral Richard Howe, an earl of the realm and a member of Parliament.

Franklin began to see just who was making the moves in this game when, on the eve of his second chess date, he received a call, at home, from an old friend who was deeply involved in London politics: David Barclay, a Quaker banker and merchant, and a sympathetic supporter of America. Barclay had close ties with an influential peer, Lord Hyde, chancellor of the Duchy of Lancaster, whom Franklin had known when he was in the post office and the diplomatic service, and whom he knew to be a friend of Lord Howe. The chess game had many players.

Barclay, Franklin noted, "spoke of the dangerous situation of American affairs, the hazard that a civil war might be brought on by the present measures, and the great merit that a person would have who could contrive some means of preventing so terrible a calamity and bring about a reconciliation."

These were the words that Franklin had been longing to hear. He almost exploded with excitement when Barclay followed up the meeting with a note informing Franklin that he had "accidentally met our mutual friend, Dr. Fothergill, in my way home, and I intimated to him the subject of our discourse." Immediately thereafter came a note from Dr. John Fothergill, asking Franklin to meet with him and Barclay the following evening "to confer on American affairs."

The name "Fothergill" was all Franklin needed to know that Barclay had been primed by others higher up. Fothergill was the personal physician of Lord Dartmouth, Secretary of State for America. Franklin did not for a minute believe they had run into each other "accidentally," almost on his doorstep. This was a political chess game for high stakes. . . .

ENCOURAGED, FRANKLIN DRAWS UP A PLAN; IT'S REJECTED

At Dr. Fothergill's that [next] evening, Fothergill told Franklin he hoped he had already "put pen to paper, and formed some plan for consideration, and brought it with me." Franklin, still moving slowly, playing the reluctant mediator, answered that he had formed no plan, for he was convinced that the ministry showed no disposition for accommodation.

Fothergill protested that this was not the case. He said "he had reason, *good reason*, to believe others differently disposed." This was as close as he dared come to saying outright that Dartmouth was of a favorable disposition. He beseeched Franklin to work with the two of them in elaborating a plan and promised it would get attention in the right hands. "And what appeared reasonable to us, two of us being Englishmen, might appear so to them."

Franklin set a date for the following Tuesday evening to bring to them a plan, and worked all through the weekend on a seventeen-point proposal, which he modestly entitled "Hints for Conversation upon the Subject of Terms that might probably produce Union between Britain and the Colonies."

Article 1 proposed that Boston pay for the tea destroyed, a

most generous proposal in the circumstances, establishing Franklin's credentials as a fair negotiator, for the first point went to the ministerial side.

Article 2, balancing the first, proposed repeal of the hated duty on tea.

Article 3 called for re-enactment of the Acts of Navigation, followed by a fourth article proposing the stationing of a Crown naval officer in each colony to supervise the Acts, another gesture of reconciliation with the other side.

Then came a series of demands that had long been put forward by Franklin on behalf of the colonies: repeal of all acts restraining manufactures; all duties to be paid into colonial treasuries; customs officers to be appointed by local governors, not by London; no military requisitions in time of peace; no quartering of troops; an agreement not to build Crown fortresses without consent of the provinces; judges to be appointed and paid by the provinces, not the Crown; finally, Article 17, a vital point: "all powers of internal legislation in the colonies to be disclaimed by Parliament." Franklin noted that Article 17 "could hardly be obtained, but might be tried."

Fothergill and Barclay, upon receiving the plan, finally revealed just who was playing the chess game.

"Suppose," said Mr. Barclay, "I were to show this paper to Lord Hyde; would there be anything amiss in so doing?"

Dr. Fothergill told Franklin what he already knew, that he saw Lord Dartmouth daily and would be pleased to communicate the paper to him as coming from persons who wished the welfare of both countries. Franklin politely told them that he had drawn the paper at their request and "it was now theirs to do with what they pleased."

On December 18, Franklin received a note from Barclay reporting Lord Hyde's "hearty wish that they might be productive," an understandably noncommittal reply, but encouraging nonetheless.

Four days later, a setback: Barclay dined with Franklin and told him that Lord Hyde thought the propositions too hard. . . .

AFTER THREE MORE MONTHS OF FAILED NEGOTIATIONS, FRANKLIN LEAVES ENGLAND

Now, on the voyage home, the weather was good. Franklin breathed deeply of the salt air; the sun warmed his old bones, eased his aches. He rubbed oil on his scaling skin and hot poultices on his boils to draw them out. The beautiful days found him at the ship's side, studying the waters. He had designed a primitive odometer to determine its speed. On starry nights, he would take short breaks from his writing and study the skies through his telescope. For the first time in years he was thoroughly indulging himself, thinking of nothing but his maritime studies and his memoirs. He was literally lost at sea without long-distance communication.

The weather in Massachusetts was very different from the calm seas in which Franklin was sailing. The worst political tempests had erupted. General Gage had replaced the hated Governor Hutchinson and things had gone from bad to worse. In the fall of 1774, just as Franklin was beginning his chess game, Gage had dissolved the local Assembly. As soon as they were dismissed, the assemblymen had met promptly at Concord and constituted themselves as a provincial Congress, presided over by John Hancock. Ignoring Gage's existence in Boston, the Assembly of Concord had appointed its own treasurer to collect its own taxes. A Committee of Safety was created to collect arms and munitions and to train a local militia, the embryo of the Minute Men. All through that dismal winter of '74–'75, while Franklin negotiated in vain in London, the forces in Massachusetts had been roaring ahead on a collision course. . . .

Nothing could more perfectly illustrate how well Franklin understood his fellow Americans, including the simplest of them. He had told British officials that it was not enough to lower duties or cut the price of tea, that Parliament must abandon pretensions to legislate for the colonies. They meant to govern themselves. King George, wrong-minded as he was, guessed correctly when he kept the tea tax on to symbolize Parliament's sovereignty, announcing: "The dye is now cast. The Colonies must either submit or triumph."

General Gage was the man to cast the die. He was unimpressed with the reports of armed men in the countryside. How could mere peasants with antiquated squirrel rifles stand up to the mightiest army on earth with the most modern weapons? He was, however, sufficiently impressed by reports of militia in training, ready to fight, building up arms depots. He did not fear them, but he would not let them grow too big. He decided to pull their teeth by sending Major John Pitcairn out on a raiding expedition to root out arms dumps. They packed to march on the night of the eighteenth of April.

Paul Revere and his scouts saw them, saddled up and rode off to warn the countryside that the redcoats were coming.

When Pitcairn and his men reached Lexington, he saw, blocking the way, a determined band of Minute Men lined up, muskets ready. "Disperse, ye rebels, disperse," came the command. Someone, no one knows who, fired a shot. In seconds, flashes came from the muzzles of all the guns facing each other on Lexington Common. As the superior British troops moved forward, bayonets fixed, the Minute Men broke ranks and ran for cover, leaving eight of their fellows dead upon the ground. . . .

It took time, but the shots were eventually heard around the world—everywhere, that is, except aboard the Pennsylvania packet in the mid-Atlantic. There, Ben Franklin was spending his days dipping his thermometer into the waters, his nights poring over the notes of his negotiations and covering sheet after sheet of foolscap with his fine copperplate hand. He was deeply engrossed in the past, a past that was already a dead letter. It no longer mattered—except to future historians—why the war could not be prevented, or who was responsible; it had already broken out. In a sense, it was symbolically fitting that Franklin was one of the few men in the world who had not heard the shot, for it was a shot he had never wanted to hear, and had labored mightily to forestall. . . .

He could see crowds gathering at the docks waiting for the ship to berth. He expected that, for the arrival of a packet was always a great event. What he did not expect was the presence of a delegation with special news for him. He was home, but he was not going to get any rest.

Franklin's Second Career and His Mission for Peace

Philip J. McFarland

In an era when people were considered senior citizens by the age of fifty, Franklin was just beginning a second career. Franklin served as the American colony's agent in England from 1757 to 1775. Then, at the age of sixty-nine, he returned to America and became a member of the Continental Congress, only to be sent abroad once more in 1776, this time as a diplomat to France. In this excerpt from his recent book, The Brave Bostonians: Hutchinson, Quincy, Franklin, and the Coming of the American Revolution, *acclaimed historian and novelist Philip J. McFarland highlights Franklin's later years, specifically his diplomatic service in France. The French highly regarded Franklin and Franklin was equally fond of the French. Such mutual respect helped Franklin in recruiting French support for American independence. Having remained in France for eight years, Franklin returned home to Philadelphia in 1785 at the age of seventy-nine, heralded as an American hero.*

[Benjamin Franklin] was over fifty and world renowned when he began a new life, in London as a provincial agent, first for interests in Pennsylvania, then for wider colonial interests. That new life, centered for the most part agreeably in Craven Street, extended from 1757 to 1775, nearly twenty years as a Londoner. When it was ended, the cosmopolitan Franklin, aboard ship bound for America, was . . . sixty-nine.

At such an age, with such full and varied accomplishments in two geographical worlds and in many more worlds of the mind and spirit behind him, the voyager was presuming that his evening had come, and the time had come for repose. But fresh challenges awaited this remarkable human being when he debarked. Soon after his arrival home in May, Franklin wrote to his sister in Boston "just to let you know I am return'd well from England; that I found my Family well; but have not found the Repose I wish'd for, being the next Morning after my Arrival delegated to the Cong[ress] by our Assembly."

A SECOND LIFE: FRANKLIN GOES ON A PEACE MISSION

He was to join those representing Pennsylvania at the Second Continental Congress, which had opened its sessions on May 10 with the regathering in Philadelphia of delegates from the various American colonies.

Franklin's was by no means an honorary appointment to that historic body. Despite his age, he attended sessions faithfully and served on numerous important committees, including a vital one to procure gunpowder and another to conduct the foreign affairs of the evolving nation. Congress elected him postmaster general, and he was charged with preparing and submitting a draft of Articles of Confederation for the united provinces. In the autumn, he was chosen as one of three delegates to journey to Cambridge, across the river from Boston, to confer with Washington on needs and regulations of the new Continental army that the general was there forging into shape. And the following spring, from late March to the end of May 1776, Franklin with three much younger delegates undertook an arduous journey overland to Montreal, in a vain effort to persuade Canadians to make common cause with their neighbors to the south against the English.

Although that last took a toll on his health, the old man persevered in serving this new collection of independent colonies moving toward nationhood. Back in Philadelphia, congress chose him in June to serve on the committee to prepare the Declaration of Independence. That done, with John Adams (and sharing a bed along the way) he journeyed in late summer to Staten Island, to meet with his old acquaintance Lord Howe, recently put in command of the British fleet in North America, now come too late as peace commissioner. Civilly, but with a proud decisiveness, the American emissaries rejected Howe's pacific overtures.

In early autumn, on September 26, 1776, Franklin found himself appointed commissioner to France—an absolutely crucial assignment, inasmuch as gaining the support of the

French might well mean the difference between the success
and failure of the Revolution. He sailed from Philadelphia in
late November. . . .

ADORED BY THE FRENCH, FRANKLIN GETS THE JOB DONE

No one, no one in all of America could have pleaded with the
French government to such good effect as did Benjamin
Franklin. In France he was to remain eight years—yet another distinct and most remarkable fife for this phenomenon
who at the start of it was seventy-one. Very soon the visitor
would learn to love these new surroundings, in "the civilest
nation upon Earth," as he described it. "'Tis a delightful
People to live with." And ever afterward his most enjoyable
dreams, he said, were set there.

But if Franklin soon came to love the French, the French
adored Franklin, and from the first. He reached Paris at the
end of 1776 and was before long established in the village of
Passy, two miles out of the city. Within a month he found

FRANKLIN USES WRITING, ESPECIALLY SATIRE, TO PROMOTE HIS CAUSE

*While working as an assistant professor of English at the
University of Michigan, Mary E. Rucker contributed an essay
on Benjamin Franklin to be included in* American Literature,
1764–1789: The Revolutionary Years, *published in 1977. In her
essay, Rucker notes that Franklin's use of satire and irony, in
the tradition of British writer Jonathan Swift, effectively promoted American views to sympathetic readers in England.*

As early as the 1720s, when he sedulously aped the *Spectator,*
Franklin gave vent to his proclivity to satire—directed to social
conduct and to political issues. He later evidenced his skill in
Swiftian irony and hoax in "The Speech of Polly Baker," "A
Witch Trial at Mount Holly," and a caustic essay on the exportation of felons. Given his conception of the value of the press
which such essays attest, Franklin naturally buttressed his official negotiations with political satire. From 1764 to 1775 he
appropriated British periodicals—primarily *The London
Chronicle; or, Universal Evening Post,* the *Public Advertiser,*
and the *Public Ledger*—as a forum from which to wage a propaganda war, explaining the American cause, defending American rights and customs, pointing out the futility of coercion,
deprecating violence, and pleading for the preservation of the

himself lionized; and the enthusiasm felt for the sage old republican, plain-clothed, unaffected, immensely knowledgeable, he who with his invention of the lightning rod had wrenched thunderbolts from the sky as he was now wrenching the scepter from the tyrant's hand—the wild enthusiasm of the French for such a one scarcely diminished in all the time that he lived among them. They hung engravings of his image over their mantels, displayed busts of him, portraits, prints; reproduced his familiar features on medallions for their rings and snuffboxes. Amazed by the fashion that persisted, the object of it felt moved two years after his arrival to write his daughter back home about the number of such reproductions, an incredible number, "copies upon copies . . . spread everywhere," with the result of having made "your father's face as well known as that of the moon, so that he durst not do any thing that would oblige him to run away, as his phiz would discover him wherever he should venture to show it."

empire either through a return to requisitioning finances or through colonial representation in Parliament. His vehicles were varied: anecdote, colloquy, query, fable, parody, fictitious controversy, hoax, and tall tale, among others. Although no single piece of his propaganda was as effective as, say, [the English-born American supporter Thomas] Paine's *Common Sense,* his numerous contributions won support among those in England who were potentially sympathetic toward the colonies, and the reprinting of this journalism in American periodicals reinforced emerging separatist attitudes. His journalism was effectively ancillary to the formal petitions of various assemblies, the protests of British merchants, the nonimportation agreements, and the riots. He defined his aim in his comment on two of his most enduring satires, "Rules by Which a Great Empire may be Reduced to a Small One" (1773) and "An Edict by the King of Prussia" (1773): "Such papers may seem to have a tendency to increase our divisions; but I intend a contrary effect, and hope by comprising in little room, and setting in a strong light the grievances of the colonies, more attention will be paid to them by our administration, and that when their unreasonableness is generally seen, some of them will be removed to the restoration of harmony between us."

Mary E. Rucker, "Benjamin Franklin," *American Literature, 1764–1789: The Revolutionary Years.* Ed. Everett Emerson. Madison: University of Wisconsin Press, 1977.

Noblewomen of Louis XVI's court vied for his time and attention, carried on flirtations to which he responded with charming bagatelles [delightful miniature essays] printed on his own press at Passy. But his new life involved much more than celebrity and fashion and the writing of bagatelles. From the start he busied himself persuading the French to support the American cause by providing the new nation overseas with loans and supplies for its ragged army. He worked hard to negotiate commercial treaties with the French, to commission privateers, to secure aid for American vessels in French waters. And triumphantly, he was able, scarcely before the first year of his stay was done—and with the success of American arms at Saratoga supporting his efforts—to pave the way for signing, on the evening of February 6, 1778, at the office of the ministry for foreign affairs in the Hôtel de Lautrec in Paris, treaties of alliance and amity between France and the United States of America. . . .

FRANCE JOINS UP; FRANKLIN'S TRIUMPHANT HOMECOMING

The news of France's entry into the war appalled the English, dumbfounded them, left them desperate. At once a peace proposal went off from Whitehall [British government headquarters] to Philadelphia, what amounted virtually to a capitulation. All American grievances were to be redressed. Commissioners would be dispatched with full authority to treat with the American congress, with authority to negotiate a truce, grant pardons, repeal all the acts of Parliament since 1763, provide for home rule within the empire—precisely what Franklin had urged three years earlier. Whatever Americans wanted, short of outright independence, was to be granted. The English vessel bearing such gladsome tidings all but raced across the Atlantic against the French ship bringing news of Franklin's diplomatic triumph. Word of the triumph arrived first. Congress approved the new alliance with France in early May 1778, and the war went on. . . .

Deliberately, ever efficient of voice and movement, the old man labored on, beseeching funds from the French treasury to support the American war effort, bargaining for more supplies, conducting himself through the labyrinths of diplomacy with unvarying tact and skill. But the long effort drained him, and in March 1781, now seventy-five years old, he sought to be relieved of further duties. "I have been engaged in public affairs," he wrote the congress in Philadelphia, "and enjoyed public confidence, in some Shape or other, during the long term of fifty years, an honour sufficient to satisfy any reasonable ambition." He pleaded that someone else represent American interests at Versailles. For answer came word in August that the minister was to remain where he was, in order to act as one of the commissioners to negotiate a peace with England. And within three months the time for peace was brought nearer, as joyous news reached Paris of a decisive French-American victory over General Cornwallis at Yorktown.

Despite victory, making peace proved a long and delicate process. Finally, preliminary articles were agreed upon toward the end of 1782; and in January 1783, Franklin and John Adams attended at the signing that led to an armistice. David Hartley, Franklin's English friend and correspondent . . . signed the definitive treaty for Great Britain that September. "We are now Friends with England and with all Mankind," the successful American diplomat exulted in writing to [his friend] Josiah Quincy Sr., within days of the signing—and added: "May we never see another War! for in my opinion *there never was a good War, or a bad Peace.*"

Even after the peace, it was not until the summer of 1785 that Franklin, now nearly eighty, at last left Passy, laden with honor, and proceeded to Le Havre to board ship for home. His long residence in France was finally ended. A brief stop at Southampton [England], a final passage across the Atlantic, and on September 14 the statesman arrived in Philadelphia, at Market Street wharf, where as a youth from Boston he had first set foot in the town on an autumn day like this, sixty-two years before.

This later landing was yet another triumph, a speedier ship having informed townspeople of their beloved Franklin's progress westward, thus allowing them time to prepare a reception. "The affectionate Welcome I met with from my Fellow Citizens," he wrote soon after, "was far beyond my Expectation." Cannon had boomed as he stepped ashore; bells had rung in all the churches as he made his slow, crowded way the four blocks to Franklin Court, to his waiting daughter and to grandchildren he had never seen. For days after the return, visitors flocked to the great man's door to pay homage and show their regard.

Efforts to Liberate American Prisoners of War

William Bell Clark

William Bell Clark is considered a preeminent authority on the subject the U.S. Navy during the revolution and is the author of numerous articles and books on naval history. In this viewpoint, Clark tells of Franklin's deep concern for the American sailors who had been captured and were being held in British prisons. Clark explains that as an American diplomat with the highest rank of Minister Plenipotentiary, it was left up to Franklin to decide if and how to arrange for prisoner exchange. Initially, Franklin's efforts seemed fruitless, but he persisted in negotiations. Eventually he achieved an agreement for a prisoner exchange, but realized that it would be necessary to take more British prisoners to trade for Americans. He hired an American-captained, French-commissioned ship, the *Black Prince*, and thereby set the stage for the freeing of prisoners, French and American, taken by the British.

Dating from shortly after he arrived in France, Dr. Benjamin Franklin had evinced solicitude for the unfortunate American prisoners of war in England. As one of the three American Commissioners to the Court of Versailles, his kindly and humane interest had been stirred by their plight to continuous efforts in their behalf. The other Commissioners had given sporadic attention to proposals for exchange, or to have the sufferings of these captives ameliorated, but had been easily discouraged when formal demands upon the British Ministry had been ignored. They had been quite willing then to let the good Doctor take the whole burden upon his aging but still vigorous shoulders. Now that he had become Minister Plenipotentiary, the burden rested there entirely.

And Franklin might well have been discouraged, too, that bleak morning in mid-March, 1779, as, recovering from a severe attack of gout, he sat before the fire in the study of the little house in the rear of M. Le Ray de Chaumont's estate in Passy. Almost nine months had elapsed since his persistency had won reluctant agreement from the Ministry in London to exchange, man for man, American prisoners in England for British prisoners in France. Tedious negotiations through his old friend, the philanthropic David Hartley, a member of Parliament, had settled the details. The first cartel ship would be sent to Nantes [France] with one hundred Americans taken from Mill Prison, at Plymouth, to be returned with a similar number of Britishers brought into France by American vessels of war. The same cartel would then bring a second load of Americans from Forton Prison, at Portsmouth [England].

FRANKLIN PURSUES PRISONER EXCHANGE

Months had passed, but no cartel ship had appeared. Franklin had about concluded that he and his friend Hartley had been deceived. Delay had been by design—of that he was sure—to give more opportunity for seducing the prisoners, through promises and hardships, to secure their liberty by serving against their country. Hired agents were continual visitors to both prisons, he had learned, telling the captives they had been neglected; that the British government was willing to exchange them, but through his fault it had not been done. These agents had boasted that the American war was about over, with the British victorious, and had threatened each prisoner: Accept the King's pardon and enter on board a man-of-war, or be hanged as a traitor.

Even should the cartel arrive belatedly, Dr. Franklin's problem would be far from solved. He feared there were many more officers and men from Continental vessels, privateers, and letters of marque [an individual licensed by the government to seize the enemy] then imprisoned in England than there were British seamen in his custody for exchange. Such fears were justified. As of mid-March there had been almost five hundred Americans in the two prisons. To offset these, he had two hundred Britishers in a jail in Brest [France], and another hundred on board a prison ship in that harbor. The latter were to be dispatched to Nantes for delivery to the British cartel ship, and, as the Doctor remarked dryly, were "not so comfortably accommodated."

Moreover, prize taking in European waters was overwhelmingly in favor of the enemy. Few American war vessels were then cruising abroad and sending prisoners into France, and most of those venturing so far from home had been taken by the enemy. The British navy and privateers were finding rich prey also among lightly armed merchantmen bringing cargoes of wheat, rice, tobacco, and indigo for the Dutch, French, and Spanish markets. Alleviating the sufferings of the few hundred he could exchange meant only that hundreds more would be looking to him for relief he could not supply.

Various and numerous efforts had been made to counteract this disparity in numbers. Until the French treaty in February, 1778, American captains could not retain their prisoners in French ports. The British Ambassador, Lord Stormont, had ignored the Commissioners' first overture for exchange. The second he had "return'd with Insult." So it had been necessary to free all British officers and seamen brought in. By the fall of 1777, some two hundred had been set at liberty, and many more had been dismissed at sea and supplied with vessels to carry them to home ports.

Having been rebuffed by Lord Stormont, the Doctor's next attempt had been through David Hartley, whose interest in reconciliation had made correspondence possible. Some act of generosity and kindness towards American prisoners, such as more humane treatment, or, better still, an exchange, the Doctor had pointed out, would go further towards an accommodation than verbal wishes for peace. "Your King will not reward you for taking this trouble," he had written, "but God will, I shall not mention the good will of America; you have what is better, the applause of your own conscience."

Before Hartley could reply, the Commissioners jointly had addressed Lord North, explaining that, as upwards of five hundred British seamen had been generously treated and set at liberty by American cruisers in European seas, they trusted he would think himself bound "to dismiss an equal number of seamen taken in the service of the United States." The result had been complete silence on the part of the Prime Minister. A second letter had been drafted, renewing the request "for an immediate exchange of prisoners in Europe," but it had not been sent because Hartley, meanwhile, had reported a proposal from the Board of Admiralty. If Franklin would forward the number and rank of Britishers ready for delivery, an equal number of Americans would be selected from Mill and Forton prisons, each party then sending their prisoners to Calais [France] for exchange.

ATTEMPTS ARE MADE TO NEGOTIATE A BETTER DEAL

In accepting this, Franklin again had sought for a broader delivery. He had urged upon Hartley that the British clear their prisons, releasing all Americans. If that should be done, he had given his "solemn Engagement" to deliver to Lord Howe in America, "a Number of your Sailors equal to the Surplus." Negotiations then had droned on; Nantes instead of Calais, one hundred only to be exchanged at a time, no distinction between men taken in Continental service or in merchant vessels, seniority to govern selection, and passports to be issued for cartel ships. But the broader proposal had been rejected. Their Lordships of the Admiralty had determined that it would "be prejudicial to his Majesty's Service to exchange prisoners upon account of Debtor & Creditor."

Refusing to be discouraged by his rebuff, Franklin had another suggestion. If their Lordships would send over two hundred and fifty Americans, he would deliver every Britisher held in France. He had explained it carefully to Hartley: "If the Number we have falls short of the 250, the Cartel ship may take back as many of those she brings as the Deficiency amounts to, delivering no more than she receives. If our Number exceed the 250 we will deliver them all nevertheless, their Lordships promising to send us immediately a Number equal to the Surplus." But their Lordships had the King's consent to the original proposal, and would not presume to ask for an alteration. It would have to be one hundred at a time, man for man, or none.

There it had stood, and the British awareness of their great advantage had again been brought to his attention by his secretary-grandson. Young William Temple Franklin had pointed out a paragraph in a London newspaper of a January date, which had found its way to Passy. A number of benevolent English gentlemen, who in December, 1777, had launched a subscription to relieve the distresses of the American prisoners, had seen their funds dwindling. Before making a new appeal for subscriptions, they had visited the

Admiralty to ask John Montagu, Lord Sandwich, whether an exchange would soon take place. The First Lord had received them with great politeness, the paragraph continued, and had informed them, "that though some of the prisoners would probably be exchanged, the greater part would remain for want of a sufficient number of English prisoners in France to exchange in return."

Sandwich's utterances brought to Franklin's mind his own caustic conclusion of a month before, that the Ministry "cannot give up the pleasant idea of having at the end of the war one thousand Americans to hang for high treason." To defeat that unpalatable prospect more prisoners would have to be carried into France. Achieving this would call for more American cruisers, or, at least, cruisers with American commissions, operating in European seas.

FINDING AN ALTERNATE PLAN FOR PRISONER EXCHANGE

One such project was under way. John Paul Jones was at L'Orient transforming an old East Indiaman, now called the *Bonhomme Richard,* into a fifty-gun ship of war. But it would be long months before this ship would be ready to sail. The Doctor knew he could commission more vessels to cruise out of French ports. He had the necessary blank commissions. True they were all signed by John Hancock as President of the Continental Congress, and Hancock had retired to Massachusetts more than a year before. That was a detail which might occasion some difficulties.

What chiefly caused him to hesitate, however, was his reluctance to become further involved in naval matters. He felt himself wholly unacquainted with maritime problems, and the distance from Passy to the various ports rendered it most inconvenient to act. Likewise, every Continental ship that had come to a French harbor had required extensive outfitting, and he was no judge either of its necessity or of its cost. Disposing of prizes had produced some tiresome and vexatious arguments in which also he had been involved. Some nine months before, while the American Commissioners still functioned, they had obtained permission from the French Minister of Marine to issue a privateering commission to a sloop fitting at Dunkirk [France], and containing a mixed crew of Frenchmen, Americans, and Englishmen. It had proved a fiasco. Poreau, Mackenzie & Co., the merchants who had proposed the privateer, had misrepresented its fitness to the Commissioners' agent. Nor had the firm the resources to carry out the equipment desired by the American captain selected to command her. Recriminations had followed. Commission, instructions, and bond, over which much time had been spent, had to be scrapped, and the captain's bill for a useless journey to Dunkirk had to be paid.

The affair had left an unpleasant taste in Franklin's mouth, and he was loathe to commit himself again. Certainly no more commissions would be issued until the cartel arrived, and the exchange was proceeding as promised. That was why he had declined a more recent request to supply a commission to the burgomaster [mayor] of Dunkirk, who was equipping a fourteen-gun brig as a privateer. Perhaps a secondary reason was the burgomaster's use of Poreau, Mackenzie & Co. as a reference. Refusal, however, Franklin had ascribed to a desire for fresh orders from Congress.

Now the matter had bobbed up again in a letter just received and lying before him on the escritoire [writing table]. The writer was Stephen Marchant, a Connecticut-born Boston shipmaster. Marchant had been in Passy in January, after escaping from England via Dunkirk. The Doctor had supplied money for living expenses and a homeward passage, and had expected to hear no more from him. Instead Marchant had returned to Dunkirk, where the burgomaster had offered him command of the brig. All this the captain explained in an atrocious hand and with much misspelling.

"I Receved a Letter that If I Wood Com to Dunkirk I shold have the command off a Priveretere and thinking It a Bad time of the yeare for to goo upon the American kost I Consented for to Com Back," he wrote, "and I Shold Be much a Blig^d. to youre honner If you Wood Send the american Commishon Witch It wood Be greatly to me and my Marchants Benafet." He added that he was "Livin at Mr. Porrows."

If Marchant's letter might have reopened the subject, the postscript with the return address closed it. Franklin wanted "nothing to do with Mr. Porrow," of Poreau, Mackenzie & Co. So he reached for his quill, dipped it in the inkstand, and scratched out a reply:

I rec^d. yours of the 27th of february requesting a Commission. I had before written to M. Dem-O'hyver [That was a pretty good essay at the burgomaster's name, which was Taverne Demond Dhiver], that it was not in my Power to grant his Request untill I have rec^d. fresh Orders from Congress

But as it is easy for that Gentleman now in time of war to obtain a Commission for you from the Admiralty of France, I wish you would explain to me why you desire rather an American one. I am Sir your humble serv^t.

THE MINISTER PLENIPOTENTIARY IS ON HIS OWN

Actually Franklin anticipated no "fresh Orders" from Congress. The American Revolution, in fact, was fought with little or no co-ordination between the efforts in the United States and those in France. It could not be otherwise with ocean crossings requiring at least four weeks eastbound, and, against the prevailing winds, often twice that time westbound; to say nothing of the hazards of storm and enemy interception.

Moreover, in the early months of 1779, the Continental Congress had other problems than instructing its Minister Plenipotentiary in Paris whether he should or should not issue commissions to French-owned, American-captained privateers. James Lovell, of the Committee of Foreign Affairs, had felt in December, 1778, that the only important struggle was with the currency. But he was reckoning without [the American lawyer and diplomat] Silas Deane, whose address to the "Free and Virtuous Citizens of America" launched a bitter struggle in Congress, which seriously retarded getting on with the war, and practically throttled naval activities. Congress was more interested in getting help from the French fleet in the West Indies for the beleaguered states of South Carolina and Georgia, than advising Franklin of anything. It was content, as Lovell put it in January, in wishing him success and satisfaction in his important agency.

While the Doctor slowly recovered from his attack of gout—even on April 8 there was still "a little remaining indisposition"—he heard that the cartel ship had at last arrived at Nantes. She had brought ninety-seven instead of one hundred Americans from Mill Prison. The reason for the discrepancy was absurd. Carrying out the conceit that the prisoners were still British subjects, George III had issued a pardon early in February to each of the one hundred designated for exchange. By March 15, when they paraded down through Plymouth to the cartel ship, two of their number had died and one was left behind dangerously ill. The three vacancies could not be filled because no others had received royal clemency! But, as Franklin observed, "This Exchange is the more remarkable, as our people were all committed as for high Treason."

Even though unconscionably slow about it, the enemy had shown good faith, so his concern began anew for the Americans who must continue to languish in prison after the supply of Britishers for exchange had been exhausted. When the French Minister of Marine requested that the frigate *Alliance,* which had brought Franklin's commission as Minister Plenipotentiary, be held abroad, he was happy to acquiesce, because "she may procure us some more prisoners to exchange the rest of our countrymen." This hope was bolstered by her reputation as an exceedingly fast sailer, and on April 28, he ordered her to join Jones at L'Orient. He had no idea when the squadron gathering there would be ready. A letter from Jones, written at the end of April, had remarked, "Be not discouraged—Our Object will not be lost tho' I Should not be able to put to Sea for two Months to come."

Franklin did not wish to wait for two months. He was in a mood for action. Hence he gave attentive ear to M. Sutton de Clonard, a nobleman of naval bent and with influence at court. M. de Clonard called at Passy early in May, following a trip to Dunkirk, and spoke of a very fine cutter he had seen in that harbor; a cutter being armed with sixteen guns, and which would make an ideal American privateer. Likewise the Count remarked that there were many Irish smugglers idling about Dunkirk. These with some of the escaped Americans, who were continually crossing from Dover, would assure a good crew. Perhaps Dr. Franklin might like to look into it? Having dropped the seed, M. de Clonard let it germinate a few days and then wrote a brief note: "Mr. Stephen Merchant [*sic*] of Boston, is come from Dunkirk to Sollicite your Excellency for an American Commission to Enable him to Command the Cutter of 16 guns which I mention'd to you—I request that you may gratify him therein. This Vessel will have a very good Crew, American & Irish, as She Sails extremely well, She must do considerable Execution."

Here was the illiterate Marchant back again. Franklin, remembering the Poreau connection and recalling that the captain never had replied to his letter, probably would have refused to consider the request. However, another visitor arrived at Passy with an endorsement of the Count's recommendation. This was Francis Jean Coffyn, Flemish broker and royal interpreter at Dunkirk. For several years Coffyn had been a trustworthy agent for the American Commissioners and had endeared himself to Franklin by the intelligent and sympathetic manner in which he had managed the small fund given him for the relief of escaped prisoners. As the Dunkirk agent had been the one to expose Poreau, Mackenzie & Co. the previous year, the Doctor accepted Coffyn's statement that Marchant was an able but simpleminded seaman, who originally had fallen into bad hands. The owners of the privateer, the agent explained, were the Torris brothers, reputable merchants of Dunkirk. Poreau had nothing to do with her. An ample crew had been recruited, and the owners desired Marchant as her commander. If Dr. Franklin decided to issue the commission, Coffyn would remain in Paris a few days to receive it, and carry it to Dunkirk and administer it personally.

FRANKLIN APPROVES THE COMMANDER AND LAUNCHES THE *BLACK PRINCE*

Marchant was given audience and supplied additional data. The cutter was of one hundred and twenty tons burden, and her sixteen carriage guns were all 4-pounders. Outfitting and provisioning were virtually completed for a crew numbering seventy men. As first lieutenant, he was happy to have his former mate in the merchant service, Jonathan Arnold, of Middletown, Connecticut. Franklin listened noncommittally, and sent the captain back to Dunkirk to await a decision.

For twenty-four hours the Doctor considered the matter. Commissioning the privateer, as he knew from past experience, would involve him in many more troubles. On the other hand, encouraging such an armament was the only way he could hope to attain the exchange of more Americans in England. Should this cutter, rejected by him, go forth under a French commission, the prizes she would take would be the property of France; the Britishers she would bring in would be exchanged for Frenchmen. That would be of no service to his countrymen in Mill and Forton prisons. He weighed the inconveniences and annoyances, which might, and most likely would, arise should he issue the commission, against the satisfaction of freeing more men from captivity. As to be expected from Dr. Franklin, his humanitarian interest tipped the scales in behalf of the prisoners.

Once decision was made, action was prompt. He called for a blank commission, a blank bond, and a copy of the oath of allegiance. Young Temple Franklin produced each and listened to his grandfather's directions. The captain's commission was filled in first, then the bond. There were spaces in each for the owners' names to be supplied later. The commission bore John Hancock's signature and was dated October 8, 1777. The Doctor overcame that by endorsing at the bottom: "This Commission is delivered by B. Franklin Minister of the United States at the Court of France to Captain Marchant at Passy, May 19th. 1779."

It was neither delivered at Passy, nor on the date specified; first, because Marchant was not there to receive it, and second, because it was sent by messenger on May 14 to Francis Coffyn, predated to allow for time to reach Dunkirk. "I am directed by my Grand father," Temple Franklin wrote Coffyn, "to transmit you the enclosed Commission for a Privateer, together with the instructions to the Commander and the bond to be signed by the Owners you are directed carefully to attend to the filling up of the Blanks both in the Commission and Bond." Temple added that the oath of allegiance should be taken by the captain in the agent's presence before the commission was delivered.

The instructions Franklin wrote himself. They were explicit and to the point. Marchant was to bring in all the prisoners possible, "because they serve to relieve so many of our Country-men from their Captivity in England." With that singleness of purpose as a benediction, the Doctor launched the *Black Prince* upon her career.

CHAPTER 4

Dr. Franklin's Legacy

Dr. Franklin's Business Lessons

Peter Baida

The late Peter Baida, a graduate of the Wharton
School of the University of Pennsylvania, and author
of *Poor Richard's Legacy: American Business Values
from Benjamin Franklin to Donald Trump*, notes in
this viewpoint Franklin's good advice can be found
in his writing, but his dealings in business offer further examples of strategies for success. Even after
his death, Franklin's business sense has helped some
people while his ghost has haunted others. Baida
himself was inspired by the ghost and concluded
that Franklin's success was due to his entrepreneurial skill, hard work, and some good luck.

Anyone who has lived in Philadelphia knows that the ghost
of its best known citizen still haunts the city. "University of
Pennsylvania—Founded by Benjamin Franklin"—so read
the sign that greeted me each morning as I pushed through
the doors of [the Wharton School's] Vance Hall. . . . At dusk
each evening, I passed beneath the statue of Franklin that
gazes toward the Van Pelt Library from the walk in front of
College Hall. My wife worked in the Franklin Building. We
drove home via the Benjamin Franklin Parkway.

All of these signs must mean something, I thought. As a
pilgrim travels to the Holy Land in search of his soul's salvation, so I had come to Wharton in search of the secret of
money. Somehow, I thought, Ben Franklin held the key. But
how? I knew about Franklin what every schoolchild knows:
he had served an apprenticeship, flown a kite, signed a declaration, and entertained the French. I knew also that it had
been Franklin who popularized the maxims about thrift and
pennies and stitches in time that an earnest teacher had
drilled into my head in the third grade; Franklin who de-

clared, with an economy of language as characteristic as the economy of the sentiment, that "Time is money"; and Franklin who taught America, in the title of his best known essay, "The Way to Wealth." What were my classmates and I doing at Franklin's university if not struggling to remake ourselves in his image, to lay hands on his legacy? . . .

FRANKLIN'S ADVICE; POOR RICHARD'S GUIDANCE

In 1748, Franklin summarized his approach to business in a remarkable two-page essay entitled "Advice to a Young Tradesman." Apart from its value as an expression of Franklin's views, the essay reflects certain crucial tendencies in American life, and it occupies a position of unusual interest as a document in the history of ideas. At the start of his classic study, *The Protestant Ethic and the Spirit of Capitalism,* the German sociologist Max Weber could find no better way to introduce his subject than to quote "Advice to a Young Tradesman" virtually in its entirety. . . .

To Weber, these paragraphs express the spirit of capitalism "in almost classical purity." Weber defines capitalism as "the pursuit of profit, and forever *renewed* profit, by means of continuous, rational, capitalist enterprise." The Puritan-capitalist ethic takes as its highest goal "the earning of more and more money, combined with the strict avoidance of all spontaneous enjoyment of life." It affirms "the idea of a duty of the individual toward the increase of his capital, which is assumed as an end in itself." Under its influence, "Man is dominated by the making of money, by acquisition as the ultimate purpose of his life."

Franklin's views "called forth the applause of a whole people," Weber observes, yet in both ancient times and the Middle Ages, these same views would have been condemned "as the lowest sort of avarice and as an attitude entirely lacking in self-respect." It is easy to show that Franklin did not lack self-respect, and easy to show that motives other than avarice guided many activities in his life. But to critics who raise these points as "problems," Weber replies testily that "the problem is just the reverse: how could such a philanthropist come to write these particular sentences . . . in the manner of a moralist?"

"Advice to a Young Tradesman" was neither the first nor the most influential of Franklin's writings on personal economy. Beginning in 1732, Franklin published annually an almanac ostensibly put together by a poor farmer and amateur astrologer named Richard Saunders, better known as Poor Richard. In an effort to make the almanac "both entertaining and useful," Franklin tells us in his autobiography, he "filled all the little spaces that occurred between the remarkable days in the calendar with proverbial sentences, chiefly such as inculcated industry and frugality. . . ." The almanac soon won a large following and "came to be in such demand that I reaped considerable profit from it, vending annually over ten thousand."

In addition to anonymous folk proverbs representing "the Sense of all Ages and Nations," Franklin packed the almanac with maxims that he himself invented and epigrams drawn from writers such as [the English poet and satirist Jonathan] Swift, [the English philosopher and statesman Francis] Bacon, and [the French author and moralist Duc Francois VI de] La Rochefoucauld. He never hesitated to polish popular wisdom. For instance, "Three may keep counsel if two of them are away" was sharpened into "Three may keep a secret if two of them are dead." The Scottish "A gloved cat was never a good hunter" and the English "A muffled cat is no good mouser" became Poor Richard's "The cat in gloves catches no mice."

In 1757, Franklin composed a narrative that brought together in a "connected discourse" approximately 100 sayings from the almanacs of the previous 25 years. The narrative unites the most worldly of Poor Richard's maxims in a speech made by a shrewd old man named Father Abraham to a crowd at a colonial auction. This piece, Franklin tells us, "being universally approved, was copied in all the Newspapers of the Continent, reprinted in Britain on a Broadside to be stuck up in Houses, two Translations were made of it in French, and great Numbers bought by the Clergy and Gentry to distribute gratis among their poor Parishioners and Tenants." Under the title "The Way to Wealth" or "Father Abraham's Speech," it was reprinted at least 145 times in seven different languages before the end of the eighteenth century, and over the next 200 years it came to be, with the autobiography, the most widely read of Franklin's writings.

"The Way to Wealth" crams so many proverbs into so few pages that it is difficult to believe that anyone has ever read it without experiencing some discomfort. Franklin is right, however, when he claims that "bringing all these scatter'd counsels thus into a Focus, enabled them to make greater Impression." The straightforward exposition of "Advice to a Young Tradesman" makes it easier to read, but the condensed wisdom of "The Way to Wealth" makes it easier to remember. . . .

FRANKLIN AS ENTREPRENEUR EXERCISES BUSINESS SAVVY

With the establishment of his own printing business, Franklin began a dazzling entrepreneurial career. An early coup presents a classic example of the self-made man making his own luck. Having noticed "a Cry among the People for more Paper-Money," Franklin wrote and published an anonymous pamphlet entitled *A Modest Enquiry into the Nature and Necessity of a Paper Currency.* When the legislature voted to issue an additional 40,000 pounds, the young publisher was hired to print the money—"a very profitable Jobb, and a great Help to me."

A second stroke paid off even more handsomely. Franklin's main competitor, Andrew Bradford, handled all the printing for the Pennsylvania Assembly. He had printed badly a message of the assembly to the governor. "We reprinted it elegantly and correctly, and sent one to every Member." The next year—and every year thereafter for as long as he wanted the job—Franklin did the printing for Pennsylvania, and in time he printed "the Votes and Laws and other Publick Business" not only for Pennsylvania but also for New Jersey, Delaware, and Maryland.

Other profitable ventures included the *Pennsylvania Gazette,* which Franklin took over from a bankrupt competitor in 1729 and turned into one of the most vigorous newspapers in the colonies, and, of course, *Poor Richard's Almanack.* Among printers in Philadelphia, two of Franklin's three main competitors left the business shortly after he entered it, and the third soon settled into semiretirement, so that when the 24-year-old Franklin bought out his partner in 1730, he had the field virtually to himself.

With success in business came, in the words of [Franklin biographer] Carl Van Doren, a "swift accumulation of offices." From 1736 until 1751, when the citizens of Philadelphia elected him their representative, Franklin served as clerk to the Pennsylvania Assembly. The position provided an "Opportunity of keeping up an Interest among the Members," and thus "secur'd to me the Business of Printing the Votes, Laws, Paper money and other occasional Jobbs for the Public, that on the whole were very profitable." In addition, beginning in 1737, Franklin served as postmaster of Philadelphia—another modest position, but it increased the demand for his newspaper, brought him new advertisers, and "came to afford me a very considerable income."

Additional income flowed in from partnerships or working arrangements with printers in the Carolinas, New York, and the British West Indies, as well as from investments in real estate. In 1748, 20 years after the formation of the partnership that launched him, Franklin retired . . . at the age of 42, exactly

Franklin, a successful businessman and civic leader, was admired and respected by his fellow citizens.

halfway through a remarkably busy life. In Carl Van Doren's 782-page biography, Franklin's retirement occurs on page 123. Ahead lies enough activity to fill the lives of half a dozen men. "Electrician," "Soldier," "Agent," "Speaker," "Agent-General," "Philosopher in England," "Postmaster-General," "Commissioner," "Minister-Plenipotentiary," "Sage in France," "Peacemaker," "President of Pennsylvania"—even a partial list of Van Doren's chapter titles suffices to suggest how little we see of Franklin if we see him only as a businessman.

Yet he began as a businessman, and his success in business paved the way for grander successes. The story of Franklin's rise has entertained and instructed generations of Americans, but its familiarity may lull us into a failure to ask one fundamental question. To what extent did Franklin owe his rise to the virtues that he recommended in the writings that made him famous? This question offers our best protection against the charm of Franklin's own voice and the temptation to take a simple view of him.

No one can reasonably deny that industry helped Franklin to gain his fortune and that frugality helped him to keep it. But luck also helped, and natural ability helped even more. Luck led to the apprenticeship as a printer that supplied him with the technical skills on which he based his business success. Natural ability led to mastery whenever he exerted himself. He would not have fared so well if he had been an industrious bumbler or a frugal knucklehead.

On the other hand, luck alone would have meant little if he had not worked to master his trade, and natural ability would have meant little if he had not worked to develop his gifts. Franklin was born with a lively intelligence, but not with the lively prose style that marked his maturity He needed luck to succeed, but he needed something more than luck—and something more than industry, frugality, and prudence—to succeed as brilliantly as he did. Imagine Franklin without his eye for entrepreneurial opportunities, or without his humor and his literary skill, and at once it becomes clear that simple economic virtues tell only part of the story. . . .

ONE CAN LEARN A LOT FROM FRANKLIN ABOUT NETWORKING

In the second half of the twentieth century, successors of Poor Richard have embraced the term "networking" to refer to an activity that they unanimously proclaim[ed] a key to business success—the cultivation and utilization of professional connections. Here as in so much else, we follow a trail that Franklin blazed. Aspiring youths of any era may usefully study Franklin's accomplishments as networker. . . .

In 1727, four years after his arrival in a city where he knew no one, the 21-year-old printer "form'd most of my ingenious Acquaintance into a Club for mutual Improvement, which we call'd Junto." The members of the Junto were young men not yet respectable or established enough to break into the clubs that served Philadelphia's business elite. Like Franklin, they were tradesmen, sometimes called Leather Aprons, and the Junto was sometimes called the Leather-Apron Club.

The Junto was a secret brotherhood that met weekly. Its rules, drafted by Franklin, required new members to "sincerely declare" that they loved mankind in general and truth for truth's sake. Meetings began with 24 "standing Queries," also drafted by Franklin, which show that the club did not so mix business with pleasure as it mixed the business of doing good with the business of getting ahead. . . .

The Junto survived for more than 30 years and was, Franklin claimed, "the best School of Philosophy, Morals and Politics that then existed in the Province." But it was also, always, an effective source of business assistance for its members, "every one of these exerting themselves in recommending Business to us." In Franklin's mind and in his life, public service and private welfare went hand in hand. As Carl Van Doren remarked, the Junto was Franklin's "benevolent lobby for the benefit of Philadelphia, and now and then for the advantage of Benjamin Franklin."

At age 25, with the assistance of the Junto, Franklin embarked upon the first in the long line of public projects. . . . This was just the start: it is unlikely that any city has ever owed as much to one man as Philadelphia owes to Franklin. After the library (1731), Franklin founded or helped to found Philadelphia's city watch (1735–1752), its first fire company (1736), its first college (1749), its first hospital (1751), and its first fire insurance company (1752). He also served as Grand Master of Pennsylvania's Freemasons (1734), founded the American Philosophical Society (1743), organized Pennsylvania's first militia (1747), and encouraged the paving and lighting of Philadelphia's streets (1751–1762).

Each project depended upon the assistance of Franklin's network of personal and professional connections, and with each project his network grew, along with his reputation as a doer of good—"a great Promoter of useful Projects." Franklin's skill as a promoter of public improvements fully matched his skill as a promoter of his personal interests. Indeed, we miss the essence of Franklin's success if we try to separate the two. . . .

Self-effacement not in the expression of his views but in the manner of the expression, self-effacement not in the promotion of public works but in the pursuit of credit—or at least the *appearance* of pursuit—those are the lessons that Franklin teaches. He would not have found anything new in Dale Carnegie's *How to Win Friends and Influence People* or in the self-help books of Carnegie's successors in our own generation. He would not have found anything new in the ten generations of self-help writers who have followed his own Poor Richard.

He was an accomplished networker and an invaluable team player—a master of what social psychologists of the twentieth century call "group dynamics.". . . His career as a team player began with the group of young tradesmen that he brought together in his Junto and ended with the teams that hammered out the Declaration of Independence and the Constitution of the United States. To anyone who wishes to function effectively in a group, his example teaches a vital lesson: other people may have been more modest, but no one has ever sounded more modest.

FRANKLIN BELONGS TO THE PUBLIC

Almost since the day he died, America has been talking back to Benjamin Franklin. Some love him, others loathe him, but few of us are neutral. He is not like anyone else, yet somehow he is representative—a figure we must understand if we want to understand the American character. All of us see ourselves in him, or see an antiself.

Franklin has been fiercely criticized, but the critics have always been in the minority. The majority have made Franklin's autobiography the most famous ever written by an American and made Franklin himself one of the two or three most popular subjects of American biography. Franklin's name has become a public possession. When citizens of nineteenth-century Boston decided to sponsor lectures to encourage young men to lead sober and industrious lives, they called them Franklin Lectures, and hundreds of savings institutions call themselves Franklin banks. . . .

Thomas Mellon, the founder of one of America's greatest fortunes, was a 14-year-old living on a farm outside Pittsburgh when he stumbled upon a copy of the autobiography. "I had not before imagined any other course of life superior to farming," he said later, "but the reading of Franklin's life led me to question this view. For so poor and friendless a boy to be able to become a merchant or a professional man had before seemed an impossibility; but here was Franklin, poorer than myself, who by industry, thrift and frugality had become learned and wise, and elevated to wealth and fame. The maxims of 'Poor Richard' exactly suited my sentiments. . . . I regard the reading of Franklin's *Autobiography* as the turning point of my life."

Not long after he discovered Franklin, Mellon set out from his home in Poverty Point, Pennsylvania for Pittsburgh, 21 miles away, with 99 cents in his pocket. Years later, the financier put a statue of Franklin in his bank, and late in life he printed 1,000 copies of the autobiography to give to the young people who flocked to him for assistance or advice.

Mark Twain took a less reverent view. Franklin, he declares, was "of a vicious disposition" and "full of animosity towards boys." He "early prostituted his talents to the invention of maxims and aphorisms calculated to inflict suffering upon the rising generation of all subsequent ages. . . . It was in this spirit that he became the son of a soap-boiler, and probably for no other reason than that the efforts of all future boys . . . might be looked upon with suspicion unless they were the sons of soap-boilers."

The general acceptance of Franklin as a model for the young offered Twain a target he could not resist. He complains that "with a malevolence which is without parallel in history," Franklin would "work all day, and then sit up at nights, and let on to be studying algebra by the light of a smouldering fire, so that all other boys might have to do that also, or else have Benjamin thrown up to them. Not satisfied with these proceedings, he had a fashion of living wholly on bread and water, and studying astronomy at meal time—a thing which has brought affliction to millions of boys since, whose fathers had read Franklin's pernicious biography.". . .

The bitterest denunciations of Franklin, as well as the most sweeping and the least conventional, have come from the American poet William Carlos Williams and the stormy Englishman D.H. Lawrence. Both of these authors associate

Franklin with values they detest, and both of them launch long, complex, vigorous attacks. Williams complains that in his experiments with lightning, Franklin "didn't dare let it go in at the top of his head and out at his toes. . . . His mighty answer to the New World's offer of a great embrace was THRIFT. Work night and day, build up, penny by penny, a wall against that which is threatening, the terror of life, poverty. Make a fort to be secure in." Franklin, Williams concludes with a sigh, is "our wise prophet of chicanery, the great buffoon, the face on the penny stamp." Like Williams, D.H. Lawrence sees Franklin as a spiritual enemy—an enemy of life itself. When Franklin says that God "governs the world by his Providence," Lawrence protests that Franklin's God is "the supreme servant of men who want to get on.". . .

The extreme responses to Franklin, whether pro or con, are more vivid and entertaining than balanced appraisals, which have nothing to recommend them except the wish to be fair. A balanced appraisal must concur with Carl Van Doren's statement that Franklin "seems to have been more than any single man," as well as his assertion that nothing seems to have been omitted from Franklin's character "except passionate desire, as in most men of genius, to be all ruler, all soldier, all saint, all poet, all scholar, all some one gift or merit or success." Franklin was indeed, as Van Doren says, "a harmonious human multitude." He might have taken as his epitaph Turgot's famous epigram: "He snatched the lightning from the sky and the sceptre from tyrants." But the grand style did not suit him, and though he stood before kings, he never forgot his roots. His will begins, "I, Benjamin Franklin, Printer. . . ."

FRANKLIN'S GHOST REIGNS SUPREME

He does not seem such an unfriendly spirit now that I know him better. Having listened to the best and the worst that posterity has said of him, I find that I prefer to listen to the ghost himself. He has saved one last story, and he will not let me go until he tells it. The year is 1755, and a retired businessman named Benjamin Franklin has gone on an excursion with friends. But let him speak for himself:

"Being in Maryland, riding with Colonel Tasker and some other gentlemen to his country seat . . . , we saw, in the vale below us, a small whirlwind beginning in the road and showing itself by the dust it raised and contained. It appeared in the form of a sugar loaf, spinning on its point, moving up the hill towards us, and enlarging as it came forward. When it passed by us, its smaller part near the ground appeared no bigger than a common barrel, but, widening upwards, it seemed at forty or fifty feet high to be twenty or thirty feet in diameter.

"The rest of the company stood looking after it, but, my curiosity being stronger, I followed it, riding close by its side, and observed its licking up in its progress all the dust that was under its smallest part. . . .

"I accompanied it about three-quarters of a mile, till some limbs of dead trees, broken off by the whirl, flying about and falling near me, made me more apprehensive of danger; and then I stopped, looking at the top of it as it went on, which was visible by means of the leaves contained in it for a very great height above the trees."

This is not the voice of Franklin the prudent aphorist or Franklin the philosopher of common sense or Franklin the self-made self-promoter. It is not even the voice of Franklin the scientist. It is the voice of Franklin the man—the most inquisitive American of his time, as well as the most versatile and the most observant.

Franklin is ours forever—in the phrase of Herman Melville, "the type and genius of his land." We may love him or hate him, but we cannot escape him: his ghost will not let us go. When we recall the familiar stories that deceive us into thinking that we know everything about him, when we recall the writings that led Weber to choose him as the embodiment of the spirit of capitalism and led others to dismiss him as "mean and thrifty" or "cheap and shabby," and when we recall the characteristics that led Lawrence to renounce him as "the sharp little man . . . middle-sized, sturdy, snuff-coloured Doctor Franklin," we should also take a moment to remember Benjamin Franklin and the whirlwind: "The rest of the company stood looking after it, but, my curiosity being stronger, I followed it, riding close by its side."

I began my inquiry with the expectation that Franklin would show me the way to wealth, but in the end I knew that to earn his blessing, I would have to follow him further. In my dreams today, it is the soapmaker's son from Boston who rides into the territory ahead of the rest, ahead of all of us.

A Will for the American People

Carl Van Doren

Carl Van Doren won a Pulitzer Prize for his biography
of Benjamin Franklin, published in 1938. From that
biography comes this explanation of Franklin's will
as well as his intellectual legacy as expressed in his
autobiography. This last chapter of Franklin's biography also highlights Franklin's attempts to settle a debt
owed to him by Congress and to dispel the rumors
that he had stolen money from Congress; frustrated
with Congress's lack of interest in the matter and
aware that his death was near, Franklin spent his last
days working on his autobiography. Carl Van Doren
taught English at Columbia University and published
work as a literary critic, editor, and historian.

In the summer of 1788 Franklin made his will (signed and
witnessed on 17 July) in language which was plainly not
only for his executors but also for the public which he knew
would be interested. He left his son William the Nova Scotia
land, the books and papers in his possession, and the debts
which had accumulated during the years when William had
lived beyond his governor's salary on money furnished by
his father. "The part he acted against me in the late war,
which is of public notoriety, will account for my leaving him
no more of an estate he endeavoured to deprive me of."
Franklin's real estate and household goods in Philadelphia
he left to Richard and Sarah Bache. Richard was given "the
lands near the Ohio" and forgiven his debt of over two thousand pounds to his father-in-law, who requested that "in
consideration thereof he would immediately after my decease manumit and set free his Negro man Bob." The miniature of Louis XVI went to Sarah, with the request "that she
would not form any of those diamonds into ornaments ei-

From *Benjamin Franklin*, by Carl Van Doren. Copyright 1938 by Carl Van Doren, renewed © 1966 by Margaret Van Doren Bevans, Anne Van Doren Ross, and Barbara Van
Doren Klaw. Used by permission of Viking Penguin, a division of Penguin Putnam Inc.

ther for herself or daughters, and thereby introduce or countenance the expensive, vain, and useless fashion of wearing jewels in this country." Franklin left his sister Jane Mecom his house and lot in Unity Street, Boston, and fifty pounds a year for life. His right to take up land in Georgia he gave to his grandson Temple, with "the bond and judgment I have against him of four thousand pounds sterling." All the types and printing materials in Philadelphia and Franklin's share in the Library Company were to go to [Sarah's son] Benjamin Franklin Bache. There were small legacies for the surviving descendants of the Boston Franklins, and precise instructions for dividing books, manuscripts, and philosophical and musical instruments among relatives, friends, the Library Company, the American Philosophical Society, and the American Academy of Arts and Sciences in Boston.

The Philanthropic Franklin Prepares for an Unknown Future

Franklin's old uncollected business debts, as "stated in my great folio ledger E," he left to the Pennsylvania Hospital, hoping that his debtors or their descendants, "who now, as I find, make some difficulty of satisfying such antiquated demands as just debts, may, however, be induced to pay or give them as charity to that excellent institution." (But seven years after his death the managers of the hospital found the bequest gave them more trouble than it was worth and returned the ledger to the executors.) To the directors of "the free schools in my native town of Boston" he left a hundred pounds, of which the interest was to be annually "laid out in silver medals and given as honorary rewards." The Franklin medals were awarded first in January 1793 and continuously after that. Always given only to boys, they have since 1867 been given only to boys in the Boston Latin School and other high schools. In 1922 the number of medals was about thirty a year, and the total from 1793 had been about four thousand.

On 23 June 1789 Franklin added the long codicil [supplement] which has made his will famous. There were a few minor changes and corrections and some further personal bequests. "My fine crab-tree walking-stick, with a gold head curiously wrought in the form of the cap of liberty, I give to my friend, and the friend of mankind, General Washington. If it were a sceptre, he has merited it and would become it." But the feature of the codicil was a scheme of progressive philanthropy meant to run two hundred years. Out of the unused salary Franklin had received as President of Pennsylvania he left a thousand pounds each to Boston and Philadelphia. These sums were to be used for loans to "such young married artificers, under the age of twenty-five years, as have served an apprenticeship in the said town, and faithfully fulfilled the duties required in their indentures, so as to obtain a good moral character from at least two respectable citizens who are willing to become their sureties." Each borrower was to pay five per cent interest and repay a tenth of the principal each year, "which sums of principal and interest, so paid in, shall be again let out to fresh borrowers. . . . It is hoped that no part of the money will at any time be dead, or be diverted to other purposes, but be continually augmented by the interest. . . . If this plan is executed, and succeeds as projected without interruption for one hundred years, the sum will then be one hundred and thirty-one thousand pounds." Of this amount the town of Boston or Philadelphia was to expend one hundred thousand on public works and to continue the remainder as loans to promising young men for another hundred years. "At the end of this second term, if no unfortunate accident has prevented the operation, the sum will be four millions and sixty-one thousand pounds sterling, of which I leave one million sixty-one thousand pounds to the disposition of the inhabitants of the town of Boston [or Philadelphia], and three millions to the disposition of the government of the state, not presuming to carry my views further."

Franklin, who owed this expansive scheme to a French correspondent Mathon de la Cour, had had it in mind ever since his return to Philadelphia. There was in 1789 hardly an American fortune so large as a million dollars, and Franklin's was perhaps no more than a fifth of that. But he had always known how to be patient, and time had served him. He would put money to work, at benevolent compound interest, for posterity. In a hundred years, and then in another hundred, his gift would be princely. Nor would the money lie idle in the meantime. Speculating on the best use to put it to, Franklin remembered that a loan to him when he was a married tradesman under twenty-five had set him on the road to success. Now he might pass the favour on to many men after him. He could—or did—not foresee the coming changes in the apprentice system and the rise of an industrialism which would make young independent tradesmen less and less common, less and less able to profit by his loans. His calculations as to the "continually augmenting" fund turned out to have been too hopeful. But by 1907 the Benjamin Franklin Fund in Philadelphia amounted to $172,350, of which $133,076.46 was transferred to the Franklin Institute; and the remainder of the Fund had grown by 1936 to $132,660.24. Boston at the end of the first hundred years of the Franklin Fund had $391,000. Part of this was withdrawn for public works, as Franklin had ruled, and with the help of Andrew Carnegie [the great American industrialist and philanthropist] it built and equipped the Franklin Union, a technical school for young men already employed and possibly able to study only in the evening. The part of the Franklin Fund which was reinvested in 1891 had grown in 1935 to $593,000, and at the . . . [time of its maturity was] expected to be in 1991 about four millions—the most munificent money gift ever made by a philosopher.

FRANKLIN SEEKS PAYMENT; EMBEZZLEMENT RUMORS CIRCULATE

Disappointment came to Franklin from Congress. At the settlement of his account in May 1785, Thomas Barclay, serving as Congress's auditor, found that Franklin had 7533 livres [old French units of money, each one equal to 20 sols] and a fraction still due him; "the difference between my statement and his," Franklin told Cyrus Griffin, president of Congress, on 29 November 1788, "being only seven sols which by mistake I had overcharged: about threepence halfpenny sterling. At my request, however, the accounts were left open for the consideration of Congress, and not finally settled, there being some equitable demands, as I thought them, for extra services which he had not conceived himself empowered to allow, and therefore I did not put them in my account. He transmitted the accounts to Congress and had advice of their being received. On my arrival in Philadelphia one of the first things I did was to dispatch my grandson, William T. Franklin, to New York to obtain a final settlement of those accounts; he, having long acted as my secretary and being well acquainted with the transactions, was able to give an explanation of the articles that might seem to require explaining, if any such there were. He returned without effecting the settlement, being told that it could not be made till the arrival of some documents expected from France. . . . It is now more than three years that those accounts have been before that honourable body, and to this day no notice of any such objection has been communicated to me. But reports have for some time past been circulated here, and propagated in the newspapers, that I am greatly indebted to the

---

PART OF THE FRANKLIN LEGACY: A TECHNOLOGY INSTITUTE IN HIS NAME

Benjamin Franklin made certain that even after his death he would still be contributing to society. One way he did this was to bequeath money for the education of apprentices. In early twentieth-century Boston, the Franklin Institute was established from the first part of the matured funds Franklin had willed to the city of his birth.

The Franklin Institute of Boston owes its existence to the vision of Benjamin Franklin. In 1789, in the codicil to his will, Benjamin Franklin bequeathed a gift of 1,000 pounds sterling to the "inhabitants of the Town of Boston" to be loaned at interest to young and needy apprentices. The interest was to augment the principal continually, and at the end of one hundred years, part of the fund was to be expended for "public works," and the balance was to be compounded for the second hundred years. When the first part of the fund matured just before the turn of the 20th century, the Board of Managers of the Franklin Fund decided that a technical college would constitute the most appropriate means of accomplishing Franklin's purposes.

The land on which the Institute stands, at the corner of Berkeley and Appleton Streets, was provided by the City of Boston in 1906. The college opened its doors on September 21, 1908. Initially, it offered only evening courses in science and technology and the necessary preparatory subjects.

After World War I the need for returning veterans for engineering education at this level justified the addition of day courses to the program of the college. These were to provide training in science and engineering.

Franklin serves more than 400 students each year and, since its founding in 1908, over 85,000 men and women have been enrolled in both day and evening courses.

The Institute continues to carry out Benjamin Franklin's legacy of providing strong technical training and education to the citizens of Boston, Massachusetts and New England.

Franklin Institute of Boston: A Short History, February 2001. Available at www.franklin-fib.edu/pages/aboutfib/short_hist.html.

United States for large sums that had been put into my hands and that I avoid a settlement. This, together with the little time one of my age may expect to live, makes it necessary for me to request earnestly, which I hereby do, that the Congress would be pleased, without further delay, to examine those accounts; and if they find therein any article or articles which they do not understand or approve, that they would cause me to be acquainted with the same, that I may have an opportunity of offering such explanations or reasons in support of them as may be in my power, and then that the accounts might be finally closed."

"I must own, I did hope," Franklin explained on 29 December to his old friend Charles Thomson, still secretary of Congress, "that, as it is customary in Europe to make some liberal provision for ministers when they return home from foreign service during which their absence is necessarily injurious to their private affairs, the Congress would at least have been kind enough to have shown their approbation of my conduct by a grant of some small tract of land in their western country, which might have been of some use and some honour to my posterity." He proudly rehearsed his services. What he most wanted was that Temple be somehow recompensed for his years as unofficial secretary to the legation in Paris. He had given up the study of law for the practice of diplomacy, but Congress had refused him a post. He had returned from Paris to a farm in New Jersey which he liked so little that he spent most of his time in Philadelphia with Franklin. Surely the young man merited a reward.

Congress neither rewarded Temple nor took notice of him. Nor did it even acknowledge Franklin's request for a further settlement of his accounts. Arthur Lee, a member of the treasury board, was not likely to be considerate towards the man he hated; nor was Richard Henry Lee, a member of Congress. John Adams had returned from England, and the Adamses were as good haters as the Lees. The animosity against Franklin in Massachusetts seemed to him "to emanate from the Brantry [Braintree] focus"—that is, from Adams. There had been delegates to the Constitutional Convention from both Massachusetts and Virginia who thought Franklin too fond of France. . . . [Supposedly] the clause which forbade any official of the United States to accept any present or emolument from any foreign king or state was aimed at Franklin on account of the portrait the king of

France had given him. And it must have been directly or indirectly through Arthur Lee that Franklin came again to be accused of having withheld money intended for Congress. There was a million livres that neither he nor Ferdinand Grand, banker for America in Paris, could account for. Franklin could only conclude that it had been paid to Beaumarchais [aka Pierre-Augustin Caron, the French dramatist and businessman] before [the American lawyer and diplomat Silas] Deane went over. Time was to justify this conclusion, but for the present Franklin was suspected by his enemies, particularly by those who opposed the Constitution in which he had had a hand.

THE GRIEVOUS FRANKLIN WORKS ON HIS AUTOBIOGRAPHY— HIS LAST DAYS

Franklin was grieved but reticent. "This is all to yourself only as a private friend," he told Charles Thomson; "for I have not, nor ever shall, make any public complaint; and even if I could have foreseen such unkind treatment from Congress as their refusing me their thanks, would not in the least have abated my zeal for their cause and ardour in support of it. For I know something of the nature of such changeable assemblies, and how little successors are informed of services that have been rendered to the corps before their admission, or feel themselves obliged for such services; and what effect in obliterating a sense of them, during the absence of the servant in a distant country, the artful and reiterated malevolent insinuations of one or two envious and malicious persons may have on the mind of members, even of the most equitable, candid, and honourable dispositions. Therefore I would pass these reflections into oblivion."

He turned to his *Autobiography,* so long postponed, about which his European friends asked in almost every letter. He explained to [his former neighbor in France and the mayor of Passy, Louis-Guillaume M.] Le Veillard that the three scientific articles had been written at sea instead of the promised memoirs because they could be done "out of my own head; the other could not so well be written there for want of the documents that could only be had here." But by 26 November 1786 Franklin had "made some progress in it," he wrote to Edward Bancroft [his American friend who later supported the British], "and hope to finish it this winter." Apparently he had done no more than go over the manuscript already written. Other matters interfered, and then the Constitutional Convention, and his third term. "I have come to the resolution," he assured Le Veillard on 22 April 1788, "to proceed in that work tomorrow and continue it daily till finished, which, if my health permits, may be in the course of the ensuing summer." Finally he did begin the delayed third part, and noted in the margin: "I am now about to write at home, August 1788." By 22 October he must have written about a fourth more of the whole book, for he that day told [the French humanitarian Duc Louis-Alexandre] La Rochefoucauld: "It is now brought down to my fiftieth year. What is to follow will be of more important transactions." He thought that the earlier years would be "of more general use to young readers; as exemplifying strongly the effects of prudent and imprudent conduct in the commencement of a life of business."

This burden of moralism was heavier on the third part than on the first, written gaily at Twyford [England, 1771], or on the second, written in a philosophic interlude at Passy [1784]. Though on the 24th Franklin believed his work should now be done in two months, he was still at his fiftieth year on 9 December. His stone had become worse. "Of late I am so interrupted by extreme pain, which obliges me to have recourse to opium," he wrote to Benjamin Vaughan [his long-time friend] on the following 3 June, "that between the effects of both I have but little time in which I can write anything." Benjamin Bache was copying what had been written and a copy would go to Vaughan by the next ship. It was not ready till 2 November, when Franklin, no longer "able to bear sitting to write," had begun to dictate to his grandson and wished he had tried the method sooner. Both the copy to Vaughan and another to Le Veillard were sent on the "express condition . . . that you do not suffer any copy to be taken of them, or of any part of them, on any account whatever." Vaughan was to consult with Richard Price [the English philosopher and American supporter], and Le Veillard with La Rochefoucauld. Franklin requested of his French friends that they should read the memoirs carefully, "examine them critically, and send me your friendly, candid opinion of the parts you would advise me to correct or expunge; this in case you should be of opinion that they are generally proper to be published; and if you judge otherwise, that you would send me that opinion as soon as possible, and prevent my taking farther trouble in endeavouring to finish them." And to his English friends: "I shall rely upon your opinions, for I am now grown so old and feeble in mind, as well as body, that I cannot place any confidence in my own judgment."

The two copies went off to England and France to set in train the complex textual history of this simple book: of which three parts appeared first in French, and of which the earliest English editions were retranslations from the French, and of which Temple Franklin published as authorized in 1818 the copy sent to Le Veillard instead of Franklin's original, which was not published entire, as Franklin wrote it, till 1868. At some time after the copies were made, Franklin, in the six painful months left to him, wrote the fragmentary fourth part and then broke off. It seems likely that he himself had made the revisions which in the copy tamed the original. He could no longer trust his taste and could now and then prefer round academic phrases to his own natural sharp, homely ones. He had lived too long, and put off writing too late, to be able to do justice to himself in a book. His greatest years would have to stay unwritten. He might truly have reflected that this was not altogether the loss it seemed. Plenty of other men could find materials for the story of his latest years. Only he had known about his obscure youth, which could never again be obscure.

Reflections on Franklin's Autobiography

Leonard W. Labaree, Ralph L. Ketcham, Helen C. Boatfield, and Helene H. Fineman

In the accompanying viewpoint, four scholars who edited *The Autobiography of Benjamin Franklin* contend that events and attitudes in the latter half of the twentieth century mean that Franklin's story of himself is still relevant. The editors also offer insights into events and people who influenced Franklin as he wrote his autobiography. At the time this viewpoint was written, the late Leonard W. Labaree was a professor of history at Yale and the editor-in-chief of *The Papers of Benjamin Franklin*, which he worked on from its instigation in 1954 until he retired in 1969. The late Helen C. Boatfield, a gifted researcher and reference librarian for the Sterling Library at Yale, also contributed fifteen years as an editor for the first fourteen volumes of the *Papers*, while the late Latin and Greek scholar Helene H. Fineman spent ten years on the editorial staff from 1956 to 1966. Ralph L. Ketcham, professor emeritus of history, public affairs, and political science at Syracuse University, was an editor for the papers from 1962 to 1963, shortly before he published several more books on Franklin.

Assessments of the autobiography reflecting the spirit of the mid–twentieth century disagree. Some people would insist that the book is now irrelevant and that it must be regarded at best as a curiosity out of a dim and very different past. Certainly in many ways the world is moving in directions uncongenial to the assumptions and temper of Franklin's times. A rapidly rising population, together with an ever more intricate technology, the consequent increase in areas where collective, even mass, action seems necessary, and a decline in the willingness and ability of individuals to manage their own destinies sometimes make the emphasis on self-reliance in the autobiography appear woefully old-fashioned. In the United States and other highly developed countries, at least, Franklin's devotion to business and his advice to cultivate the simple virtues no longer seem to capture the imagination as they once did. Those who deem themselves "free spirits," in the mood of [the English writer] D.H. Lawrence, explicitly repudiate what they conceive to be the narrow morality of the autobiography; for them it kills the human spirit. Finally, Franklin's optimistic belief that complex problems will yield to reason, cooperation, and good will seems too simple for the dilemmas, paradoxes, and horrors of today. To some people, Franklin's dismissal by a popular comedian seems justified: who cares about "the weirdo with the square glasses?"

THE AUTOBIOGRAPHY IS STILL RELEVANT, PROMOTING SELF-IMPROVEMENT

Others hold that in important ways the autobiography is as relevant to our times as ever. Industry and self-reliance, they contend, are still necessary if society is to be strong and healthy. Franklin's example of self-education is still significant, whether one's formal schooling has been as brief as his was or has extended to the highest levels of a modern university curriculum. He reminds us of the satisfactions to be derived from good reading and from continually broadening and deepening our knowledge and our mental skills. To keep intelligently aware of developments in current thought and of its backgrounds in the past, as Franklin did, has never been more important than it is in the present era of rapid development and change. [Franklin's] Poor Richard pointed out in the almanac for 1755 that "The Doors of Wisdom are never shut," and, as the autobiography makes clear, Franklin placed high on his scale of values the pleasure and the benefits to be derived both from private study and from the exchange of ideas with other men, even during those years when he was most busily engaged in making a living.

Unlike most Americans of his time, Franklin was an urbanite; he lived his entire life in or very close to cities: Boston, Philadelphia, London, Paris. His urban outlook is implicit throughout his autobiography and explicit in many of the activities he describes, activities which would have been impossible for an eighteenth-century American farmer or dweller in a rural village. Our twentieth-century America is becoming increasingly urbanized, the suburbs are no longer small country towns but growing municipalities with problems of police and fire protection, street paving and lighting, local government, schools, and the like, in many ways akin to those Franklin recognized and helped to solve in Philadelphia. As a citizen of a rapidly growing urban community he had much in common with a majority of present-day Americans.

This is also an age of voluntary cooperation and organization, and for much of our effort in this direction Franklin has helped to point the way. Our community chests, the Red Cross, the associations to alleviate various diseases, and the countless other undertakings for civic welfare are modern expressions of the same sense of community responsibility

Franklin's Autobiography *contains insights on education, community responsibility, and the exchange of ideas among citizens that are still relevant today.*

that influenced Franklin and his associates. Far from killing the human spirit, his accounts of founding the Library, the Academy, and the Hospital, for example, and of raising funds for them, reflect an attitude toward society in full harmony with the most altruistic undertakings of our own times. Even though the scale of these actions and the number of people sharing in them have increased and many of them reach out to a far wider area than a single city, Franklin's concern for the welfare of the community in which he lived was as strong and as generous as that which influences so many people today. And he sought to advance that welfare, just as in large measure we continue to do, by voluntary cooperation and organization.

These are but a few ways in which his autobiography is still relevant in the mid–twentieth century. It is true that the book is seldom now included in school reading assignments, as it once was, primarily to help mold "stronger fibred boys and girls." Yet its values, both for young people and for adults, have not disappeared but have simply changed. It is increasingly used in schools and colleges as literature and as a document in American social and cultural history, and older people continue to read it for pure enjoyment. Modern commentaries contain little about its didactic potential [meant for instructional purposes], but are full of praise for its language, its picture of life in colonial America, its place in the development of American thought, and its insight into the mind and character of one of the greatest of the Founding Fathers. . . .

BEGINNING THE MEMOIRS

Franklin worked on his autobiography at four different times during a period of nearly nineteen years. He began it in August 1771 while on a visit of about two weeks at Twyford, the country home of his friend Jonathan Shipley, Bishop of St. Asaph. The house, which is still standing, is near the southern coast of England, about six miles south of Winchester and nine miles from Southampton. The bishop was politically a liberal. Probably influenced in part by Franklin, he became an outspoken defender of the American colonies in the House of Lords, and after the war began he vigorously opposed the British ministry for continuing it. The friendship between the two men continued until the bishop's death in 1788. His wife, Anna Maria Mordaunt, was a niece of the third Earl of Peterborough; their family consisted of one son (away from home at the time of Franklin's visit) and five girls ranging in age from twenty-three to eleven. There is a tradition that while at Twyford Franklin wrote for several hours each day and then during the evening the family gathered around and listened with delight while he read aloud what he had put down about his boyhood and early career in America, a setting so different from the comfortable English country house the Shipleys called their home.

If Franklin completed all of Part I of the autobiography during these two weeks he must have written very rapidly; possibly he added some of the last pages when he was back in London and before he became absorbed again in other activities. In any case, about thirteen years passed before he resumed this account of his life, and much had happened to Franklin personally and to the English-speaking world during that interval. He was now in France, the world-famous minister of the newly independent United States, waiting for orders that would permit him to return to spend his last years in his Philadelphia home. The tone and purpose of his writing in the rest of the autobiography reflect that change. The first part—begun in the form of a long letter to his son William (then royal governor of New Jersey), but actually addressed to all his "Posterity"—is an highly personal account of the first twenty-five years or so of his life: his humble beginnings, his progress down to the firm establishment of his printing business, his marriage, and the formation of his club of like-minded fellow tradesmen. In it he reveals a good deal—but by no means all—of what the distinguished scientist and political leader of sixty-five thought of the boy and young man he had been.

In the remaining three installments that he succeeded in writing before his final illness, he was consciously addressing a much wider public than his own descendants. He was no longer, even in form, writing to his son. William and he were now completely estranged, for the younger man had supported the British cause during the Revolution, while the father was giving every effort to help win American independence. These three parts of the work deal almost exclusively with Franklin's external, rather than his inner, life. The one important exception is in Part Two, where he included a description of his project for attaining "moral Perfection." He had long planned to give it a more extended treatment in a separate book to be called *The Art of Virtue*, which he had promised his friends to write but never did. An urgent reminder of this intention by Benjamin Vaughan perhaps explains why he devoted so much space to the subject when he resumed writing. With this exception, the last three parts reveal little of the inner man; the "private Franklin" virtually disappears as he becomes in the continuing narrative more and more the public figure, concerned with civic and political affairs and with his scientific pursuits.

AFTER MUCH TIME ELAPSES, FRANKLIN IS URGED TO RESUME HIS MEMOIRS

Public service so completely engaged Franklin's thought and energies between 1771 and 1784 that it was not until the end of the Revolutionary War that he found time to resume work on the autobiography. And even then it took the stimulus of two friends to set him writing again. Meanwhile he had lost possession of the part he had already set down. When he was preparing to set sail in October 1776 as one of the American commissioners to France, he packed many of his papers in a trunk which he placed for safekeeping at Trevose, the country home of his trusted friend Joseph Galloway a few miles outside Philadelphia. To Franklin's distress, Galloway soon went over to the British; and during the enemy occupation of the city, 1777–78, Trevose was raided, the trunk was broken into, the papers were scattered, and many were lost.

When the British evacuated Philadelphia, Mrs. Galloway remained in the city, where she died in 1782. Whether the sheets containing the completed section of the autobiography had been in the trunk at Trevose or were in her personal possession is not certainly known. In either case, a well-known Philadelphia Quaker merchant, Abet James, who was one of the executors of her estate, wrote Franklin some time in 1782 a letter . . . telling him that the manuscript and the original outline for the whole had come into his hands. He enclosed a copy of the outline and begged his friend to complete the memoirs if he had not already done so. He did not send the manuscript itself to France but evidently returned it to its writer after Franklin came back to Philadelphia in 1785.

On receiving James's letter, Franklin sent a copy of the

outline to his friend Benjamin Vaughan, who had published in London in 1779 the first extensive edition of his nonscientific writings, and asked for advice on whether to continue the autobiography. Vaughan was then in Paris; his reply . . . was an enthusiastic and urgent recommendation that Franklin take "the work most speedily into hand." Negotiation of the definitive treaty of peace with Great Britain and other public business kept him for a while from adopting these recommendations, but in 1784 he found time to write a second, much shorter, section, designated . . . as Part Two.

Soon after reaching Philadelphia in September 1785, Franklin was elected president of the Supreme Executive Council of Pennsylvania and served for three years in this post, which corresponded in a general way to that of governor in the other states. This and other responsibilities, such as membership in the Federal Constitutional Convention of 1787, together with poor health, explain why he was unable to go on vigorously with the autobiography until 1788, although he may have spent some time in 1786 going over the first part and making some changes and additions at various points. At last in August 1788 he settled down to work and wrote Part Three. This section, about the same length as the first, carries the narrative to Franklin's arrival in England in July 1757.

The fourth part is very short and describes only his negotiations with the Proprietors as agent of the Pennsylvania Assembly. Except for the very last pages, which briefly mention incidents in 1759 and 1760, the account stops in 1758. He probably composed this section in the winter of 1789–90, and the manuscript shows, as do his letters of that time, that his hand was losing some of its firmness and control, though the writing remains perfectly legible. By early 1790 he was dictating nearly all his correspondence to his grandson Benjamin Franklin Bache, and it is doubtful that he was strong enough to write even these last few pages any later than January or February. A few short additions and corrections elsewhere in the manuscript, written in a very shaky hand, suggest that he may also have made some final revisions during these last few months before his death on April 17, 1790.

Franklin's Contributions to the Field of Science

Paul K. Conkin

Emeritus history professor Paul K. Conkin of Vanderbilt University is the author and coauthor of nearly two dozen books. In this viewpoint, Conkin explores Benjamin Franklin's approach to natural science, noting that his primary value was utility. Alongside Franklin's practical contributions should be placed his intelligence and imagination. Furthermore, as Conkin explains, Franklin's work with electricity would prove to be valuable in helping future scientists understand the nature of matter itself.

Franklin never doubted either the beautiful and harmonious economy and perfection of nature or its infinite utility for man. He was always a natural philosopher, with an unquenchable curiosity about the workings of his universe, with an unsurpassed brilliance in formulating ingenious explanations for its heretofore unexplained "riddles," and with a complete dedication to bettering the lot of mankind through a more rational utilization of its beneficent but too often misunderstood gifts. Here he found the most rewarding outlet for his superior intelligence, although he was never able to give as much time to science as he wished. In the study of nature, Franklin never found the frustrations, the meaningless abstractions, the unacceptable conclusions that plagued his few endeavors in theology. Here there was the unquestioned truth. As long as he speculated about the physical world, Franklin knew that he could ultimately appeal his most imaginative hypothesis to the unbiased test of experience. Here the subjective ultimately had to give way before the objective. For Franklin, quite naturally in his day and perhaps yet in ours, joined most scientists and most

Excerpted from "Benjamin Franklin: Science and Morals," in *Puritans and Pragmatists: Eight Eminent American Thinkers*, by Paul K. Conkin (New York: Dodd, Mead, 1968). Reprinted by permission of the author.

people in holding to a simple realism. He assumed an existent and knowable world to which we must submit our opinions if we would know truth. Unlike many of his religious contemporaries, Franklin limited the real and knowable world to the physical universe. His Creator was knowable only through it.

FRANKLIN'S GREATEST CONTRIBUTION TO SCIENCE

Contrary to many unfair criticisms, Franklin was not an early Edison, or a mere tinker and inventor. Neither was he solely or even primarily concerned with applied science or technology. Because of his determined anti-intellectualism and anti-obscurantism in religion and philosophy, it is too easy to make an erroneous judgment about his scientific work. In actuality, Franklin's greatest contribution to science, in electricity and related fields, was his highly imaginative hypotheses to explain phenomena often discovered and described as much by other people as by himself. As a scientist, his great gifts included a lucid intelligence, a vivid imagination, and enough detachment from his theories to be willing to test them and freely reject them when they proved inadequate. As much as Franklin loved to perform experiments, he loved even more to speculate about the causes of observed phenomena.

But Franklin never separated science from other aspects of his life and particularly never tried to sever it from his moral commitments. Never too concerned over immortality, never pious enough to make love of God a compelling moral motive, Franklin still felt a tremendous, a Puritan-like responsibility. The call of duty was always a clanging cymbal. He felt that life, enjoyable and wonderful as he found it to be, was not self-justifying. He lived for something above and beyond himself. Perfectly fulfilling one theme so aptly applied to the Enlightenment . . . he lived for the betterment of mankind and struggled to win praise and honor from his contemporaries and from posterity. He wanted to leave his good mark upon his world. As much as he loved his experiments, as enjoyable as were his speculations about nature, he could never have wholeheartedly embraced science if he had not also believed, and in most cases known through tangible evidence, that science did have utility. When he could find a partner good enough to challenge him, Franklin played chess. For years he amused himself and friends with magical number squares. But these enjoyable mental exercises could only be justified as needed recreation, and both created a bit of guilt.

Franklin loved to know about things, to comprehend their workings, but he wanted to use his understanding for some improvement in the human condition. He pursued his early work in electricity out of complete fascination; despite hope and expectation, there were no early practical returns from his experiments. Rather pathetically, some of his friends tried to show that chickens killed electrically yielded a better meat, but Franklin was too skeptical to find solace in their empty hopes. But later he did find a specific use in the lightning rod and in it a balm for his demanding conscience and a new and brilliant star in posterity's crown. In terms of his ultimate commitments, here was justification for all his enjoyment and his international fame. From the perspective of today, it seems that Franklin put undue emphasis upon his lightning rod and possibly even helped obscure the

TECHNOLOGICAL SETBACKS DID NOT DISCOURAGE FRANKLIN

Samuel Florman, a civil engineer and builder as well as the author of several books and numerous articles regarding technology and society, explains that in researching an essay on "American Know-How" he learned how Franklin worked to put technology to work solving problems that advances in technology had caused.

House & Garden magazine, in celebration of the American Bicentennial, devoted its July 1976 issue to the topic "American Know-How." The editors invited me to contribute an article, and enticed by the opportunity to address a new audience, plus the offer of a handsome fee, I accepted. We agreed that the title of my piece would be "Technology and the Human Adventure," and I thereupon embarked on a strange adventure of my own.

I thought that it would be appropriate to begin my Bicentennial-inspired essay with a discussion of technology in the time of the Founding Fathers, so I went to the library and immersed myself in the works of Benjamin Franklin, surely the most famous technologist of America's early days. Remembering stories from my childhood about Ben Franklin the clever tinkerer, I expected to find a pleasant recounting of in-greater significance of his electrical theories for later generations. But this judgment of today is based upon something Franklin could not know—the eventual practical significance of electricity itself. Thus, the contemporary evaluation is often based on his own standard of utility.

The conclusion to all this is quite clear. Franklin was a *practical* scientist. But so what? He was also, to suggest various categories, an able scientist, a speculative scientist, and an experimental scientist. There is a dangerous sophistry [faulty reasoning disguised as accurate reasoning] and a perverted type of snobbery in the tendency to give the higher value to pure philosophy, pure science, or pure art. There may be single-minded scientific investigation unrelated, in terms of motivation, to any immediate utilitarian purpose apart from the satisfaction of curiosity, or the fulfillment of a personal desire for simplicity and order. Franklin knew this type of science. But he believed the usual order—from curious investigation to personal satisfaction to social use-

ventions and successful experiments, a cheering tale of technological triumphs. I found such a tale, to be sure, but along with it I found a record of calamities *caused by* the technological advances of his day.

In several letters and essays, Franklin expressed concern about fire, an ever-threatening scourge in Colonial times. Efficient sawmills made it possible to build frame houses, more versatile and economical than log cabins—but less fire-resistant. Advances in transport made it possible for people to crowd these frame houses together in cities. Cleverly conceived fireplaces, stoves, lamps, and warming pans made life more comfortable, but contributed to the likelihood of catastrophic fires in which many lives were lost.

To deal with this problem, Franklin recommended architectural modifications to make houses more fireproof. He proposed the licensing and supervision of chimney sweeps and the establishment of volunteer fire companies, well supplied and trained in the science of firefighting. As is well known, he invented the lightning rod. In other words, he proposed technological ways of coping with the unpleasant consequences of technology. He applied Yankee ingenuity to solve problems arising out of Yankee ingenuity.

Samuel C. Florman, "Technology and the Tragic View," *Blaming Technology: The Irrational Search for Scapegoats.* New York: St. Martin's Press, 1981.

fulness—was desirable, and was disappointed when the last step was missing. He saw, correctly, that it is logically absurd to conclude that any scientific investigation that is motivated by the hope for, or that actually leads to, practical results—to lightning rods or reactors—is somehow poor science or, at least, inferior to completely disinterested science that has no obvious practical application to human problems. Franklin sought fulfillment in science, but he sought moral as well as intellectual fulfillment.

FRANKLIN'S METHODOLOGY AND MORALITY ARE OFTEN MISUNDERSTOOD

Critics in a more cynical age may, at some peril, ridicule Franklin, or Jefferson, or their colonial predecessors, for seeking a moral dimension in all areas of life. But they must realize that the condemnation is a condemnation of the men, not of their science, their art, or their political ideals. Moral commitments and practical goals underlie much, if not most, creativity and discovery. The result of creative endeavor must be evaluated in terms of some standard of beauty. The product of scientific investigation must be judged by how well it meets clear rules of verification. Neither can be fairly judged by what motivated them.

Of course, there may be valid criticisms of any undue emphasis upon applied science at the expense of theoretical science. It is unlikely that there would have been any lightning rods unless there was some understanding of electricity itself. Throughout the nineteenth century, Americans generally relied upon Europeans for their theoretical science, but gradually assumed the leadership in several areas of technology. Both are important, but one—technology—is usually but not always dependent. In this sense, at least, Americans might rightly feel inferior. But Franklin fulfilled both functions. He took the lead in developing a theoretical understanding and then pointed to practical applications.

There is another possible area of confusion concerning Franklin's scientific interest. To mention theoretical science today is to implicate the highly technical and formalistic theorems of relativity or quantum theory. Even in Franklin's day there was the imposing, highly technical, and largely mathematical mechanics of the *Principia* [by the great English mathematician and physicist, Isaac Newton]. If by pure science, one means the very abstract and necessarily mathematical hypotheses of modern physics, then Franklin could not qualify. He had no training in mathematics and could express himself exactly and symbolically only with the simplest equations. But unless one confers literal truth upon the formal structures of modern science, mathematics and logic have to be regarded as very effective and exact tools for dealing with very subtle and complex areas of experience. This is true whether experience is related to an objective reality (as Franklin and the Enlightenment always did) or is accepted simply as experience without an assumption about an underlying reality. If this view is accepted, the tool can only be judged in terms of its adequacy. Franklin could not read the *Principia*; he floundered completely in trying to comprehend Cadwallader Colden's attempt to outdo Newton by describing the various powers in matter. But he had the tools he needed—a logical mind attuned to quantitative thinking, a broad knowledge of eighteenth-century science, and an almost perfect ability to communicate his ideas. Electricity was a new field of scientific investigation. The first theoretical formulations were relatively simple, yet adequate to the existing phenomena. To have wrapped his theories in needless mathematical symbols, to have invented a new technical vocabulary, would have been to succumb to the very obscurantism that Franklin so often deplored in other fields.

AVOIDING MATHEMATICAL PROOFS, FRANKLIN ADVANCES THE EMPIRICAL TECHNIQUE OF OBSERVATION AND EXPERIMENT

Had Franklin attempted to do constructive work in developed scientific fields, such as in mechanics or astronomy, he would have been forced to learn more mathematics. Similarly, he could never have coped with later developments in his own field. His scientific speculation remained closely tied to simple experiments. The verification was always one step removed from the theory and required only simple types of observation. As soon as more elaborate hypotheses were advanced, logical bridges would have to connect the theory with possible areas of factual observation, and at that point science becomes too complex for the untrained layman, for it requires complex mathematical equations, more knowledge and training on the part of the scientist, and usually more complicated mechanical aids for the senses. If Franklin had a serious weakness in his conception of science, it was in his ambivalence about the role of mathematics. He often regretted his own lack of mathematical training. Yet, with real pride he communicated one of his experiments with this note: "If my Hypothesis is not the Truth itself it is at least as naked: For I have not with some of our learned Moderns, disguis'd my Nonsense in Greek, cloth'd it in Algebra or adorn'd it with Fluxions.". . .

Most colonial science was in the empirical tradition of [the English philosopher and statesman Francis] Bacon and often consisted of no more than the collection and description of new natural objects or the performance of simple experiments. Only in Franklin or in a daring theorist like Colden did it reach the level of bold new explanatory hypotheses. Most eighteenth-century scientists, in England and America, were scientists by avocation and not by profession; they were scientists because of lively curiosity, not because of extensive education or training. They collected and speculated out of sheer enjoyment and cooperated because of their common interests and delightful fellowship. Science was fun and never more so than in the thrill of discovering some new object never before described or in proposing some logical explanation that could account for new phenomena and reconcile it with what was already known and with an ordered, rational universe the existence of which was beyond doubting. For gentlemen who had some leisure and who possessed either curiosity or a desire for social advancement, natural philosophy was an absorbing hobby and an excellent substitute for the divisive theological debates that had occupied earlier generations. Never again would science offer the dedicated layman, or even the dilettante [amateur], so much opportunity or pleasure. In many vast areas, man's knowledge of and control over nature was in its infancy in the eighteenth century. Only in one of these virgin areas could an untrained Franklin virtually revolutionize a whole new area of investigation and win international fame. And he did it in his spare time. Although science was his greatest love, he never made it a profession nor gave it his single-minded attention. Even here he was not irretrievably committed. He never served his greatest mistress with the devotion or the undivided attention of Isaac Newton or Albert Einstein. If he had, he would have been a much greater scientist; but possibly he would have been a lesser man.

Franklin never tried to elaborate any scientific methodology, but he did frequently express himself concerning certain requirements for establishing scientific truth. Nature was a rational entity which man experienced through his senses and comprehended by his mind. To Franklin, good science depended on careful and patient accuracy in observation and on humble, tentative, explanatory hypotheses. His great strength was his recognition that speculative hypotheses must stand the test of both logical and experimental verification. He was able to remain almost completely aloof from the unending personal jealousies and recriminations that plagued so many of his scientific colleagues. He believed that the process of experiment and reflection could lead to an ever expanding body of knowledge, to unending scientific progress. For in back of the recorded changes, the observed motions, were eternal laws, permanent and invariant. Here was the ultimate corrective of human error. A hypothesis was not a call for some scientific crusade against opposing hypotheses, but an invitation and a few preliminary directions for a voyage of discovery. A hypothesis justified itself when it launched a voyage, even when new directions had to be chosen because of the exigencies of the trip.

FRANKLIN SUCCESSFULLY MARKETS SCIENCE

Franklin's scientific interests were boundless, but his contributions were somewhat restricted. He joined Peter Collinson, the English Quaker merchant and benefactor of most colonial scientists, in raising a subscription to finance the individualistic John Bartram in his far-ranging trips to collect American flora. He corresponded with Cadwallader Colden, a physician and botanist as well as an aspiring physicist, and eventually became a friend of virtually every scientist in the colonies. It was in part through the influence of Bartram that Franklin took a leading role in forming the first, abortive American Philosophical Society in 1743. His own proposals for the society were slanted toward natural history, agriculture, medicine, invention, and applied chemistry, with hardly a mention of physical science. In the early 1740's *Poor Richard* became increasingly interested in plant descriptions for medicinal purposes.

From his early work with chimneys and stoves, Franklin developed a permanent interest in problems of heat and ventilation. At various times he investigated the fascinating

subject of evaporative cooling and suggested various ingenious uses for this phenomenon. Just prior to his absorption in electrical experiments he began his elaborate attempts to explain the shorter time consumed by a ship
traveling from America to England than from England to
America. He tried to explain this by the earth's motion, but
later found the correct answer in the Gulf Stream. Some of
his earliest speculations concerned geological upheavals in
the past, which Franklin justified as beneficial to man because they exposed many valuable minerals. He com-
mended the more specialized research in both geology and
astronomy carried out by John Winthrop and made some of
his own lay observations in astronomy. The weather continually fascinated Franklin from his earliest speculations
in *Poor Richard* until his death. His speculations concerning whirlwinds, the path of hurricanes, and the causes of
waterspouts led, after his identification of natural electricity in clouds, to complex but often erroneous speculations
concerning all areas of climatology.

Franklin began his electrical experiments in the last
months of 1746. He utilized some electrical tubes given to
the library company by Peter Collinson, along with descriptions of experiments already being performed in Europe.
Franklin's first letter back to Collinson revealed his early
and complete absorption in the new area of research: "For
my own part, I never was before engaged in any study that
so totally engrossed my attention and my time as this has
lately done; for what with making experiments when I can
be alone, and repeating them to my Friends and Acquaintances, who, from the novelty of the thing, come continually
in crowds to see them, I have, during some months past, had
little leisure for any thing else.". . . Not only did Collinson
provide the first equipment, but he subsequently communicated Franklin's finding and theories to English scientists
and to the Royal Society. It was also Collinson who collected
the communications and had them published in book form.

Franklin's reputation in the field of electricity rests on two
main achievements. He began his speculations in an area of
experimental ferment and theoretical confusion and contributed simple theoretical principles that successfully explained or predicted all but one of the existing electrical phenomena. Second, by proving the electrification of clouds, he
made electricity a respected branch of natural science. For-

merly, it had been considered an unusual, isolated side show of physical science, conducted by faddists largely for personal amusement. These two solid achievements were timely, and they were made by an authentic American. The popular interest in electricity insured quick recognition of Franklin, while his Americanism added an extra degree of interest and curiosity. Other scientists, particularly in England, contributed significantly to the understanding of electricity, but never received a fraction of the recognition given Franklin, whose contribution was greater, but it was not so much greater as his fame soon seemed to indicate.

FRANKLIN'S SINGLE-FLUID THEORY SPARKED THE FUTURE

As he performed more and more fascinating electrical experiments, Franklin formulated tentative explanations for each observed phenomenon. Since many of the experiments were performed together with several of his interested friends, the whole endeavor had a communal flavor, with Franklin simply assuming a position of leadership. He formulated his theories within the larger framework of an economical and harmonious universe. He also worked in the shadow of Newton and among such concepts as the atomic and porous nature of matter and the probable existence of an elastic, fluid substance called ether, capable of accounting for the transmission of light. Using a simple friction machine to produce electricity, and Leyden jars [a "condenser" or "capacitor" made by coating a glass jar inside and out with tinfoil and having a brass chain stuck inside the jar through a stopper], or variations of them, to hold the accumulated charge, he found only one satisfactory explanation for the mysterious effects. There must be an electrical fire or matter (later called fluid) evenly distributed throughout ponderable matter [what would be a significant amount worth considering]. Normally in a state of balance or equilibrium, the even distribution can be altered by friction (rubbing), and either an object or a part of an object (as the glass in a Leyden jar) can have an excess or a deficiency of electrical matter. But since there is a constant amount of electricity in the universe, every excess requires a proportionate deficiency. The most obvious (and most dangerous) electrical phenomenon, the spark that seemed to jump from one object to another, is accounted for by excess electricity jumping to fill a deficiency in another object. Franklin and his fellow experimenters used plus and minus to denominate either an excess or deficiency of electricity, and charge to designate any quantity of electrical energy.

The single-fluid theory satisfactorily explained almost all the experimental phenomena. It accounted for the attraction between plus and minus and for the great potential energy in an electrical discharge between two oppositely charged bodies. Franklin assumed that electrical matter was atomic, strongly attracted by ponderable matter, but elastic in itself, i.e., that unattached electrical atoms repelled each other. Thus was explained the mutual repulsion between two positively charged bodies. But his theory did not account for the unexpected repulsion between negatively charged bodies, a weakness in his theory that Franklin could never resolve, and which could only be rationalized later by *ad hoc* hypotheses [formed specifically for the situation at hand] about the elastic nature of matter, but an elasticity normally neutralized by a full portion of electricity and only visibly present when there was a deficiency of electricity. Although the flow of electrons is the reverse of what was indicated by Franklin's experiments and hence his plus and minus misleading, the single-fluid theory remains a very workable and simple explanation of electrical phenomena, particularly for the layman. Within a few years it, or a more elaborate but related two-fluid (one minus and one plus) theory, was accepted by all but a few scientists.

By submitting the first clear, workable hypothesis to account for electricity, Franklin placed himself in the tradition of all great scientists. Like Newton before him, and Darwin and Einstein later, he brought harmony, simplicity, and predictability to a confused and underdeveloped field of science. But unlike these greatest scientists, he suggested an explanatory hypothesis without working out rigorous quantitative concepts to aid in control and prediction. His was a theoretical skeleton, capable of endless elaboration by better mathematicians and more dedicated scientists than Franklin. He recognized the existence of measurable factors (charge and conductivity) in electricity and established simple ratios or proportions, but never defined an exact unit of measurement. Without the slightest awareness or comprehension, Franklin was helping open the door to a new, now all-important area of investigation. To an extent unappreciated by anyone in the eighteenth century, electricity became a means of investigating and understanding matter itself. The long journey of exploration into the microcosm was beginning, but Franklin never pushed the exploration very far. He was a Copernicus but never a Newton; he opened a door for an Alessandro Volta, a Michael Faraday, or a James Maxwell, but never uncovered much of the darkness within.

DISCUSSION QUESTIONS

CHAPTER 1

1. Explain how the general religious atmosphere of Boston at the time of Franklin's childhood affected him through his family and his familial obligations.

2. The eighteenth-century period known as the Age of Enlightenment revamped ideas dating back to the Greeks of the fifth and fourth centuries B.C. How does the Enlightenment's concept of self-knowledge vary from the Greeks' idea of self-awareness and why did life stories, especially autobiographical writing like Franklin's, become important? Why is Franklin's *Autobiography* exemplary of these eighteenth-century ideas?

3. Describe the various influences on Franklin's journalistic style and how those influences are reflected in Franklin's work. Include a discussion on Franklin's development and employment of literary devices, specifically his use of varied personae.

4. How is Franklin exemplary of the cultural ideals and developments of his lifetime? Consider his roles as a writer, a scientist, and a leader.

CHAPTER 2

1. Describe Franklin's contributions to the 1787 Constitutional Convention, including the role he played, his views on government, and others' opinions of him.

2. Explain how Franklin used marketing techniques in the structuring of his autobiography. Who is his audience supposed to be?

3. Discuss the evidence that supports the theory that Franklin was a British spy. Why is this theory about Franklin frequently overlooked?

4. What was the practice of medicine like in the eighteenth century and how did this affect Franklin? Also describe Franklin's views of medicine, health, and treatment. How

do you think contemporary medical practitioners might view Franklin's practices?

CHAPTER 3

1. It seemed only natural for Franklin to move into politics. Describe some of his actions, undertakings, or plans that helped him prepare for a political career.

2. What were Franklin's feelings and thoughts about government and unions and why did he feel that way? What might Franklin think about government today? Support your speculation with examples.

3. Franklin was a fan of chess. Why did he partake in a "political chess game"? What did he hope to achieve and did he succeed?

4. Describe the problems Franklin faced in arranging for prisoner exchange. What were some of his solutions?

CHAPTER 4

1. What are some of the secrets of Franklin's success and how can others learn from them? How might you apply them to your own life?

2. Do you think there are connections between Franklin's successes and his enemies' opinions of him? Include a discussion of your answer.

3. Consider some of Franklin's reasons for composing his autobiography. What purposes does it fulfill and how does it reflect Franklin's intentions? Is the autobiography still relevant today? How?

4. Discuss Franklin's attitude regarding science. What contributions did he make to the field of science?

APPENDIX OF DOCUMENTS

DOCUMENT 1: REGARDING WOMEN: LETTERS FROM FRANKLIN AS SILENCE DOGOOD AND EPHRAIM CENSORIOUS

In 1722, at the age of sixteen, Benjamin Franklin began his literary career. At the time, he was working as an apprentice to his brother James, publisher of a Boston newspaper, the New England Courant. *Unbeknownst to James, Benjamin began submitting letters "To the Author of the* New England Courant," *under the pseudonym Silence Dogood. In this excerpt from letters dated Monday, May 21 to Monday, May 28, 1722, Mrs. Dogwood responds to Ephraim Censorious's letter to the* New England Courant *regarding women. Censorious was another pseudonym used by Franklin, but as Mrs. Dogood he gave his views on the education of women.*

SIR,

I shall here present your readers with a letter from one, who informs me that I have begun at the wrong end of my business, and that I ought to begin at home, and censure the vices and follies of my own sex, before I venture to meddle with yours: Nevertheless, I am resolved to dedicate this speculation to the fair tribe, and endeavour to show, that Mr *Ephraim* charges women with being particularly guilty of pride, idleness, etc. wrongfully, inasmuch as the men have not only as great a share in those vices as the women, but are likewise in a great measure the cause of that which the women are guilty of. I think it will be best to produce my antagonist, before I encounter him.

To Mrs DOGOOD

MADAM,

My design in troubling you with this letter is, to desire you would begin with your own sex first: Let the first volley of your resentments be directed against *female* vice; let female idleness, ignorance and folly, (which are vices more peculiar to your sex than to ours,) be the subject of your satyrs, but more especially female pride, which I think is intollerable. Here is a large field that wants cultivation, and which I believe you are able (if willing) to improve with advantage; and when you have once reformed the women, you will find it a much easier task to reform the men, because women are the prime causes of a great many male enormities. This is all at present from

Your Friendly Wellwisher,
EPHRAIM CENSORIOUS

After thanks to my correspondent for his kindness in cutting out work for me, I must assure him, that I find it a very difficult matter to reprove women separate from the men; for what vice is there in which the men have not as great a share as the women? . . .

And now for the ignorance and folly which he reproaches us with, let us see (if we are fools and ignoramuses) whose is the fault, the men's or ours. An ingenious writer, having this subject in hand, has the following words, wherein he lays the fault wholly on the men, for not allowing women the advantages of education.

'I have (says he) often thought of it as one of the most barbarous customs in the world, considering us as a civilized and Christian country, that we deny the advantages of learning to women. We reproach the sex every day with folly and impertinence, while I am confident, had they the advantages of education equal to us, they would be guilty of less than ourselves. One would wonder indeed how it should happen that women are conversible at all, since they are only beholding to natural parts for all their knowledge. Their youth is spent to teach them to stitch and sew, or make baubles. They are taught to read indeed, and perhaps to write their names, or so; and that is the height of a woman's education. And I would but ask any who slight the sex for their understanding, What is a man (a gentleman, I mean) good for that is taught no more? If knowledge and understanding had been useless additions to the sex, God Almighty would never have given them capacities, for he made nothing needless. What has the woman done to forfeit the priviledge of being taught? Does she plague us with her pride and impertinence? Why did we not let her learn, that she might have had more wit? Shall we upbraid women with folly, when 'tis only the error of this inhumane custom that hindred them being made wiser.'

So much for female ignorance and folly; and now let us a little consider the pride which my correspondent thinks is *intolerable.* By this expression of his, one would think he is some dejected swain, tyrannized over by some cruel haughty nymph, who (perhaps he thinks) has no more reason to be proud than himself. *Alas-a-day!* What shall we say in this case! Why truly, if women are proud, it is certainly owing to the men still; for if they will be such *simpletons* as to humble themselves at their feet, and fill their credulous ears with extravagant praises of their wit, beauty, and accomplishments (perhaps where there are none too,) and when women are by this means perswaded that they are something more than human, what wonder is it, if they carry themselves haughtily, and live extravagantly. Notwithstanding, I believe there are more instances of extravagant pride to be found among men than among women, and this fault is certainly more hainous in the former than in the latter.

Upon the whole, I conclude, that it will be impossible to lash any vice, of which the men, are not equally guilty with the women, and consequently deserve an equal (if not a greater) share in the censure. However, I exhort both to amend, where both are culpable, otherwise they may expect to be severely handled by

Sir, Your Humble Servant,

SILENCE DOGOOD

"Dogood Papers, No. V" in "A Likely Lad for an Apprentice," *Benjamin Franklin: His Life as He Wrote It.* Ed. Esmond Wright. Cambridge: Harvard University Press, 1990, pp. 37–40.

DOCUMENT 2: "THE *FIXT NATURE* OF PLEASURE AND PAIN"

Odd circumstances found the young Franklin stranded in London on Christmas Eve, 1724. The enterprising youth quickly secured employment at Samuel Palmer's well-known printing house, and his first assignment was to typeset William Wollaston's third edition of The Religion of Nature Delineated. *Finding fault with Wollaston's reasoning, the nineteen-year-old Franklin wrote his metaphysical response,* A Dissertation on Liberty and Necessity, Pleasure and Pain, *from which this excerpt is taken. Palmer was impressed with Franklin's argument, but he found Franklin's conclusions "abominable." Franklin himself later disavowed this essay and destroyed most of the copies.*

V. *Therefore the Sensation of* Pleasure *is equal, or in exact proportion to the Sensation of* Pain.

As the *Desire* of being freed from Uneasiness is equal to the *Uneasiness,* and the *Pleasure* of satisfying that Desire equal to the *Desire,* the *Pleasure* thereby produc'd must necessarily be equal to the *Uneasiness* or *Pain* which produces it: Of three Lines, *A, B,* and *C,* if *A* is equal to *B,* and *B* to *C, C* must be equal to *A.* And as our *Uneasinesses* are always remov'd by some Means or other, it follows that *Pleasure* and *Pain* are in their Nature inseparable: So many Degrees as one Scale of the Ballance descends, so many exactly the other ascends; and one cannot rise or fall without the Fall or Rise of the other: 'Tis impossible to taste of *Pleasure,* without feeling its preceding proportionate *Pain;* or to be sensible of *Pain,* without having its necessary Consequent *Pleasure:* The *highest Pleasure* is only Consciousness of Freedom from the *deepest Pain,* and Pain is not Pain to us unless we ourselves are sensible of it. They go Hand in Hand; they cannot be divided.

You have a View of the whole Argument in a few familiar Examples: The *Pain* of Abstinence from Food, as it is greater or less, produces a greater or less *Desire* of Eating, the Accomplishment of this *Desire* produces a greater or less *Pleasure* proportionate to it. The *Pain* of Confinement causes the *Desire* of Liberty, which accomplish'd, yields a *Pleasure* equal to that *Pain* of Confinement. The *Pain* of Labour and Fatigue causes the *Pleasure* of Rest, equal to that *Pain.* The *Pain* of Absence from Friends, produces the *Pleasure* of Meeting in exact proportion. *&c.*

This is the *fixt Nature* of Pleasure and Pain, and will always be found to be so by those who examine it.

Part V "Therefore the Sensation of *Pleasure* Is Equal, or in Exact Proportion to the Sensation of *Pain*," Sect. II. "Of *Pleasure* and *Pain*," in "A Dissertation on Liberty and Necessity, Pleasure and Pain," *Benjamin Franklin: Writings.* Ed. J.A. Leo Lemay. New York: The Library of America-Literary Classics of the United States, 1987, p. 65.

DOCUMENT 3: ENTRIES FROM FRANKLIN'S JOURNAL FROM HIS 1726 VOYAGE FROM LONDON TO PHILADELPHIA

Eighteen months after he found himself stranded in London in July 1726, Ben Franklin finally set sail for home on the ship Berkshire. *During the voyage, Franklin took care to keep busy and interact with others. When a shipmate accused of cheating at cards was punished by being placed in solitary confinement, Franklin was prompted to write in his journal about the human need for companionship to help maintain sanity.*

Monday, August 22d.—This morning I saw several flying-fish, but they were small. A favorable wind all day.

Tuesday, August 23d; Wednesday, 24th.—Fair winds, nothing remarkable.

Thursday, August 25th.—Our excommunicated shipmate thinking proper to comply with the sentence the court passed upon him, and expressing himself willing to pay the fine, we have this morning received him into unity again. Man is a sociable being, and it is, for aught I know, one of the worst of punishments to be excluded from society. I have read abundance of fine things on the subject of solitude, and I know 't is a common boast in the mouths of those that affect to be thought wise, *that they are never less alone than when alone.* I acknowledge solitude an agreeable refreshment to a busy mind; but, were these thinking people obliged to be always alone, I am apt to think they would quickly find their very being insupportable to them. I have heard of a gentleman, who underwent seven years' close confinement, in the Bastille, at Paris. He was a man of sense, he was a thinking man; but, being deprived of all conversation, to what purpose should he think? for he was denied even the instruments of expressing his thoughts in writing. There is no burden so grievous to man as time that he knows not how to dispose of. He was forced at last to have recourse to this invention; he daily scattered pieces of paper about the floor of his little room, and then employed himself in picking them up and sticking them in rows and figures on the arm of his elbow-chair; and he used to tell his friends, after his release, that he verily believed, if he had not taken this method he should have lost his senses. One of the philosophers, I think it was Plato, used to say, that he had rather be the veriest stupid block in nature, than the possessor of all knowledge without some intelligent being to communicate it to.

What I have said may in a measure account for some particulars in my present way of living here on board. Our company is, in general, very unsuitably mixed, to keep up the pleasure and spirit of conversation; and, if there are one or two pair of us that can sometimes entertain one another for half an hour agreeably, yet perhaps we are seldom in the humor for it together. I rise in the morning and read for an hour or two, perhaps, and then reading grows tiresome. Want of exercise occasions want of appetite, so that eating and drinking afford but little pleasure. I tire myself with playing at drafts, then I go to cards; nay, there is no play so trifling or childish, but we fly to it for entertainment. A contrary wind, I know not how, puts us all out of good humor; we grow sullen, silent, and reserved, and fret at each other upon every little occasion. 'T is a common opinion among the ladies, that, if a man is ill-natured, he infallibly discovers it when he is in liquor. But I, who have known many instances to the contrary, will teach them a more effectual method to discover the natural temper and disposition of their humble servants. Let the ladies make one long sea-voyage with them, and, if they have the least spark of ill-nature in them, and conceal it to the end of the voyage, I will forfeit all my pretensions to their favor. The wind continues fair.

"Journal of Occurrences in My Voyage to Philadelphia on Board the Berkshire, Henry Clark, Master, from London," in "Journal of a Voyage from London to Philadelphia," *The Works of Benjamin Franklin.* Vol. 1. Ed. Jared Sparks. Boston: Hilliard Gray, 1840, pp. 557–58.

DOCUMENT 4: BENEFITS OF WRITING AND PAPER CURRENCY

In this excerpt from his autobiography, Franklin explains how in 1729 Philadelphians were in need of more paper money, and he answered the call. By anonymously publishing The Nature and Necessity of a Paper Currency, *he not only promoted the idea of paper money but also secured the job of printing the bills.*

About this time there was a cry among the people for more paper money, only fifteen thousand pounds being extant in the province, and that soon to be sunk. The wealthy inhabitants oppos'd any addition, being against all paper currency, from an apprehension that it would depreciate, as it had done in New England, to the prejudice of all creditors. We had discuss'd this point in our Junto, where I was on the side of an addition, being persuaded that the first small sum struck in 1723 had done much good by increasing the trade, employment, and number of inhabitants in the province, since I now saw all the old houses inhabited, and many new ones building: whereas I remembered well, that when I first walk'd about the streets of Philadelphia, eating my roll, I saw most of the houses in Walnut-street, between Second and Front streets, with bills on their doors, "To be let;" and many likewise in Chestnut-street and other streets, which made me then think the inhabitants of the city were deserting it one after another.

Our debates possess'd me so fully of the subject, that I wrote and printed an anonymous pamphlet on it, entitled "*The Nature and Necessity of a Paper Currency.*" It was well receiv'd by the common people in general; but the rich men dislik'd it, for it increas'd and strengthen'd the clamor for more money, and they happening to have no writers among them that were able to answer it, their opposition slacken'd, and the point was carried by a majority in the House. My friends there, who conceiv'd I had been of some service, thought fit to reward me by employing me in printing the money; a very profitable jobb and a great help to me. This was another advantage gain'd by my being able to write.

"Printing Experiences," *English and American Memoirs.* Rev. ed. El Cajon, CA: Immaculate Heart Seminary, 1901, pp. 217–18.

DOCUMENT 5: FRANKLIN'S BATTLE TO ACHIEVE THE VIRTUE OF ORDER

Once back in Philadelphia, Franklin delineated the thirteen moral virtues which he planned to follow so as to reach moral perfection. Franklin accompanied each of the thirteen virtues with brief explanations such as this one for Order: "Let all your things have their places; let each part of your business have its time." Franklin later noted that he personally found Order especially difficult to achieve.

My scheme of ORDER gave me the most trouble; and I found that, tho' it might be practicable where a man's business was such as to leave him the disposition of his time, that of a journeyman printer, for instance, it was not possible to be exactly observed by a master, who must mix with the world, and often receive people of business at their own hours. *Order,* too, with regard to places for things, papers, etc., I found extreamly difficult to acquire. I had not been early accustomed to it, and, having an exceeding good memory, I was not so sensible of the inconvenience attending want of method. This article, therefore, cost me so much painful attention, and my faults in it vexed me so much, and I made so little progress in amendment, and had such frequent relapses, that I was almost ready to give up the attempt, and content myself with a faulty character in that respect, like the man who, in buying an ax of a smith, my neighbour, desired to have the whole of its surface as bright as the edge. The smith consented to grind it bright for him if he would turn the wheel; he turn'd, while the smith press'd the broad face of the ax hard and heavily on the stone, which made the turning of it very fatiguing. The man came every now and then from the wheel to see how the work went on, and at length would take his ax as it was, without farther grinding. "No," said the smith, "turn on, turn on; we shall have it bright by-and-by; as yet, it is only speckled." "Yes," says the man, "*but think I like a speckled ax best.*" And I believe this may have been the case with many, who, having, for want of some such means as I employ'd, found the difficulty of obtaining good and breaking bad habits in other points of vice and virtue, have given up the struggle, and concluded that *"a speckled ax was best";* for something, that pretended to be reason, was every now and then suggesting to me that such extream nicety as I exacted of myself might be a kind of foppery in morals, which, if it were known, would make me ridiculous; that a perfect character might be attended with the inconvenience of being envied and hated; and that a benevolent man should allow a few faults in himself, to keep his friends in countenance.

In truth, I found myself incorrigible with respect to Order; and now I am grown old, and my memory bad, I feel very sensibly the want of it. But, on the whole, tho' I never arrived at the perfection I had been so ambitious of obtaining, but fell far short of it, yet I was, by the endeavour, a better and a happier man than I otherwise should have been if I had not attempted it; as those who aim at perfect writing by imitating the engraved copies, tho' they never reach the wish'd-for excellence of those copies, their hand is mended by the endeavor, and is intolerable while it continues fair and legible.

The Autobiography of Benjamin Franklin. Ed. William MacDonald. London: J.M. Dent; New York: E.P. Dutton, 1905, pp. 105–107.

DOCUMENT 6: THE PRINTER TO THE READER

In 1735, Franklin published James Logan's translation of Cato's Moral Distichs—*the first time a classical work had been translated and printed in the colonies. Logan, a Pennsylvania statesman and leading man of letters, so impressed Franklin that he attached the following preface to Logan's work.*

THE Manuscript Copy of this Translation of *Cato's Moral Distichs,* happened into my Hands some Time since, and being my self extreamly pleased with it, I thought it might be no less acceptable to the Publick; and therefore determined to print it as soon as I should have convenient Leisure and Opportunity. It was done by a Gentleman amongst us (whose Name or Character I am strictly forbid to mention, tho' it might give some Advantage to my Edition) for the Use of his Children; But in my Opinion, it is no unfit or unprofitable Entertainment for those of riper Years. For certainly, such excellent Precepts of Morality, contain'd in such short and easily-remember'd Sentences, may to Youth particularly be very serviceable in the Conduct of Life, since there can scarce happen any Affair of Importance to us, in which we may need Advice, but one or more of these Distichs suited to the Occasion, will seasonably occur to the Memory, if the Book has been read and studied with a proper Care and Attention.

When I obtained Leave to make this Publication, I procured also the following Account of the Author and his Work; for I thought something of the kind necessary to be prefix'd to it.

In most Places that I am acquainted with, so great is the present Corruption of Manners, that a Printer shall find much more Profit in such Things as flatter and encourage Vice, than in such as tend to promote its contrary. It would be thought a Piece of Hypocrisy and pharisaical Ostentation in me, if I should say, that I print these *Distichs* more with a view to the Good of others than my own private Advantage: And indeed I cannot say it; for I confess, I have so great Confidence in the common Virtue and Good Sense of the People of this and the neighbouring Provinces, that I expect to sell a very good Impression.

"The Printer to the Reader," *Benjamin Franklin's Autobiographical Writings.* Ed. Carl Van Doren. New York: Viking Press, p. 37.

DOCUMENT 7: PREFACE TO *POOR RICHARD'S ALMANACK*, 1738

Franklin published Poor Richard's Almanack *from 1733 to 1758. Writing as Richard Saunders, a poor man prodded by his wife to earn his living, Franklin sought to instruct "the common people" and, as noted in the second part of his autobiography, filled any available space between the calendar dates with proverbs, maxims, witticisms, and more, usually borrowed from other sources. Generally, it was Mr. Saunders who wrote the preface, but Franklin opted to write as Mrs. Saunders for the 1738 preface.*

Dear Readers,

My good man set out last week for *Potowmack,* to visit an old stargazer of his acquaintance, and see about a little place for us to settle and end our days on. He left a copy of his Almanack seal'd up, and bid me send it to the press. I suspected something, and therefore as soon as he was gone, I open'd it, to see if he had not been flinging some of his old skitts at me. Just as I thought, so it was. And truly, (for want of something else to say, I suppose,) he had put into his preface, that his wife Bridget—was this, and that, and t'other.— What a peasecods! cannot I have a little fault or two, but all the country must see it in print! They have already been told, at one time that I am proud, another time that I am loud, and that I have got a new petticoat, and abundance of such kind of stuff; and now, forsooth! all the world must know that *Poor Dick's* wife has lately taken a fancy to drink a little tea now and then. A mighty matter, truly, to make a song of! 'Tis true, I had a little tea of a present from the printer last year; and what, must a body throw it away? In short, I thought the preface was not worth a printing, and so I fairly scratch'd it all out, and I believe you'll like our Almanack never the worse for it.

Upon looking over the months, I see he has put in abundance of foul weather this year; and therefore I have scatter'd here and there, where I could find room, some *fair, pleasant, sunshiny,* &c. for the good-women to dry their clothes in. If it does not come to pass according to my desire, I have shown my goodwill, however;

and I hope they'll take it in good part.

I had a design to make some other corrections; and particularly to change some of the verses that I don't very well like; but I have just now unluckily broke my spectacles; which obliges me to give it you as it is, and conclude

Your Loving Friend,
BRIDGET SAUNDERS.

You will excuse me, dear readers, that I afford you no eclipses of the moon this year. The truth is, I do not find they do you any good.

When there is one you are apt in observing it to expose yourselves too much and too long to the night air, whereby great numbers of you catch cold. Which was the case last year, to my very great concern. However, if you will promise to take more care of yourselves, you shall have a fine one to stare at the year after next.

"Preface by Mistress Saunders," *Poor Richard's Almanack.* Ed. Benjamin E. Smith. New York: Century, 1898, pp. 23–26.

DOCUMENT 8: ADVICE TO A YOUNG TRADESMAN

In 1748, Franklin formed a printing partnership with David Hall, giving Hall control over the shop, allowing Franklin to retire and pursue other interests. Franklin's business advice to Hall exemplifies the same sort of proverbial wit as utilized in the almanacs.

As you have desired it of me, I write the following hints, which have been of service to me, and may, if observed, be so to you.

Remember, that *time* is money. He that can earn ten shillings a day by his labour, and goes abroad, or sits idle, one half of that day, though he spends but sixpence during his diversion or idleness, ought not to reckon *that* the only expense; he has really spent, or rather thrown away, five shillings besides.

Remember, that *credit* is money. If a man lets his money lie in my hands after it is due, he gives me the interest, or so much as I can make of it during that time. This amounts to a considerable sum where a man has good and large credit, and makes good use of it.

Remember, that money is of the prolific, generating nature. Money can beget money, and its offspring can beget more, and so on. Five shillings turned is six, turned again it is seven and three-pence, and so on till it becomes an hundred pounds. The more there is of it, the more it produces every turning, so that the profits rise quicker and quicker. He that kills a breeding sow, destroys all her offspring to the thousandth generation. He that murders a crown, destroys all that it might have produced, even scores of pounds. . . .

Remember this saying, *The good paymaster is lord of another man's purse.* He that is known to pay punctually and exactly to the time he promises, may at any time, and on any occasion, raise all the money his friends can spare. This is sometimes of great use. After industry and frugality, nothing contributes more to the raising of a young man in the world than punctuality and justice in all his dealings; therefore never keep borrowed money an hour beyond the time you promised, lest a disappointment shut up your friend's purse for ever.

The most trifling actions that affect a man's credit are to be regarded. The sound of your hammer at five in the morning, or nine at night, heard by a creditor, makes him easy six months longer; but, if he see you at a billiard table, or hears your voice at a tavern, when you should be at work, he sends for his money the next day; demands it, before he can receive it, in a lump.

It shows, besides, that you are mindful of what you owe; it makes you appear a careful as well as an honest man, and that still increases your credit.

Beware of thinking all your own that you possess, and of living accordingly. It is a mistake that many people who have credit fall into. To prevent this, keep an exact account for some time, both of your expenses and your income. If you take the pains at first to mention particulars, it will have this good effect: you will discover how wonderfully small, trifling expenses mount up to large sums, and will discern what might have been, and may for the future be saved, without occasioning any great inconvenience

In short, the way to wealth, if you desire it, is as plain as the way to market. It depends chiefly on two words, *industry* and *frugality;* that is, waste neither *time* nor *money,* but make the best use of both. Without industry and frugality nothing will do, and with them every thing. He that gets all he can honestly, and saves all he gets (necessary expenses excepted), will certainly become *rich,* if that Being who governs the world, to whom all should look for a blessing on their honest endeavors, doth not, in his wise providence, otherwise determine.

AN OLD TRADESMAN.

"Advice to a Young Tradesman," *Autobiography and Other Writings.* Ed. Russel B. Nye. Boston: Riverside Press-Houghton Mifflin, 1958, pp. 166–67.

DOCUMENT 9: FRANKLIN'S VENOMOUS RETALIATION AGAINST ENGLAND'S EXPORTATION OF CRIMINALS

Colonial efforts to end the practice of transporting convicts from England to the colonies proved unsuccessful. In the April 11, 1751, edition of the newspaper Franklin published, the Pennsylvania Gazette, he printed a horrifying list of murders and other crimes committed by convicts employed as servants in the colonies. Following up in the May 9 Gazette, Franklin, under the pseudonym "Americanus," sarcastically proposed that the colonies repay England in kind.

To the Printers of the Gazette.

By a Passage in one of your late Papers, I understand that the Government at home will not suffer our mistaken Assemblies to make any Law for preventing or discouraging the Importation of Convicts from Great Britain, for this kind Reason, *"That such Laws are against the Publick Utility, as they tend to prevent the* IMPROVEMENT *and* WELL PEOPLING of the Colonies."

Such a tender *parental* Concern in our *Mother Country* for the *Welfare* of her Children, calls aloud for the highest *Returns* of Gratitude and Duty. This every one must be sensible of: But 'tis said, that in our present Circumstances it is absolutely impossible for us to make *such* as are adequate to the Favour. I own it; but nevertheless let us do our Endeavour. 'Tis something to show a grateful Disposition.

In some of the uninhabited Parts of these Provinces, there are Numbers of these venomous Reptiles we call RATTLE-SNAKES; Felons-convict from the Beginning of the World: These, whenever we meet with them, we put to Death, by Virtue of an old Law, *Thou shalt bruise his Head.* But as this is a sanguinary Law, and may seem too cruel; and as however mischievous those Creatures are with us, they may possibly change their Natures, if they were to change the Climate; I would humbly propose, that this general Sentence of *Death* be changed for *Transportation.*

In the Spring of the Year, when they first creep out of their Holes, they are feeble, heavy, slow, and easily taken; and if a small Bounty were allow'd *per* Head, some Thousands might be collected annually, and *transported* to Britain. There I would propose to have them carefully distributed in St. James's Park, in the Spring-Gardens and other Places of Pleasure about London; in the Gardens of all the Nobility and Gentry throughout the Nation; but particularly in the Gardens of the *Prime Ministers,* the *Lords of Trade* and *Members of Parliament;* for to them we are *most particularly* obliged.

There is no human Scheme so perfect, but some inconveniencies may be objected to it: Yet when the Conveniencies far exceed, the Scheme is judg'd rational, and fit to be executed. Thus Inconveniencies have been objected to that *good* and *wise* Act of Parliament, by virtue of which all the Newgates and Dungeons in Britain are emptied into the Colonies. It has been said, that these Thieves and Villains introduc'd among us, spoil the Morals of Youth in the Neighbourhoods that entertain them, and perpetrate many horrid Crimes: But let not *private Interests* obstruct *publick Utility.* Our *Mother* knows what is best for us. What is a little *Housebreaking, Shoplifting,* or *Highway Robbing;* what is a *Son* now and then *corrupted* and *hang'd,* a Daughter *debauch'd* and *pox'd,* a Wife *stabb'd,* a Husband's *Throat cut,* or a Child's *Brains beat out* with an Axe, compar'd with this "IMPROVEMENT and WELL PEOPLING of the Colonies!". . .

I would only add, That this Exporting of Felons to the Colonies, may be consider'd as a *Trade,* as well as in the Light of a *Favour.* Now all Commerce implies *Returns:* Justice requires them: There can be no Trade without them. And *Rattle-Snakes* seem the most *suitable Returns* for the *Human Serpents* sent us by our *Mother*

Country. In this, however, as in every other Branch of Trade, she will have the Advantage of us. She will reap *equal* Benefits without equal Risque of the Inconveniencies and Dangers. For the *Rattle-Snake* gives Warning before he attempts his Mischief; which the Convict does not. I am Yours, &c.

AMERICANUS

"Felons and Rattlesnakes," *The Papers of Benjamin Franklin.* Vol. 4. Ed. Leonard W. Labaree et al. New Haven: Yale University Press, 1961, pp. 130–33.

DOCUMENT 10: FRANKLIN'S THOUGHTS ON THE SOUL

Although raised among Puritans and Quakers, Franklin's religious beliefs extended beyond the strict dogma of any one faith. Still, Franklin believed in God and immortality. After receiving the news of the death of John Franklin, his brother, he sent John's stepdaughter, Elizabeth Hubbard this condolence letter, which conveys some of Ben Franklin's beliefs.

Philadelphia, February 22, 1756

Dear Child,

I condole with you, we have lost a most dear and valuable relation, but it is the will of God and Nature that these mortal bodies be laid aside, when the soul is to enter into real life; 'tis rather an embrio state, a preparation for living: a man is not completely born until he be dead: Why then should we grieve that a new child is born among the immortals? A new member added to their happy society? We are spirits. That bodies should be lent us, while they can afford us pleasure, assist us in acquiring knowledge, or doing good to our fellow creatures, is a kind and benevolent act of God. When they become unfit for these purposes and afford us pain instead of pleasure—instead of an aid, become an incumbrance and answer none of the intentions for which they were given, it is equally kind and benevolent that a way is provided by which we may get rid of them. Death is that way. We ourselves prudently choose a partial death. In some cases a mangled painful limb, which cannot be restored, we willingly cut off. He who plucks out a tooth, parts with it freely since the pain goes with it, and he that quits the whole body, parts at once with all pains and possibilities of pains and diseases it was liable to, or capable of making him suffer.

Our friend and we are invited abroad on a party of pleasure—that is to last forever. His chair was first ready and he is gone before us. We could not all conveniently start together, and why should you and I be grieved at this, since we are soon to follow, and we know where to find him.

Adieu.

B. F[ranklin]

"To Elizabeth Hubbard," in "A Philosopher Looks at Death," *Mr. Franklin: A Selection from His Personal Letters.* Ed. Leonard W. Labaree and Whitfield J. Bell Jr. New Haven: Yale University Press; London: Geoffrey Cumberlege, Oxford University Press, 1956, pp. 10–12.

DOCUMENT 11: LETTER TO FRANKLIN'S WIFE ON THEIR DAUGHTER'S MARRIAGE

Franklin included both frugality and moderation in his list of thirteen virtues. In a letter to Deborah written from London on June 22, 1767, Franklin expresses his faith in her ability to determine the suitability of their daughter's engagement, but reminds his wife to watch her spending on the wedding. Deborah approved Sarah "Sally" Franklin's marriage to Richard Bache, which occurred later that year on October 29.

It SEEMS now as if I should stay here another winter, and therefore I must leave it to your judgment to act in the affair of our daughter's match, as shall seem best. If you think it a suitable one, I suppose the sooner it is completed the better. In that case I would advise, that you do not make an expensive feasting wedding, but conduct every thing with frugality and economy, which our circumstances now require to be observed in all our expenses. For, since my partnership with Mr. Hall is expired, a great source of our income is cut off; and, if I should lose the postoffice, which, among the many changes here, is far from being unlikely, we should be reduced to our rents and interest of money for a subsistence, which will by no means afford the chargeable housekeeping and entertainments we have been used to.

For my own part, I live here as frugally as possible not to be destitute of the comforts of life, making no dinners for anybody and contenting myself with a single dish when I dine at home; and yet such is the dearness of living here in every article, that my expenses amaze me. I see, too, by the sums you have received in my absence, that yours are very great; and I am very sensible that your situation naturally brings you a great many visitors, which occasions an expense not easily to be avoided, especially when one has been long in the practice and habit of it. But, when people's incomes are lessened, if they cannot proportionably lessen their outgoings, they must come to poverty. If we were young enough to begin business again, it might be another matter; but I doubt we are past it, and business not welt managed ruins one faster than no business. In short, with frugality and prudent care we may subsist decently on what we have, and leave it entire to our children; but without such care we shall not be able to keep it together; it will melt away like butter in the sunshine, and we may live long enough to feel the miserable consequences of our indiscretion.

I know very little of the gentleman or his character, nor can I at this distance. I hope his expectations are not great of any fortune to be had with our daughter before our death. I can only say, that, if he proves a good husband to her and a good son to me, he shall find me as good a father as I can be; but at present, I suppose you would agree with me, that we cannot do more than fit her out handsomely in clothes and furniture, not exceeding in the whole five hundred pounds of value. For the rest, they must depend, as you and I did, on their own industry and care, as what remains in our hands will be barely sufficient for our support, and not enough for them when it comes to be divided at our decease.

I suppose the blue room is too blue, the wood being of the same color with the paper, and so looks too dark. I would have you finish it as soon as you can, thus; paint the wainscot a dead white; paper the walls blue, and tack the gilt border round just above the surbase and under the cornice. If the paper is not equally colored when pasted on, let it be brushed over again with the same color, and let the *papier mâché* musical figures be tacked to the middle of the ceiling. When this is done, I think it will look very well.

I am glad to hear that Sally keeps up and increases the number of her friends. The best wishes of a fond father for her happiness always attend her.

"To his wife, London, 22 June, 1767," in "Domestic Matters," *The Life and Letters of Benjamin Franklin.* Eau Claire, WI: E.M. Hale, n.d., pp. 158–59.

DOCUMENT 12: NO TAXATION WITHOUT REPRESENTATION

Franklin was not opposed to taxation, but he was concerned that England's proposed Stamp Act of 1765 would gravely affect the poor; there was also the issue that these taxes were being levied by English Parliament rather than by American colonial assemblies. In the following letter of October 2, 1770, from Franklin, then residing in London as an elected official representing Pennsylvania, Georgia, and New Jersey, to Jacques Barbeu-Dubourg, Franklin's French editor and friend, Franklin expresses himself on behalf of the colonies.

I SEE with pleasure, that we think pretty much alike on the subject of English America. We of the colonies have never insisted, that we ought to be exempt from contributing to the common expenses necessary to support the prosperity of the empire. We only assert, that, having Parliaments of our own, and not having representatives in that of Great Britain, our Parliaments are the only judges of what we can and what we ought to contribute in this case; and that the English Parliament has no right to take our money without our consent. In fact, the British empire is not a single state; it comprehends many; and, though the Parliament of Great Britain has arrogated to itself the power of taxing the colonies, it has no more right to do so, than it has to tax Hanover. We have the same King, but not the same legislatures.

The dispute between the two countries has already lost England many millions sterling, which it has lost in its commerce, and America has in this respect been a proportionable gainer. This commerce consisted principally of superfluities; objects of luxury and fashion, which we can well do without; and the resolution we have formed of importing no more, till our grievances are redressed, has enabled many of our infant manufactures to take root; and it will not be easy to make our people abandon them in future, even should a connexion more cordial than ever succeed the present troubles. I have, indeed, no doubt that the Parliament of England will finally abandon its present pretensions, and leave us to the peaceable enjoyment of our rights privileges.

Chapter 2 "To M. Dubourg, dated London, Oct. 2, 1770," *The Life of Benjamin Franklin, Written by Himself.* Vol. 2. Ed. John Bigelow. Philadelphia: J.B. Lippincott; London: Trübner, 1875, pp. 62–63.

DOCUMENT 13: FRANKLIN'S CLEVER HOAX

While residing in London as a colonial agent, Franklin's "An Edict by the King of Prussia" was printed in the Gentlemen's Magazine, *October 1773. The edict, which is excerpted here, satirizes England's treatment of her colonies. So convincing was Franklin's spoof that his English friends were actually convinced of the validity of the edict. Eventually, the notable satirist Paul Whitehead realized the truth and observed, looking directly at Franklin, "I'll be hanged if this is not some of your American jokes upon us."*

Dantzic, Sept. 5, 1773

We have long wondered here at the supineness of the English nation, under the Prussian impositions upon its trade entering our port. We did not, till lately, know the claims, ancient and modern, that hang over that nation; and therefore could not suspect that it might submit to those impositions from a sense of duty or from principles of equity. The following edict, just made public, may, if serious, throw some light upon this matter.

FREDERICK, by the grace of God, King of Prussia, etc., etc., etc., to all present and to come (*à tous présens et à venir*), health. The peace now enjoyed throughout our dominions, having afforded us leisure to apply ourselves to the regulation of commerce, the improvement of our finances, and at the same time the easing our domestic subjects in their taxes: for these causes, and other good considerations us thereunto moving, we hereby make known, that, after having deliberated these affairs in our council, present our dear brothers, and other great officers of the state, members of the same, we, of our certain knowledge, full power, and authority royal, have made and issued this present Edict, viz.,

Whereas it is well known to all the world, that the first German settlements made in the island of Britain, were by colonies of people, subject to our renowned ducal ancestors, and drawn from their dominions, under the conduct of Hengist, Horsa, Hella, Uff, Cerdicus, Ida, and others; and that the said colonies have flourished under the protection of our August house for ages past; have never been emancipated therefrom; and yet have hitherto yielded little profit to the same: And whereas we ourself have in the last war fought for and defended the said colonies, against the power of

France, and thereby enabled them to make conquests from the said power in America, for which we have not yet received adequate compensation: And whereas it is just and expedient that a revenue should be raised from the said colonies in Britain, towards our indemnification; and that those who are descendants of our ancient subjects, and thence still owe us due obedience, should contribute to the replenishing of our royal coffers as they must have done, had their ancestors remained in the territories now to us appertaining: We do therefore hereby ordain and command, that, from and after the date of these presents, there shall be levied and paid to our officers of the *customs*, on all goods, wares, and merchandizes, and on all grain and other produce of the earth, exported from the said island of Britain, and on all goods of whatever kind imported into the same, a duty of four and a half per cent *ad valorem*, for the use of us and our successors. And that the said duty may more effectually be collected, we do hereby ordain, that all ships or vessels bound from Great Britain to any other part of the world, or from any other part of the world to Great Britain, shall in their respective voyages touch at our port of Köningsberg, there to be unladen, searched, and charged with the said duties.

"An Edict by the King of Prussia" in "A Clever Hoax," *A Benjamin Franklin Reader.* Ed. Nathan G. Goodman. New York: Thomas Y. Crowell, 1945, pp. 624–28.

DOCUMENT 14: ONE CAN LEARN MUCH BY PLAYING AT CHESS

Franklin was a great fan of chess. Because playing the game required certain moral qualities, chess was for Franklin a model of diplomacy, evident in the following excerpt from "The Morals of Chess," written in 1779.

The game of Chess is not merely an idle amusement. Several very valuable qualities of the mind, useful in the course of human life, are to be acquired or strengthened by it, so as to become habits, ready on all occasions. For life is a kind of chess, in which we have often points to gain, and competitors or adversaries to contend with, and in which there is a vast variety of good and ill events, that are, in some degree, the effects of prudence or the want of it. By playing at chess, then, we may learn:

1. *Foresight,* which looks a little into futurity, and considers the consequences that may attend an action: for it is continually occurring to the player, "If I move this piece, what will be the advantages of my new situation? What use can my adversary make of it to annoy me? What other moves can I make to support it, and to defend myself from his attacks?"

2. *Circumspection,* which surveys the whole chess-board, or scene of action, the relations of the several pieces and situations, the dangers they are respectively exposed to, the several possibilities of their aiding each other; the probabilities that the adversary may make this or that move, and attack this or the other piece; and

what different means can be used to avoid his stroke, or turn its consequences against him.

3. *Caution,* not to make our moves too hastily. This habit is best acquired by observing strictly the laws of the game, such as, *If you touch a piece, you must move it somewhere; if you set it down, you must let it stand.* And it is therefore best that these rules should be observed, as the game thereby becomes more the image of human life, and particularly of war; in which, if you have incautiously put yourself into a bad and dangerous position, you cannot obtain your enemy's leave to withdraw your troops, and place them more securely; but you must abide all the consequences of your rashness.

And, lastly, we learn by chess the habit of *not being discouraged* by *present* bad appearances in the state of our affairs, the habit of *hoping for a favorable change,* and that of *persevering in the search of resources.* The game is so full of events, there is such a variety of turns in it, the fortune of it is so subject to sudden vicissitudes, and one so frequently, after long contemplation, discovers the means of extricating one's self from a supposed insurmountable difficulty, that one is encouraged to continue the contest to the last, in hopes of victory by our own skill, or, at least, of giving a *stale mate,* by the negligence of our adversary. And whoever considers, what in chess he often sees instances of, that particular pieces of success are apt to produce *presumption,* and its consequent, inattention, by which more is afterwards lost than was gained by the preceding advantage; while misfortunes produce more care and attention, by which the loss may be recovered, will learn not to be too much discouraged by the present success of his adversary, nor to despair of final good fortune, upon every little check he receives in the pursuit of it.

"Benjamin Franklin's *The Morals of Chess," Benjamin Franklin and Chess in Early America.* Philadelphia: University of Pennsylvania Press, 1958, pp. 16–18.

DOCUMENT 15: FRANKLIN'S BIFOCALS

Prompted by reading problems brought on by aging, the elderly Franklin devised his "double spectacles," now called bifocals. Franklin's ingenuity and practicality are quite obvious in this letter to his longtime friend, the English economist George Whately. Franklin eloquently demonstrates how a little bit of thought can yield a simple solution to a common problem.

Passy, May 23, 1785.

By Mr. Dollond's saying, that my double spectacles can only serve particular eyes, I doubt he has not been rightly informed of their construction. I imagine it will be found pretty generally true, that the same convexity of glass, through which a man sees clearest and best at the distance proper for reading, is not the best for greater distances. I therefore had formerly two pair of spectacles, which I shifted occasionally, as in travelling I sometimes read, and often wanted to regard the prospects. Finding this change troublesome, and not always sufficiently ready, I had the glasses cut, and half of each kind associated in the same circle, thus,

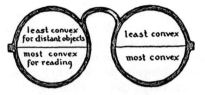

By this means, as I wear my spectacles constantly, I have only to move my eyes up or down, as I want to see distinctly far or near, the proper glasses being always ready. This I find more particularly convenient since my being in France, the glasses that serve me best at table to see what I eat, not being the best to see the faces of those on the other side of the table who speak to me; and when one's ears are not well accustomed to the sounds of a language, a sight of the movements in the features of him that speaks helps to explain; so that I understand French better by the help of my spectacles.

B. FRANKLIN

"Bifocals" in "Practical Schemes and Suggestions," *The Ingenious Dr. Franklin: Selected Scientific Letters of Benjamin Franklin.* Ed. Nathan G. Goodman. Philadelphia: University of Pennsylvania Press, 1956, pp. 54–55.

DOCUMENT 16: IN HIS LAST YEARS, FRANKLIN BECAME AN ABOLITIONIST

Throughout his life, Franklin demonstrated insight, ingenuity, and civic-mindedness. Unfortunately, for the majority of his lifetime, he did not exercise these gifts on behalf of slaves. In fact, Franklin kept slaves for thirty years and even printed ads for the selling of slaves. In his twilight years, however, Franklin became active in promoting the abolition of slavery. Just months before his death, Franklin, who was serving as the president of the Pennsylvania Society for Promoting the Abolition of Slavery, wrote this appeal for the employment and education of freed slaves, which he hoped would become national policy.

AN ADDRESS TO THE PUBLIC;

FROM THE PENNSYLVANIA SOCIETY FOR PROMOTING

THE ABOLITION OF SLAVERY, AND THE RELIEF OF

FREE NEGROES UNLAWFULLY HELD IN BONDAGE.

It is with peculiar satisfaction we assure the friends of humanity, that, in prosecuting the design of our association, our endeavours have proved successful, far beyond our most sanguine expectations.

Encouraged by this success, and by the daily progress of that luminous and benign spirit of liberty, which is diffusing itself throughout the world, and humbly hoping for the continuance of the divine blessing on our labors, we have ventured to make an important addition to our original plan, and do therefore earnestly solicit the support and assistance of all who can feel the tender emotions of sympathy and compassion, or relish the exalted pleasure of beneficence.

Slavery is such an atrocious debasement of human nature, that its very extirpation, if not performed with solicitous care, may sometimes open a source of serious evils.

The unhappy man, who has long been treated as a brute animal, too frequently sinks beneath the common standard of the human species. The galling chains, that bind his body, do also fetter his intellectual faculties, and impair the social affections of his heart. Accustomed to move like a mere machine, by the will of a master, reflection is suspended; he has not the power of choice; and reason and conscience have but little influence over his conduct, because he is chiefly governed by the passion of fear. He is poor and friendless; perhaps worn out by extreme labor, age, and disease.

Under such circumstances, freedom may often prove a misfortune to himself, and prejudicial to society.

Attention to emancipated black people, it is therefore to be hoped, will become a branch of our national police; but, as far as we contribute to promote this emancipation, so far that attention is evidently a serious duty incumbent on us, and which we mean to discharge to the best of our judgment and abilities.

To instruct, to advise, to qualify those, who have been restored to freedom, for the exercise and enjoyment of civil liberty, to promote in them habits of industry, to furnish them with employments suited to their age, sex, talents, and other circumstances, and to procure their children an education calculated for their future situation in life; these are the great outlines of the annexed plan, which we have adopted, and which we conceive will essentially promote the public good, and the happiness of these our hitherto too much neglected fellow-creatures.

A plan so extensive cannot be carried into execution without considerable pecuniary resources, beyond the present ordinary funds of the Society. We hope much from the generosity of enlightened and benevolent freemen, and will gratefully receive any donations or subscriptions for this purpose, which may be made to our treasurer, James Starr, or to James Pemberton, chairman of our committee of correspondence.

Signed, by order of the Society,

B. FRANKLIN, *President.*

"An Address to the Public; From the Pennsylvania Society for Promoting the Abolition of Slavery, and the Relief of Free Negroes Unlawfully Held in Bondage" in "Political Economy," *The Works of Benjamin Franklin.* Vol. 2. Ed. Jared Sparks. Boston: Hilliard Gray, 1836, pp. 515–16.

CHRONOLOGY

1683

Josiah Franklin emigrates from Banbury, in Oxfordshire, England, to Boston, Massachusetts.

1687

Sir Isaac Newton publishes *Philosophiae naturalis principia mathematica.*

1701

Yale College is founded in New Haven, Connecticut.

1704

Newton's *Opticks* is published.

1706

Benjamin Franklin is born in Boston on January 17 at the Milk Street residence opposite the Old South Church.

1711

First appearance of the *Spectator* by Joseph Addison and Richard Steele.

1714–1716

Franklin attends the Boston Grammar School and George Brownell's English school.

1718–1720

Benjamin is apprenticed to his brother, James Franklin, in James's print shop; Benjamin writes and distributes his ballads "The Lighthouse Tragedy" and "On the Taking of *Teach* or Blackbeard the Pirate"; he studies the writings of John Locke, Addison and Steele, Cotton Mather, John Bunyan, and Daniel Defoe.

1721

James Franklin sets up his newspaper, the *New England Courant.*

1722

Benjamin Franklin submits letters to his brother's paper, written under the pseudonym of Mrs. Silence Dogood, which receive high acclaim.

1723–1724

Franklin leaves Boston; he arrives in New York, but finding no work, he continues to Philadelphia; Franklin goes to work for Samuel Keimer, one of two Philadelphia printers; Franklin takes lodgings with Deborah Read's family, and they begin a courtship.

1724

Convinced that Governor Keith of Pennsylvania will assist him in setting up his own printing business, Franklin leaves for London to obtain necessary equipment, but he first visits his family in Boston; Josiah Franklin refuses to help finance his son's printing enterprise.

1725–1726

Franklin is stranded in London and obtains employment with two printing houses, first with Palmer, then with Watts; while at Palmer's, Franklin writes *A Dissertation on Liberty and Necessity, Pleasure and Pain*, presenting an argument against free will; Deborah Read marries John Rogers.

1726

Franklin leaves London for Philadelphia on July 23 with the merchant Thomas Denham, who has offered him a job in Philadelphia as a shopkeeper and bookkeeper; Franklin writes *Journal of a Voyage from London to Philadelphia*, which includes his "Plan of Conduct."

1727

Seriously ill with pleurisy, Franklin composes his own epitaph; he returns to work for Keimer, who exploits Franklin's superior skill as a printer to carry out an official job printing paper money for New Jersey; Franklin forms the Junto club.

1728

Franklin forms a partnership with Hugh Meredith, opening a printing house in Philadelphia with money from Meredith's father.

1729

Franklin contributes to Bradford's the *American Weekly* as the "Busy-Body"; he purchases Keimer's unsuccessful newspaper and shortens the name to *Pennsylvania Gazette;* he anonymously writes the pamphlet *A Modest Enquiry into the Nature and Necessity of a Paper Currency.*

1730

Franklin is appointed public printer by the Pennsylvania Assembly; he dissolves his partnership with Hugh Meredith; Franklin and Deborah (Rogers) Read form a common-law union. William, Franklin's son from an earlier relationship, comes to live with them; Franklin studies French and German.

1731

Franklin founds the first North American subscription library; he begins partnerships and similar associations to establish other printing houses beyond Philadelphia.

1732

Franklin publishes the *South Carolina Gazette* with his business partner, Thomas Whitemarsh; Francis Folger Franklin, Franklin's second son, is born; Franklin publishes *Poor Richard's Almanack.*

1733

Franklin develops a method for achieving what he considers moral perfection; he takes up the study of Italian, Spanish, and Latin.

1735

Franklin prints *Protection of Towns from Fire* in the *Gazette;* he proposes a system for paid night watchmen.

1736

The Union Fire Company is established by Franklin; he is appointed clerk of the Pennsylvania Assembly.

1737

Franklin is appointed postmaster of Philadelphia.

1739

War breaks out between England and Spain.

1740

War breaks out between England and France.

1740–1741

Franklin's *General Magazine and Historical Chronicle, for All the British Plantations* begins publication; Franklin designs the Pennsylvania fireplace (also know as the Franklin stove).

1742

Franklin establishes a printing house in New York with James Parker.

1743

Franklin sends out a letter to his friends including *A Proposal for Promoting Useful Knowledge Among the British Plantations in America*, which leads to the establishment of the American Philosophical Society; he attends Archibald Spencer's electrical demonstrations; daughter, Sarah "Sally" Franklin, is born on August 31.

1745

Franklin's father, Josiah, dies.

1746

Reflections on Courtship and Marriage by Franklin is the first of his writings reprinted in Europe; Franklin begins experimenting with electricity.

1747

Franklin promotes the idea of forming a colonial militia in his anonymously published *Plain Truth; or Serious Considerations on the Present State of the City of Philadelphia, and Province of Pennsylvania.*

1749

Franklin founds the Academy, which later becomes the University of Pennsylvania; he notes similarities between lightning and electricity and calls for an experiment to prove their identities.

1750

Franklin devises experiment to prove lightning is a form of electricity.

1751

Franklin's *Experiments and Observations on Electricity, Made at Philadelphia in America* is published; Franklin serves as a member of the Pennsylvania Assembly; he works with Dr. Thomas Bond to help establish the first public hospital in Pennsylvania.

1752

Franklin performs his famous kite experiment; he invents the lightning rod; Franklin's mother, Abiah Folger Franklin, dies; Franklin helps establish the first fire insurance company in the colonies.

1753

Along with William Hunter, Franklin is jointly appointed deputy postmaster general of North America; he surveys northern colony roads and post offices; both Harvard and Yale Universities grant master's degrees to Franklin; he receives the Copley medal from the Royal Society of London.

1754

Franklin proposes the Albany Plan of Union at the Albany Congress, which he attends as a commissioner; a second edition of his *Experiments and Observations on Electricity* is published.

1757

As colonial agent for the province of Pennsylvania, Franklin travels to London, arriving July 26, to pursue concerns over taxation in the colony.

1759

Receives law doctorate from the University of St. Andrews and is thereafter known as "Dr. Franklin"; he writes the *Parable Against Persecution*; Franklin is named an honorary member of the Philosophical Society of Edinburgh.

1761

Franklin visits Holland and Belgium; witnesses coronation of George III of England.

1762

Oxford University bestows honorary civil law doctorate on Franklin; Franklin invents the glass armonica; in August he leaves England for America and arrives in October.

1764

On behalf of the province of Pennsylvania, Franklin petitions King George III for a change from a proprietary to a royal government; Franklin departs for London in November.

1765

Franklin presents First Minister George Grenville the resolution of the Pennsylvania Assembly opposing the Stamp Act, which still passes; Franklin nominates John Hughes as Pennsylvania's stamp distributor, leading to rumors that Franklin supports the Stamp Act.

1766

Franklin is examined in the House of Commons pertaining to the Stamp Act appeal; his *Physical and Meteorological Observations* is published.

1771

Franklin begins writing the first part of his memoirs.

1772

The Royal Academy of Sciences of Paris elects Franklin as a foreign member.

1774

Franklin loses his post as deputy postmaster general of North America; Deborah Franklin dies on December 19; the first Continental Congress opens in Philadelphia.

1775

Franklin returns to America in May and becomes the first U.S. postmaster general, a member of the Philadelphia Committee of Safety, and a delegate to the second Continental Congress; he prints his pamphlet *An Account of Negotiations in London for Effecting a Reconciliation Between Great Britain and the American Colonies.*

1776

Thomas Paine's *Common Sense* is published in America on January 9; Franklin is appointed to the Committee of Five to frame the Declaration of Independence; in September he is appointed one of three commissioners from Congress to visit France and negotiate a treaty, leaving Philadelphia on October 27 and arriving in Paris on December 21.

1777

King Louis XVI of France approves response to commissioners' formal request for French aid to the American colonies in their rebellion against England.

1778

France and Britain go to war; Franklin is elected America's sole minister plenipotentiary to France.

1779

Spain declares war on Britain.

1781

Franklin is chosen as a fellow of the American Academy of Arts and Sciences; he is appointed one of the commissioners to negotiate a peace treaty between England and the United States; General Charles Cornwallis surrenders to General George Washington at Yorktown, Virginia, on October 19.

1783

Franklin, along with John Adams and John Jay, signs peace treaty between Great Britain and the United States.

1784

Franklin serves on the committee to investigate German physician Franz Mesmer's animal magnetism theory; he writes and publishes *Remarks Concerning the Savages of North America* and *Advice to Such as Would Remove to America*; he resumes work on the second part of his memoirs.

1785

Franklin describes his invention of bifocals; he returns home to Philadelphia, where he is met by cannon salutes and cheering crowds; he is elected to the Supreme Executive Council of Pennsylvania on October 11 and becomes its president on October 18.

1788

Franklin continues his memoirs, working on the third part; he writes his last will and testament; Franklin ends his career in public office when he resigns as president from the Supreme Executive Council of Pennsylvania.

1789

Franklin writes and publishes several papers promoting the abolition of slavery; he writes and signs the first appeal ever made to Congress to abolish slavery.

1790

Franklin dies on April 17 in Philadelphia.

FOR FURTHER RESEARCH

THE AUTOBIOGRAPHY, LETTERS, AND OTHER WRITINGS OF BENJAMIN FRANKLIN

John Hardin Best, ed., *Benjamin Franklin on Education.* New York: Bureau of Publications, Teachers College, Columbia University, 1962.

I. Bernard Cohen, ed., *Benjamin Franklin's Experiments: A New Edition of Franklin's* Experiments and Observations on Electricity. Cambridge, MA: Harvard University Press, 1941.

Verner W. Crane, ed., *Benjamin Franklin's Letters to the Press, 1758–1775.* Chapel Hill: University of North Carolina Press, for the Institute of Early American History and Culture, 1950.

Max Farrand, ed., *Benjamin Franklin's Memoirs.* Berkeley and Los Angeles: University of California Press, 1949.

Benjamin Franklin, *The Bagatelles from Passy.* New York: Eakins, 1967.

Nathan Goodman, ed., *The Ingenious Dr. Franklin: Selected Scientific Letters of Benjamin Franklin.* Philadelphia: University of Pennsylvania Press, 1956.

Randolph Goodman, ed., *An Apology for Printers.* New York: Book Craftsmen Associates, 1955.

Ralph L. Ketcham, ed., *The Political Thought of Benjamin Franklin.* Indianapolis: Bobbs-Merrill, 1965.

Leonard W. Labaree et al., eds., *The Autobiography.* New Haven, CT: Yale University Press, 1964.

J.A. Leo Lemay and P.M. Zall, eds., *Benjamin Franklin's Autobiography: An Authoritative Text.* New York: W.W. Norton, 1986.

William Greene Roelker, ed., *Benjamin Franklin and Catharine Ray Greene: Their Correspondence, 1755–1790.* Philadelphia: American Philosophical Society, 1949.

Carl Van Doren, ed., *Benjamin Franklin's Autobiographical Writings.* New York: Viking, 1945.

————, *Letters and Papers of Benjamin Franklin and Richard Jackson, 1753–1785.* Philadelphia: American Philosophical Society, 1947.

————, *The Letters of Benjamin Franklin and Jane Mecom.* Princeton, NJ: Princeton University Press for the American Philosophical Society, 1950.

GENERAL COLLECTIONS OF FRANKLIN'S WRITING

Leonard W. Labaree et al., eds., *The Papers of Benjamin Franklin.* 35 vols. to date. New Haven, CT: Yale University Press and the American Philosophical Society, 1959–.

J.A. Leo Lemay, ed., *Benjamin Franklin: Writings.* New York: Library of America—Literary Classics of the United States, 1987.

Frank Luther Mott and Chester E. Jorgenson, eds., *Benjamin Franklin: Representative Selections.* New York: American Book, 1936.

Albert H. Smyth, ed., *The Writings of Benjamin Franklin.* 10 vols. New York: Macmillan, 1905–1907.

Jared Sparks, ed., *The Works of Benjamin Franklin.* 10 vols. Boston: Hilliard, Gray, 1836–1840.

GENERAL BIOGRAPHIES

Carl L. Becker, *Benjamin Franklin: A Biographical Sketch.* Ithaca, NY: Cornell University Press, 1946.

Catherine Drinker Bowen, *The Most Dangerous Man in America: Scenes from the Life of Benjamin Franklin.* Boston: Little, Brown, 1974.

H.W. Brands, *The First American: The Life and Times of Benjamin Franklin.* New York: Doubleday-Random House, 2000.

Verner W. Crane, *Benjamin Franklin and a Rising People.* Boston: Little, Brown, 1954.

Thomas Fleming, *The Man Who Dared the Lightning: A New Look at Benjamin Franklin.* 1970. Reprint, New York: William Morrow, 1971.

Paul Leicester Ford, *The Many-Sided Franklin.* New York: Century, 1899.

Claude-Anne Lopez and Eugenia W. Herbert, *The Private Franklin: The Man and His Family.* New York: W.W. Norton, 1975.

Carl Van Doren, *Benjamin Franklin.* New York: Viking, 1938.

Esmond Wright, *Franklin of Philadelphia.* Cambridge, MA: Harvard University Press, 1986.

BIOGRAPHICAL AND CRITICAL STUDIES

Thomas Perkins Abernethy, "The Origin of the Franklin-Lee Imbroglio," *North Carolina Historical Review,* January 1938.

Charles Maclean Andrews, "A Note on the Franklin-Deane Mission to France," *Yale University Library Gazette,* 1928.

Peter Baida, "Flying Kites with Ben Franklin," *Harvard Business Review,* 1986.

William Bell Clark, *Ben Franklin's Privateers: A Naval Epic of the American Revolution.* Baton Rouge: Louisiana State University Press, 1956.

I. Bernard Cohen, *Benjamin Franklin's Science.* Cambridge, MA: Harvard University Press, 1990.

———, *Franklin and Newton.* Cambridge, MA: Harvard University Press, 1966.

Paul W. Conner, *Poor Richard's Politicks: Benjamin Franklin and His New American Order.* New York: Oxford University Press, 1965.

Cecil B. Currey, *Code Number 72/Ben Franklin: Patriot or Spy?* Englewood Cliffs, NJ: Prentice-Hall, 1972.

———, *Road to Revolution: Benjamin Franklin in England, 1765–1775.* Garden City, NY: Anchor Books, 1968.

Malcolm R. Eiselen, *Franklin's Political Theories.* Garden City, NY: Doubleday, Doran, 1928.

J. Philip Gleason, "A Scurrilous Colonial Election and Franklin's Reputation," *William and Mary Quarterly,* 1961.

William S. Hanna, *Benjamin Franklin and Pennsylvania Politics*. Stanford, CA: Stanford University Press, 1972.

John H. Lienhard, "Franklin and Mesmer," February 2001. www.uh.edu/engines/epi710htm.

Claude-Anne Lopez, *Mon Cher Papa: Franklin and the Ladies of Paris*. 1966. Reprint, New Haven, CT: Yale University Press, 1990.

Robert Middlekauff, *Benjamin Franklin and His Enemies*. Berkeley and Los Angeles: University of California Press, 1996.

David Schoenbrun, *Triumph in Paris: The Exploits of Benjamin Franklin*. New York: Harper & Row, 1976.

Ormond Seavey, *Becoming Benjamin Franklin: The Autobiography and the Life*. University Park: Pennsylvania State University Press, 1988.

Charles Coleman Sellers, *Benjamin Franklin in Portraiture*. New Haven, CT: Yale University Press, 1962.

Sheila L. Skemp, *Benjamin and William Franklin: Father and Son, Patriot and Loyalist*. Boston: Bedford Books, 1994.

Gerald Stourzh, *Benjamin Franklin and American Foreign Policy*. 2nd ed. Chicago: University of Chicago Press, 1969.

EXAMINING FRANKLIN THE WRITER

Alfred Owen Aldridge, "The First Published Memoir of Franklin," *William and Mary Quarterly*, 1967.

Elizabeth C. Cook, *Literary Influences in Colonial Newspapers, 1704–1750*. New York: Columbia University Studies in English and Comparative Literature, 1912.

Bruce Ingham Granger, *Benjamin Franklin: An American Man of Letters*. Ithaca, NY: Cornell University Press, 1964.

Max Hall, *Benjamin Franklin and Polly Baker: The History of a Literary Deception*. Chapel Hill: University of North Carolina Press, 1960.

Ralph K. Hornberger, *Benjamin Franklin*. Minneapolis: University of Minnesota Press—"Pamphlets on American Writers, No. 10," 1962.

J.A. Leo Lemay, "Franklin and the *Autobiography:* An Essay on Recent Scholarship," *Eighteenth-Century Studies,* 1967–1968.

David Levin, "The Autobiography of Benjamin Franklin, Puritan Experimenter in Life and Art," *Yale Review,* 1963.

Margaret MacLaurin, *Franklin's Vocabulary.* Garden City, NY: Doubleday, Doran, 1928.

Mary E. Rucker, "Benjamin Franklin," in *American Literature, 1764–1789: The Revolutionary Years.* Ed. Everett Emerson. Madison: University of Wisconsin Press, 1977.

James A. Sappenfield, *A Sweet Instruction: Franklin's Journalism as a Literary Apprenticeship.* Carbondale and Edwardsville: Southern Illinois University Press, 1973.

Robert F. Sayre, *The Examined Self: Benjamin Franklin, Henry Adams, Henry James.* Princeton, NJ: Princeton University Press, 1964.

THE AMERICAN REVOLUTION

Thomas Perkins Abernethy, *Western Lands and the American Revolution.* New York: Russell and Russell, 1959.

Samuel Flagg Bemis, *The Diplomacy of the American Revolution.* 1935. Reprint, Bloomington: Indiana University Press, 1967.

George Athan Billias, ed., *The American Revolution: How Revolutionary Was It?* 4th ed. New York: Holt, Rinehart, and Winston, 1990.

Philip Grant Davidson, *Propaganda and the American Revolution.* Chapel Hill: University of North Carolina Press, 1941.

Vincent T. Harlow, *The Founding of the Second British Empire, 1763–93.* 2 vols. London: Longmans, 1952.

Bruce E. Johansen, *Forgotten Founders: Benjamin Franklin, the Iroquois, and the Rationale for the American Revolution.* Ipswich, MA: Gambit, 1982.

Michael G. Kammen, *A Rope of Sand: The Colonial Agents, British Politics, and the American Revolution.* New York: Random House Vintage Books, 1974.

Pauline Maier, *From Resistance to Revolution: Colonial Radicals and the Development of American Opposition to Britain, 1765–1776.* New York: Knopf, 1972.

Philip McFarland, *The Brave Bostonians: Hutchinson, Quincy, Franklin, and the Coming of the American Revolution.* Boulder, CO: Westview/HarperCollins, 1998.

Edmund S. Morgan and Helen M. Morgan, *The Stamp Act Crisis: Prologue to Revolution.* Chapel Hill: University of North Carolina Press, 1953.

Gary B. Nash, *The Urban Crucible: Social Change, Political Consciousness, and the Origins of the American Revolution.* Cambridge, MA: Harvard University Press, 1979.

Alison Gilbert Owen, "The British Government and Colonial Union, 1754," *William and Mary Quarterly*, January 1960.

David Ramsey, *The History of the American Revolution.* New York: Russell and Russell, 1789.

Jack M. Sosin, *Agents and Merchants: British Colonial Policy and the Origins of the American Revolution.* Lincoln: University of Nebraska Press, 1965.

ADDITIONAL RESOURCES

Whitfield J. Bell Jr., *The Colonial Physician and Other Essays.* New York: Science History Publications/Neale Watson Academic, 1975.

Carl Bridenbaugh and Jessica Bridenbaugh, *Rebels and Gentlemen: Philadelphia in the Age of Franklin.* 1970. Reprint, Westport, CT: Greenwood, 1978.

Paul K. Conkin, *Puritans and Pragmatists: Eight Eminent American Thinkers*, New York: Dodd, Mead, 1968.

Richard Deacon, *A History of the British Secret Service.* Rev. ed. London: Grafton, 1991.

J.T. Desaguliers, *A Course of Experimental Philosophy.* 3rd ed. London: A. Millar, 1763.

Stephen Jay Gould, *Bully for Brontosaurus: Reflections in Natural History.* New York: W.W. Norton, 1991.

Richard M. Gummere, *The American Colonial Mind and the Classical Tradition.* Cambridge, MA: Harvard University Press, 1963.

Brooke Hindle, *The Pursuit of Science in Revolutionary America, 1735–1789.* Durham, NC: Duke University Press, 1956.

Adrienne Koch, *Power, Morals, and the Founding Fathers: Essays in the Interpretation of the American Enlightenment.* Ithaca, NY: Cornell University Press, 1961.

Edmund S. Morgan, *The Puritan Family: Religion and Domestic Relations in Seventeenth-Century New England.* Rev. ed. Westport, CT: Greenwood, 1980.

J. Thomas Scharf and Thompson Westcott, *History of Philadelphia, 1609–1884.* 3 vols. Philadelphia: L.H. Everts, 1884.

Daniel B. Shea, *Spiritual Autobiography in Early America.* Madison: University of Wisconsin Press, 1988.

INDEX